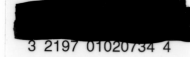

RELIGIOUS SEMINARIES
IN AMERICA

GARLAND REFERENCE LIBRARY
OF SOCIAL SCIENCE
(Vol. 539)

RELIGIOUS SEMINARIES
IN AMERICA
A Selected Bibliography

Thomas C. Hunt, *1930-*
James C. Carper

GARLAND PUBLISHING, INC. • NEW YORK & LONDON
1989

Library of Congress Cataloging-in-Publication Data

Hunt, Thomas C., 1930–
    Religious seminaries in America : a selected bibliography / Thomas
C. Hunt, James C. Carper.
        p.   cm. — (Garland reference library of social science; v.
539)
    ISBN 0–8240–7732–6 (alk. paper)
    1. Theological seminaries—United States—Bibliography.
2. Rabbinical seminaries—United States—Bibliography.   I. Carper,
James C.   II. Title.   III. Series.
Z7848.H86 1989
[BV4030]
016.2'07'73—dc20   89–7815
                                                                CIP

Printed on acid-free 250-year-life paper
Manufactured in the United States of America

DEDICATION AND ACKNOWLEDGMENTS

We respectfully dedicate this book to all those who have devoted their lives to the service of God and/or their fellow humans.

We acknowledge with thanks the assistance of many people, whose help was indispensable in the publication of this book. In particular, we wish to thank: Professor Hunt's graduate assistant, Barbara Bellefeuille, who helped in many ways, including the preparation of the indexes; David Starkey, of the Word Processing Center of the College of Education at Virginia Tech for printing the text; Marilyn Norstedt, of Virginia Tech's Newman Library, who guided the indexing process; and Linda Wilson, also of Newman Library, who aided in obtaining needed references. Finally, the editors wish to express their gratitude to the Division of Curriculum and Instruction and to the College of Education at Virginia Tech for the support they provided.

Thomas C. Hunt
Blacksburg, Virginia

James C. Carper
Mississippi State, Mississippi

v

CONTENTS

INTRODUCTION

Scholars and the general public alike have recently rediscovered the role of religion in the origin and development of the American educational enterprise. Most of the attention has been focused on questions regarding religion and precollegiate and collegiate education. For example, scholars have explored the crucial role played by evangelical Protestantism in the genesis of public schooling during the middle decades of the nineteenth century. Historians, such as Colin Burke, have also described how religion influenced the development of higher education in America during the nineteenth century. The general public, on the other hand, has grappled frequently with issues such as prayer in the public schools, government funding and regulation of religious schools, and free exercise of religion on college campuses.

Though often overlooked, the influence of religion on the configuration of education in the United States has reached beyond the collegiate level as well. As historian Natalie Naylor has pointed out, the theological seminary, a post-collegiate educational institution, was established in the United States by Protestants in the early 1800s. Supplanting both the parsonage seminary and private divinity study, the theological seminary not only enhanced the process of educational diffusion by providing more opportunities for intellectual training for ministers, but also served as the prototype of the graduate professional school.

Very quickly the theological seminary became a permanent fixture on the American educational landscape. Naylor asserts that by 1840 more than fifty of these institutions had been established by thirteen Protestant denominations. Thirty-three of these are among the more than 200 seminaries in existence today. Varying in enrollment from several dozen to over 4,000 students, theological seminaries currently provide professional and graduate education for more than 60,000 students.

This selected bibliography deals with seminaries that are either affiliated with the various denominations or nondenominational or independent. This affiliation may be close-knit; or it may be rather "loose," depending on the traditions of the several denominations.

The book has two sections. The first consists of but one chapter, which considers the relationships between civil government and the seminaries. The second section constitutes the overwhelming thrust of this book. Here the reader will find fifteen chapters, organized by denominations with the exception of the *Independent* chapter. Some of these denominations, *e.g.*, Baptist, Catholic, Episcopalian, Lutheran, have a rather extensive involvement in the establishment and support of seminaries. For others, such as the Independent, there were but few entries. Indeed, several denominations which maintain colleges and universities, *e.g.*, the Church of Jesus Christ of the Latter-Day Saints and Society of Friends, have no seminaries *per se*.

This volume is the third, and last, in a series. It follows the publication of *Religious Schools* (1986) and *Religious Colleges and Universities* (1988), each of which was also published by Garland Press. To our knowledge, no other set of reference works addresses the topics contained in these three volumes.

This work, as is the case with its predecessors, pulls together a wealth of reference material and through selection identifies the salient works, whether book, article, dissertation, or essay. It therefore provides a much-needed resource for those interested in seminary education in the United States, whether scholar, student, policy-maker or interested citizen.

Thomas C. Hunt
Blacksburg, Virginia

James C. Carper
Mississippi State, Mississippi

RELIGIOUS SEMINARIES

IN AMERICA

CHAPTER 1
GOVERNMENT RELATIONSHIPS TO SEMINARIES
Ralph Mawdsley

Preface

Seminaries are by definition usually religious institutions actively involved in the training of young men and women for ministry. Although seminaries are generally less vulnerable to government intrusions than other religious higher education, they are nevertheless affected by such issues as tax exemption, religious standards in employment and admissions and the nature of protection under the First Amendment of the United States Constitution. Because of the nature of ministerial clientele served by seminaries, issues pertaining to the rights and responsibilities of those in religious ministries as well as churches or other places of worship are of special concern to seminaries. Since some seminaries may be affiliated with religious colleges or universities, bibliographic entries are included which address the religious rights of the larger religious institution.

Law Cases

1.   *Amos v. Corporation of Presiding Bishop.* 107 S. Ct. 2862 (1987).

Upholds, against a strong Establishment Clause attack, the right of a church under a Title VII exemption to extend religious requirements to forms of work (in this case a janitor in a gymnasium) that is not ministerial in nature. Limits the rationale for the decision to legislative intent and does not reach the Free Exercise issue.

2.   *City and County of Denver v. Colorado Seminary.* 41, P.2d 1109 (Colo. 1934).

Upholds claim by the seminary that various pieces of property received as the result of a gift were entitled to tax exemption, even though for several prior years the seminary had leased the same facilities and had paid property taxes.

3.   *Equal Employment Opportunity Commission v. Southwestern Baptist Theological Seminary.* 651 F.2d 277 (5th Cir. 1981).

Determines that the Seminary does not have to complete EEOC's routine information EEO-6 form as to its faculty and administrative positions that are traditionally ecclesiastical or ministerial but must complete the form as to other administrative and support staff.

4.   *Lexington Theological Seminary v. Vance.* 596 S.W.2d 11 (Ky. App. 1979).

Upholds decision of Board of Trustees of a seminary to deny Master of Divinity degree to practicing homosexual when his homosexuality was not known by the seminary at admission but was later revealed to the seminary president. Focuses on language in seminary materials such as "Christian ministry", "gospel transmitted through the Bible", "firmly committed to the role and mission with which they will begin their ministry", "fundamental character", and "display traits of character and personality which indicate probable effectiveness in the Christian ministry."

5.   *Little v. United Presbyterian Theological Seminary.* 74 N.E. 193 (Ohio 1905).

Reversed decision of tax assessor who had levied property tax against the seminary's endowment fund. Although an older case, may be of interest regarding interpretation of state taxation statutes granting mandatory versus discretionary exemptions for religious institutions.

6.   *National Labor Relations Board v. Catholic Bishop.* 440 U.S. 490 (1979).

Rules on narrow statutory grounds that the NLRB does not have jurisdiction under the NLRA over Catholic archdiocese schools, including a seminary. Contains helpful dicta on possible Establishment Clause problems.

7.   *State ex rel. McLemore v. Clarksville School of Theology.* 636 S.W.2d 706 (Tenn. 1982).

Upholds an injunction prohibiting defendant school from offering degrees without first obtaining a state license. Rejects the school's argument that inability to award degrees violates the Religion Clauses by regulating its beliefs, practices or teaching for the reason that awarding degrees is a secular activity while the religious activity is training ministers.

8.   *Tilton v. Richardson.* 403 U.S. 672 (1971).

Upholds state funding to nonpublic institution that excluded those awarding only seminaries or theological degrees and upholds capitation grant formula excluding students enrolled in seminarian or theological programs.

Books, Pamphlets and Monographs

9.   Bird, Wendell R. "Exempt Organizations and Discriminations." In *Tax-Exempt Organizations.* Vol. 1, pp. 3295-3302. Paramus, NJ:

Prentice-Hall, 1984.

Summarizes federal legislation prohibiting discrimination on the basis of gender, religion, age and handicap and how religious exempt organizations are affected.

10. Bromberg, Robert S. "Unrelated Business Income of Museums, Hospitals, Hospital Association, and Universities." In *Tax-Exempt Organizations*, Vol. 1, pp. 3485-3500. Paramus, NJ: Prentice-Hall, 1984.

Explores ways in which tax exempt colleges and universities can generate taxable income under the unrelated business income tax (UBIT) through rental or lease of their facilities, equipment and personnel.

11. Dutile, Fernand N. and Edward McGlynn Gaffney, Jr. *State and Campus: State Regulation of Religiously Affiliated Higher Education.* Notre Dame, IN: University of Notre Dame Press, 1984.

Contains a state-by-state analysis of state regulations affecting religiously affiliated colleges and universities with a special "overview" of important state policies. Addresses eight categories of state regulation: corporate status, state financial aid, personnel policies and practices, student admission and student discipline, use of publicly funded facilities, taxation, charitable solicitation and fund-raising, and miscellaneous provisions.

12. Gaffney, Edward McGlynn, Jr. and Philip R. Moots. *Government and Campus: Federal Regulation of Religiously-Affiliated Higher Education.* Notre Dame, IN: University of Notre Dame Press, 1982.

Begins with the results of studies revealing the increasing frequency of legal problems in church-related colleges and universities and the extent to which government subsidies and regulations have undercut religious commitment on some campuses. Explores the statutory exemption and exception available to religiously affiliated colleges under Title VII and judicial and EEOC decisions restricting the exemption and exception. Includes a discussion of alcoholism and drug addicts as handicapped persons and the nature of their protection under the Handicapped Act of 1973. Discusses tax problems of unrelated business income, and the college as an integrated auxiliary of a church for purposes of filing the detailed financial Form 990. Analyzes the extent of NLRB jurisdiction over religious schools against the protection of the First Amendment Religion clauses. Concludes with a pre-*Grove City College* Supreme Court decision analysis of Title IX and its impact on relationships among the sexes.

13. Gumper, Lindell L. *Legal Issues in the Practice of Ministry.*

Franklin Village, MI: Psychological Studies and Consultation Program, Inc., 1981.

Addresses the state statutory and common law problems encountered where persons performing in a ministerial capacity furnish advice to counselors. Considers such matters as duty of confidentiality, torts like negligence, malpractice, libel and slander, invasion of privacy, and what to expect at trial.

14.   Hammar, Richard R. *Pastor, Church, and Law.* Springfield, MO: Gospel Publishing House, 1983.

Contains thorough discussion of legal areas pertinent to higher educational institutions that maintain a close church affiliation. Included are chapters on such matters as Privacy Act of 1974, taxation, social security and federal anti-discrimination statutes.

15.   Henzke, Leonard J. "Taxation of Churches, Ministers and Church Employees Under The Social Security Act." In *Tax-Exempt Organizations.* Vol. 1, pp. 3681-3685. Paramus, NJ: Prentice-Hall, 1984.

Explains the 1984 Tax Reform Act FICA exemption for churches and qualified church-controlled organizations. Also discusses the problems when persons identified as ministers are exempt under either FICA or SECA.

16.   Hopkins, Bruce. *Charity Under Siege: Government Regulations of Fund Raising.* New York: John Wiley and Sons, 1980.

Focuses on both federal and state legislative, administrative and judicial efforts to regulate charitable fund raising. Of special importance to religious organizations in general, and seminaries in particular, because of the enormous sums of money donated annually and the increased public awareness of religious fund-raising efforts.

17.   Hopkins, Bruce. *The Law of Tax-Exempt Organizations.* 3d ed. New York: John Wiley & Sons, 1978.

Discusses comprehensively the tax-exempt status of every kind of tax exempt organization including those of a religious nature. Includes helpful information on such related concerns as legislative activities, political activities and regulation of public charities.

18.   Howard, A. E. Dick. *State Aid to Private Higher Education.* Charlottesville, VA: Michie & Co., 1977.

Presents in comprehensive form constitutional issues and policy concerns related to state and to private (including religious)

higher education. Discusses separately the relevant law of each
state. Well worth reading, as coming from one of America's
preeminent authorities on the First Amendment.

19.   Kaplan, Michel G. and Mark W. Cockran. "Unrelated Business
       Income Problems of Churches and Other Organizations." In
       Tax-Exempt Organizations. Vol. 1, pp. 3649-3664. Paramus, NJ:
       Prentice-Hall, 1984.

       Details the source of taxable unrelated business income for
religious organizations, how to compute and report the income for
tax purposes and the effect such income might have on an
organization's tax-exempt status.

20.   Mawdsley, Ralph D. and Steven Permuth. "Faculty Dismissal:
       Comparison of Public and Private Higher Education." In *School
       Law Update 1985*, pp. 138-161. Edited by Thomas N. Jones and
       Darel P. Semler. Topeka, KS: National Organization on Legal
       Problems of Education, 1985.

       Compares public and private (including religious) higher
educational institutions and the constitutional and contractual
constraints on the termination of tenured and nontenured faculty
members. Also includes a discussion of financial exigency as it
applies to both kinds of institutions.

21.   Mawdsley, Ralph D. and Steven Permuth. *Legal Problems of
       Religious and Private Schools.* Topeka, KS: National Organization
       on Legal Problems of Education, 1983.

       Comprehensive treatment of critical legal problems faced by
all non-public educational institutions and especially religious
higher education. Covers topics such as tort liability, government
regulations, anti-discrimination legislation, governing board liability
and copyright.

22.   Moots, Philip R. and Edward McGlynn Gaffney, Jr. *Church and
       Campus.* Notre Dame, IN: University of Notre Dame, 1979.

       Functions as legal primer on a variety of issues applicable to
any religious affiliated organization, including the imposition of
legal liability, eligibility of students for public financial assistance,
constitutional and non-constitutional problems raised by
government regulations and problems of property ownership and
control.

23.   Oaks, Dallin H. *Trust Doctrines in Church Controversies.* Atlanta,
       GA: Mercer University Press, 1984.

       Examines the applicability of common law concepts of
charitable trusts to controversies among members of a religious
body and the government. Includes an analysis of the

constitutional problems of applying the "implied trust" doctrine to church controversies.

24.   Worth, B. J. *Income Tax Law for Ministers and Religious Workers.* Winona Lake, IN: Worth Tax Service, 1988.

Published annually and includes explanations of important tax matters such as professional expense deductions and housing allowances. Also includes sample filled-in forms and helpful checklists. Especially useful for employees of religious colleges and universities who claim ministerial status as a result of their teaching religious subjects.

Periodicals

25.   Albert, James A. "Federal Investigation of Video Evangelism: The FCC Probes The PTL Club." *Oklahoma Law Review* 33 (1980): 782-823.

Considers and rejects PTL arguments that the FCC does not have jurisdiction to investigate allegations of misleading or deceptive fund raising even though the television station investigated is an integral part of a larger religious ministry.

26.   Byers, David F. "Title VII and Sectarian Institutions of Higher Education: Congress Shall Make No Law Prohibiting The Free Exercise of Religion." *Cumberland Law Review* 14 (1983-84): 597-641.

Surveys religious employment cases involving Title VII and concludes that a proper constitutional construction requires no further review of a religious educational institution when its sincerely held religious belief is demonstrated.

27.   Comment. "A New Approach to NLRB Jurisdiction Over the Employment Practices of Religious Institutions." *University of Chicago Law Review* 54 (1987): 243.

Discusses the differing interpretations of *National Labor Relations Board v. Catholic Bishop of Chicago*, 440 U.S. 490(1979) regarding jurisdiction of the NLRB over religious institutions. Distinguishes between the Supreme Court decision which concentrated on the nature of the employee's activity and subsequent courts of appeal decisions which have analyzed accommodation of religiously affiliated organization by reference to the organization as a whole, distinguishing between "pervasively religious" and secular institutions.

28.   Durrant, Matthew B. "Accrediting Church-Related Schools: A First Amendment Analysis." *Journal of Law and Education* 14 (April 1985): 147-79.

Analyzes the problem of accreditation through several issues:

whether the accrediting agency is engaged in state action; whether accreditation represents a form of state aid; and whether accreditation through imposition of standards and possible denial of accreditation represents an infringement of free exercise of religion.

29.   Friedland, Jerold A. "Constitutional Issues In Revoking Religious Tax Exemption: *Church of Scientology of California v. Commissioner.*" *University of Florida Law Review* 85 (1985): 565-89.

Argues that there is evidence of IRS hostility toward a religious organization. IRS should be required to produce evidence that its audit was based on factors other than protected religious activity. Represents an application and extension of *Bob Jones University* v. *U.S.*

30.   Grosch, Carla A. "Church-Related Schools and the Section 504 Mandate of Nondiscrimination In Employment on the Basis of Handicap." *DePaul Law Review* 31 (1981-82): 69-113.

Argues persuasively that, following the reasoning in *NLRB v. Catholic Bishop*, the absence of any affirmatively expressed intention of Congress to include religious schools under Section 504 should mean they are excluded. Suggests the absence of establishment problems by excluding religious schools because of the schools' contervailing free exercise concerns.

31.   Johnson, Edward A. and Kent M. Weeks. "To Save A College: Independent College Trustees And Decisions On Financial Exigency, Endowment Use, And Closure." *The Journal of College and University Law* 12 (Spring 1986): 455-88.

Chronicles the legal issues concerning the effects of financial crises on institutional decisions such as reduction in staff or school closures. Examines the standard of care for trustee decisions to lay off staff, close the institution or merge with another institution and reviews the *cy pres* doctrine where restricted gifts or endowment funds can no longer be used for the specific purposes for which they were given.

32.   Lacey, Linda J. "*Gay Rights Coalition v. Georgetown University*: Constitutional Values on a Collision Course." *Oregon Law Review* 64 (1986): 409-55.

Considers the difference between individual and institutional right to alleged free exercise rights in the context of a university that has received federal funds to construct buildings for secular education. Argues that prohibition of sexual preference discrimination is a compelling government interest and that courts must act aggressively to prevent powerful religious institutions from infringing on individual freedom.

33.   Laycock, Douglas. "Civil Rights and Civil Liberties." *Chicago-Kent Law Review* 54 (1977): 390-435.

Contains section reviewing cases involving regulation of church labor relations in light of *NLRB v. Catholic Bishop.* Suggests four categories distinguishing among regulations that: increase the expense of operation; interfere with the way church activities are conducted; control who will perform church functions; and interfere with decisions to conduct the activity at all.

34.   Laycock, Douglas. "Towards a General Theory of the Religion Clauses: The Case of Church Labor Relations and the Right to Church Autonomy." *Columbia Law Review* 81 (1981): 1373-1417.

Presents a strong free exercise argument for church autonomy based not on claims of conscientious objection but on the right of organizations to develop religious doctrine. Would make the intensity of relationship between a church and its employees a barometer as to whether a church should be insulated from government regulation.

35.   Mawdsley, Ralph D. "God and The State: Freedom of Religious Universities to Hire and Fire." *West's Education Law Reporter* 36 (1987): 1093-1113.

Discusses the depth and the leading employment litigation involving religious institutions especially under the Title VII religious exemptions. Addresses applicable statutory and constitutional provisions and identifies policy concerns on both sides of the issue. Concludes with some practical advice regarding the use of religious criteria for employment.

36.   Mawdsley, Ralph D. "Religious Universities and Title VII: The Right to Discriminate On Religious Grounds." *Education Law Reporter* 43 (1988): 491.

Chronicles the U.S. Supreme Court decision of *Amos v. Corporation of Presiding Bishop*, 107 S. Ct. 2862 (1987) which upheld discharge of a Mormon janitor working in a gymnasium because he could not meet the church's "temple recommend" requirements. Agrees with the Court's treatment of a Title VII religious exemption as not violating the Establishment Clause and argues that the hiring policy of the church should be upheld under the Free Exercise Clause, even without the Title VII exemption.

37.   Miller, Charles R. "Rendering Unto Caesar: Religious Publishers And The Public Benefit Rule." *University of Pennsylvania Law Review* 134 (January 1986): 433-568.

Reviews Third Circuit decision in *Presbyterian and Reformed Publishing Co. v. Commissioner* overruling IRS efforts to revoke tax exempt status because the company was nondenominational and not owned by a particular church and because the company had accumulated net profits over several years. Summarizes significant cases interpreting Sec. 501(c)(3) requirements that a tax-exempt organization be "operated exclusively" for exempt purposes. Argues that after the *Bob Jones University* decision, tax-exempt status can be revoked where no public benefit can be proved.

38.   Note. "Development in the Law -- Religion and the State: Government Regulation of Religious Organizations." *Harvard Law Review* 100 (1987): 1740.

Analyzes the difficulties courts have in deciding religious practices of individuals as opposed to religious practices of organizations. Considers such relevant concerns as regulation of sectarian schools, application of antidiscrimination laws to religious organizations, and the power of churches to define group belief. Concludes that individual rights are the product of conscience whereas the beliefs of an organization are the product of the collective will of its members.

39.   Note. "Financial Exigency As Cause For Termination of Tenured Faculty Members in Private Post Secondary Educational Institutions." *Iowa Law Review* 62 (1976-77): 481-521.

Analyzes termination of tenured faculty in light of contract law developed in litigation involving commercial contracts for lifetime employment. Suggests that a specific definition of financial exigency be stated and that procedure be established to make certain exigency decisions are based on sound educational considerations.

40.   Note: "Mandamus -- Courts will not Interfere with Discretions Exercised in Expelling Student on Ecclesiastical Grounds." *Fordham Law Review* 31 (1962): 215.

Reviews an older case where two students who were married in a civil ceremony were considered by the Roman Catholic Church to be guilty of a serious sin and a breach of canon law. Discusses the judiciary's upholding of student dismissals against a backdrop of issues such as application of constitutional definition of capricious and arbitrary conduct by a religious institution.

41.   Note. "Serving God or Caesar: Constitutional Limits on the Regulation of Religious Employers." *Missouri Law Review* 51 (1986): 779.

Considers the case of *Ohio Civil Rights Commission v. Dayton Christian Schools*, 106 S. ct. 2718 (1986) in light of Title VII as well as broader First Amendment concerns. Raises the salient issue whether the Title VII exemption for religious discrimination applies to gender discrimination on the basis of religion and whether the First Amendment's protection is equal to or broader than the Title VII exemption.

42.   Read, George E. "Origin and Impact of Government Regulations." *The Catholic Lawyer* 24 (Winter 1978): 232-35.

        Reviews the basic procedures in assisting regulatory agencies to produce regulations not harmful to religious organizations, from developing a good legislative history to establishing good contacts.

43.   Reynolds, Laurie. "Zoning The Church: The Police Power Versus The First Amendment." *Boston University Law Review* 64 (1984): 767-819.

        Concludes that zoning ordinances may exclude religious issues if adequate alternative sitting possibilities are provided and that judicial exemption of religious uses of land from religiously neutral land use regulation violates the establishment clause.

44.   Richardson, Elizabeth Cameron. "Applying Historic Preservation Ordinance to Church Property: Protecting the Past and Preserving the Constitution." *North Carolina Law Review* 63 (1984-85): 404-29.

        Analyzes the free exercise, establishment and due process problems that can arise when permission is sought by owners of buildings used for religious purposes and designated as historic landmarks to alter the buildings and the conflict that can result with local or state land use agencies.

45.   Sciarrino, Alfred J. "*United States v. Sun Myung Moon*: Precedent for Tax Fraud Prosecution of Local Pastors?" *Southern Illinois University Law Journal* 1984: 237-81.

        Reviews thoroughly the trial and appellate decisions and the arguments raised by the defendant and numerous *amici curiae*. Determines that the effect of Moon's criminal conviction was to disregard donor's intent under the law of trusts, to allow a jury to substitute its judgement of use of funds for the churches and to subject any religious organization where one person owns the religion or has a dominant role in its use to the possibility of IRS harassment. Raises the possibility that this case may affect church behavior if IRS enforcement of its regulations compels loss of some autonomy in church structure and spending practices by church leaders.

46.   Silverman, Debra A. "Defining The Limits of Free Exercise: The Religion Clause Defenses in *United States v. Moon*." *Hastings Const. Law Quarterly* 2 (1984-85): 515-28.

        Concurs with tax evasion conviction of Reverend Sun Myung Moon despite defendant's free exercise claim that church practice was to treat defendant as the church itself. Concludes that governmental interest in collecting revenue outweighs a church's right to allocate property however it chooses.

47.   Tewes, R. Scott. "Religion, Education and Government Regulation: Implications of *Bob Jones University v. United States* For Congressional Decisionmaking." *South Carolina Law Review* 34 (1982-83): 885-930.

        Discusses public policy arguments for denying tax exemption to racially segregated schools in light of the first, fifth and thirteenth amendments. Argues that denial of tax exemption would not further the state interest of eliminating discrimination; therefore such denial should be a violation of the free exercise clause.

48.   Warren, Alvin C., Jr., Thomas G. Kruttenmaker, and Lester B. Snyder. "Property Tax Exemptions for Charitable, Educational, Religious and Governmental Institutions in Connecticut." *Connecticut Law Review* 4 (1971): 181.

        Discusses an issue of vital importance to all religious institutions and that is the importance of state and local property tax exemptions. Considers against a background of constitutional issues the practical financial problems in one state where a significant portion of exempt property is owned by religious institutions, including colleges and seminaries. Concludes, at least in Connecticut, that lack of thoughtful analysis regarding a state tax exemption policy has resulted in inequitable decisions at local levels.

49.   West, Ellis M. "The Free Exercise and the Internal Revenue Code's Restrictions on the Political Activity of Tax-Exempt Organizations." *Wake Forest Law Review* 21 (1986): 395-429.

        Discusses problems that arise when religious organizations, which can include post secondary institutions, become actively involved in the political process. Analyzes the issues by explaining: the relevant Internal Revenue Code provisions; constitutional challenges in *Regan v. Taxation Without Representation* under free speech, right to assemble and right to petition clauses; likelihood of future free exercise clause protection and the possibility of constitutional exemption from the Code of religious groups but not for secular groups.

50.   Whelan, Charles M. "Origin and Impact of Government Regulations." *The Catholic Lawyer* 24 (Winter 1978): 228-31.

        Discusses the three fundamental arguments against government regulation of church affairs: church objection, constitutional objection, and public policy objection. Declares that no new applications of excessive entanglement be developed which decrease the church's contact with governmental agencies and political processes.

CHAPTER 2
BAPTIST SEMINARIES
Jerry M. Self

51.   Anderson, Park H. *New Orleans Baptist Theological Seminary: A Brief History.* New Orleans, LA: Bound mimeographed book, 1949.

         A sketch of the origin and development of the Baptist Bible Institute of New Orleans to the present institution the New Orleans Baptist Theological Seminary (1946), as a report to the Seminary's Historical Society in February.

52.   Aulick, Amos Lindsey. *B. H. Carroll: Promoter of Christian Education.* Fort Worth, TX: 1941. Typescript.

         This annual Founder's Day Address was given January 30, 1941.

53.   Baker, Robert Andrew. *Tell the Generations Following: A History of Southwestern Baptist Theological Seminary, 1908-1983.* Nashville, TN: Broadman Press, 1983.

         This 75th anniversary history by Dr. Robert A. Baker, Professor of Church History, Emeritus, is a thorough treatment of the history of Southwestern beginning with its roots at Baylor in Independence, Texas, in 1845.

54.   Barnhart, Joe Edward. *The Southern Baptist Holy War.* Austin, TX: Texas Monthly Press, 1986.

         Includes a brief mention of the Elliott controversy at Midwestern Seminary, seen from an unusual point of view.

55.   Beale, David O. *S.B.C.: House on the Sand?* Greenville, SC: Unusual Publications, 1985.

         Includes an eight-page chapter on Midwestern, focusing on certain persons associated with the seminary over the years.

56.   Blackburn, John Glenn. "The Years of Beginning -- an Evaluation, Luke 10:27; Founders Day Address, February 10, 1960." Southeastern Baptist Theological Seminary, 1960. Typescript.

Dr. Blackburn, pastor and chaplain of Wake Forest College, was an eye-witness to the early days when the college shared its campus with the new seminary in the town of Wake Forest, North Carolina, before the college moved in 1956 to Winston-Salem. Here he gives his impressions of the spirit and dreams of the first faculty and students as they began to arrive in 1951.

57.   Blackmore, James H. "Preparing Men to Match the Times." *The Baptist Program*, June 1969, pp. 14-15.

This capsule history of the campus from 1834 to 1968 by the Director of Public Relations concludes with statistics as the end of Southeastern Seminary's eighteenth year.

58.   Boone, Joseph P. *Founder's Day Address, March 14, 1955.* Fort Worth, TX: 1955. Typescript.

J. P. Boone traces the life of the Southwestern Seminary back to 1880 when B. H. Carroll first began theological lectures for ministerial students at Baylor.

59.   Bowen, Claud Ballard. "A Dream Come True: Founder's Day Address, February 12, 1959." Southeastern Baptist Theological Seminary, 1959. Typescript.

Dr. Bowen served as a member of the committee appointed in 1949 by the Southern Baptist Convention to study needs regarding theological education. He was also on the subcommittee to select a site for a seminary in the east. As such, his Founder's Day address brings first-person freshness to the specific facts involved in the Southeastern story from around 1949 until the opening in 1951.

60.   Bowman, Robert C. "Bible Teachers at Bethany -- Mentors and Models." *Brethren Life and Thought*, Winter 1983, pp. 49-56.

Surveys the Seminary's Bible teachers from its founding in 1905 to 1983, describing the unique characteristics of each one and their influence upon Bible teaching at Bethany.

61.   *A Brief History; Founders Day, February 16, 1961, Tenth Anniversary Year.* Wake Forest, NC: Southeastern Baptist Theological Seminary, 1961.

This pamphlet gives a year by year summary of major events during the Seminary's first ten years, including enrollment growth, additions to the faculty, developments in the library, and new constructions or renovations.

62.   Brown, Henry Clifton, Jr. and Charles Price Johnson, eds. *J. Howard Williams: Prophet of God and Friend of Man.* San Antonio, TX: The Naylor Company, 1963.

J. Howard Williams served as Southwestern's fourth president from 1953 until his sudden death in 1958. H. C. Brown, Professor of Preaching, and Charles Johnson, Seminary Librarian, compiled this tribute written by eleven friends of Dr. Williams.

63.   *The Bulletin of the Baptist Bible Institute, A Decade of History, 1917-1927.* New Orleans, LA: September 1927, p. 16.

Four articles dealing with the first ten years of the Institute's history and the status of the school at the beginning of the 1927-1928 session.

64.   *The Bulletin of the Baptist Bible Institute, Description and Historical Number.* New Orleans, LA: January 1929, p. 24.

Five articles discussing the progress of the school in the second five years and the status of the school in the 1928-29 session.

65.   *The Bulletin of the Baptist Bible Institute, Memorial and Historical Number.* New Orleans, LA: January 1929. p. 16.

A survey of the first five years of the institute, two memorials for Dr. E. Y. Mullins, and a listing of Bible Institute matters of concern by the president.

66.   *The Bulletin of the Baptist Bible Institute, Memorial Number.* New Orleans, LA: January 1933. p. 18.

Four memorials for Dr. Byron H. Decent, the first president, at his death, March 17, 1933.

67.   *The Bulletin of the Baptist Bible Institute, News and Historical Number.* New Orleans, LA: October 1928. p. 16.

A sketch of the Institute, a survey of the practical work department, and a report of the Institute in the fall of 1928.

68.   Burroughs, Prince Emanuel. "B. H. Carroll, The Greatest Teacher I Ever Knew." Southwestern Theological Seminary. 1935. Typescript.

This Founder's Day address was given on March 14, 1935, at Southwestern Seminary.

69.   Carroll, Benajah Harvey. "Our Seminary; or the Southwestern Baptist Theological Seminary, Fort Worth, TX." Southwestern Baptist Theological Seminary, 1954. Typescript.

B. H. Carroll, founding president of Southwestern, wrote numerous lectures, articles and appeals in the early days of the Seminary. These were compiled and arranged by Professor J. W. Crowder forty years after Carroll's death.

70.   Carroll, James Milton, et al. *Dr. B. H. Carroll, the Colossus of Baptist History, Pastor First Baptist Church, Waco, Texas, and First President of the S. W. B. T. Seminary, Fort Worth, Texas.* Complied and edited by J. W. Crowder. Fort Worth, TX: Seminary Hill Press, 1946.

    J. M. Carroll began this biography of his brother, but did not finish it before his own death in 1931. J. W. Crowder took Carroll's material and added a number of other articles. This is not a true biography.

71.   Cates, John Dee. "B. H. Carroll: The Man and His Ethics." Th.D. dissertation. Southwestern Baptist Theological Seminary, 1962.

    The first chapter of this Th.D. dissertation deals with Carroll's life and the formation of Southwestern Seminary.

72.   "Certain Facts Concerning the History of the Southwestern Baptist Theological Seminary." Southwestern Baptist Theological Seminary, 1934. Typescript.

    L. R. Scarborough wrote to L. R. Elliott, Seminary Librarian, that "these are the facts that I judge have not been published and would not be, but are vital and important in connection with certain incidents in the history of the seminary."

73.   Churchill, Ralph Dees. "History and Development of Southwestern's School of Religious Education to 1956." Southwestern Baptist Theological Seminary, 1956. Typescript.

    The school of Religious Education was begun as a department of the Seminary in 1915 by J. M. Price who was the guiding spirit for over forty years. Ralph Churchill, a student under Dr. Price as well as a faculty member from 1944-1970, wrote this history for his D.R.E. dissertation.

74.   Copass, Mrs. Benjamin Andrew. *Woman's Missionary Training School of the Southwestern Baptist Theological Seminary.* Fort Worth, TX: Southwestern Seminary, 1948.

    Mrs. Copass, wife of a member of the theological faculty, was prominent in Texas Baptist Woman's Missionary Union. Her history of the Woman's Missionary Training School begins with an earlier such school started by R. C. Buckner in Dallas around 1904.

75.   Crouch, W. Perry. *The Beginnings of Southeastern Seminary.* Wake Forest, NC: Southeastern Baptist Theological Seminary, 1951.

    Dr. Crouch chronicles, in this pamphlet, the growing realization for the need for an additional seminary for Southern Baptists and then highlights the committees, persons and decisions influential in the fulfillment of the plans at Southeastern in Wake Forest. Dr. Crouch was chairman of the committee to nominate the first president, Dr. Sydnor L. Stealey, who began work officially June 1, 1951, prior to the opening of the Seminary on September 11, 1951.

76.   Dana, Harvey Eugene. *Lee Rutland Scarborough: A Life of Service.* Nashville, TN: Broadman Press, 1942.

        This biography of the second president of Southwestern was written the year he retired after thirty-four years of association with the Seminary, including twenty-seven years as president. The introduction is by George W. Truett.

77.   Emrick, Ernestine Hoff. "The Bethany They Remember." *Brethren Life and Thought*, Summer 1966, pp. 4-36.

        Reminiscences of early students and faculty members in response to a questionnaire designed to obtain eyewitness accounts of Bethany's first twenty years. Not only wonderfully personal accounts of the sacrifices and dedication of the people, but also deep insights into the backgrounds from which they came and the surrounding city in which they involved themselves are presented.

78.   *Encyclopedia of Southern Baptists.* 4 vols. Nashville, TN: Broadman Press, 1958-1982.

        Contains articles on each of the six Southern Baptist Convention-affiliated seminaries as well as an article on the Criswell Center for Biblical Studies.

79.   Evans, Perry F. "Measure of the Man." Southwestern Baptist Theological Seminary, 1953. Typescript.

        This Founder's Day Address is about the founding president of Southwestern Seminary, B. H. Carroll, as were all the early Founder's Day addresses.

80.   Farrell, Frank. "Southern Baptist Crisis -- Climax Awaited." *Christianity Today*, April 26, 1963, pp. 30-32.

        Centers on the upcoming Southern Baptist Convention annual meeting, and the Elliott controversy at MBTS.

81.   Garrett, James Leo. "The Bible at Southwestern During Its Formative Years: A Study of H. E. Dana and W. T. Conner." Southwestern Baptist Theological Seminary, 1985. Typescript.

        Dr. Garrett, an outstanding theologian in his own right, chose as the topic for his March 7, 1985 Founder's Day address at Southwestern two of the early theological faculty at Southwestern: Dr. Dana and Dr. Conner who are considered today to be among the best theological minds Southern Baptists have produced.

82.   Graves, Harold K. *Into the Wind.* Nashville, TN: Broadman Press, 1983.

       Undoubtedly the definitive history of Golden Gate Seminary, this book was undertaken by the man who served the longest tenure as president of the Seminary, twenty-five years.

83.   Grijalva, Joshua. *A History of Mexican Baptists in Texas, 1881-1981.* Dallas, TX: Office of Language Mission, Baptist General Convention of Texas, in cooperation with the Mexican Baptist Convention of Texas, 1982.

       Includes information on the Hispanic Baptist Theological Seminary.

84.   Gustavus, A. C. *Late Developments in South Fort Worth and On Seminary Hill.* Fort Worth, TX: Southwestern Seminary, 1913.

       This early public relations leaflet shows the division of the land around Southwestern Seminary three years after the school moved to Fort Worth from Waco.

85.   Hefley, James C. *The Truth in Crisis: The Controversy in the Southern Baptist Convention. Updating the Controversy.* Hannibal, MO: Hannibal Books, 1987.

       Includes several pages which chronicle the controversy over the writing and teachings of MBTS professor G. Temp Sparkman.

86.   Hester, H. I. *The Founding of Midwestern Baptist Theological Seminary.* Kansas City, MO: Midwestern Baptist Theological Seminary, 1964.

       This little book covers the history of the seminary from 1953 (pre-Midwestern) to the time of publication.

87.   Houghton, George. "The Founding and Philosophy of Conservative Baptist Theological Seminary." B.D. thesis. Central Baptist Seminary, 1966.

88.   Kieffaber, Alan. "Peace Studies at Bethany Theological Seminary." *Brethren Life and Thought,* Winter 1978, pp. 45-46.

       A brief description of the graduate-level peace studies program and the outside influences which have shaped its development.

89.   Mexican Baptist Bible Institute. "San Antonio: The Institute." San Antonio, TX: Mexican Baptist Bible Institute, 1979.

       An institutional self-study of Mexican Baptist Bible Institute, San Antonio, Texas, prepared by joint efforts of faculty, students and trustees, submitted to the American Association of Bible

Colleges.

90.   *Modern School of the Prophets: A History of the Southwestern*
        Baptist Theological Seminary, A Product of Prayer and Faith, Its
        First Thirty Years, 1907-1937. Nashville, TN: Broadman Press,
        1939.

        This earliest history of Southwestern is seen through the eyes
        of L. R. Scarborough, president during many years of bitter
        theological controversy and economic depression.

91.   Mosteller, James D. "Something Old -- Something New: The First
        Fifty Years of Northern Baptist Theological Seminary."
        Foundations, January 1965, pp. 26-48.

        Traces the school's first fifty years from the standpoint of the
        historical influences which shaped it, excluding "the more pleasant
        and romantic aspects as well as personalities and limiting the
        material to the most important areas."

92.   Mueller, William A. *A History of Southern Baptist Theological*
        Seminary. Nashville, TN: Broadman Press, 1959.

        The comprehensive history on Southern Seminary.

93.   Mueller, William A. *The School of Providence and Prayer: A*
        History of the New Orleans Baptist Theological Seminary. New
        Orleans, LA: New Orleans Baptist Theological Seminary, 1969.

        A detailed history of the seminary from the first suggestion
        of the school in 1817 to its founding in 1917 as the Baptist Bible
        Institute of New Orleans, and a survey of its development up to
        1969, including detailed information on the first president and early
        professors.

94.   Newman, Stewart Albert. *W. T. Conner: Theologian of the*
        Southwest. Nashville, TN: Broadman Press, 1964.

        W. T. Conner taught theology at Southwestern from 1910 to
        1949. Stewart Newman studied under Conner and also taught at
        Southwestern from 1936 to 1952. Newman left the Seminary in
        1952, the same year Conner died.

95.   Pinson, William M., Jr., compiler. *An Approach to Christian*
        Ethics: The Life, Contribution, and Thought of T. B. Maston.
        Nashville, TN: Broadman Press, 1979.

        T. B. Maston taught at Southwestern from 1922 to 1963.
        This book is composed of numerous articles written by former
        students describing Maston's views on various subjects related to
        his life and work in the field of Christian ethics.

96.   Price, John Milburn, ed. *Southwestern Men and Their Messages.*

Kansas City, KS: Central Seminary Press, 1948.

Sermons and biographical sketches are included from Charles T. Ball, W. W. Barnes, B. H. Carroll, W. T. Conner, B. A. Copass, J. W. Crowder, J. B. Gambrell, A. H. Newmann, Jeff D. Ray, I. E. Reynolds, L. R. Scarborough and C. B. Williams, all of whom taught at Southwestern.

97.   Ray, Georgia Miller. *The Jeff Ray I Knew: A Pioneer Preacher in Texas*. Introduction by Dr. W. R. White. San Antonio, TX: The Naylor Company, 1952.

Jeff Ray taught at Southwestern from 1910 until 1944 when he was eighty-four years old. Georgia Miller Ray served as secretary to President L. R. Scarborough from 1915 to 1938 when she resigned to marry Dr. Ray.

98.   Ray, Jefferson Davis. *B. H. Carroll*. Nashville, TN: Sunday School Board of the Southern Baptist Convention, 1927.

Jeff Ray knew B. H. Carroll intimately for over thirty years, joining with many Texas Baptist promotions. Their final project was Southwestern Seminary. This biography is a first-hand chronicle of their enduring relationship.

99.   Ray, Jefferson Davis. "The First Faculty of the Seminary, Fortieth Anniversary, the Southwestern Baptist Theological Seminary." March 8, 1948. Southwestern Baptist Theological Seminary. Typescript.

Jeff Ray was associated with Southwestern from its beginning as a professor of preaching as well as a close friend of B. H. Carroll. His recollections give first-hand biographical information about the intellectual giants who were attracted to Southwestern.

100. Ray, Joel Dillard. "A Study of the Curriculum Development of the New Orleans Baptist Theological Seminary." Th.D. dissertation. New Orleans, LA: Baptist Theological Seminary, 1960.

A study of the curriculum of the Seminary and its development, including a survey of the history of the school describing the establishment of various departments.

101. Rice, John R., ed. *Southern Baptists Wake Up!: As Reproduced from America's Foremost Revival Weekly, The Sword of the Lord*. Murfreesboro, TN: Sword of the Lord, 1963.

Printed with a particular bias, it includes several copies of articles about MBTS throughout the book, mostly from the early sixties.

102. Routh, Eugene Coke. *Life Story of Dr. J. B. Gambrell*. Dallas, TX:

Baptist Book Store, 1929.

Dr. Gambrell, in addition to his duties as Executive Director of the Baptist General Convention of Texas, also taught at Southwestern from 1912 to 1914 and from 1917 until his death in 1921. One chapter in the biography deals with his years on the faculty.

103.   Sandusky, Fred. "Southeastern Seminary: Evaluation and Projection." Founder's Day Address, March 10, 1987. Southeastern Baptist Theological Seminary. Typescript.

Dr. Sandusky, retired registrar who served under the first three presidents, set the Seminary's beginnings in the broader context of the demographical and cultural shifts of of the 1940s as well as in response to visionary leaders of that area. He then gives the personal qualifications and contributions made by each of the three presidents. In closing, he contrasts the local, national, and world conditions of 1951 with those facing graduates in 1987.

104.   Scarborough, Lee Rutland. "Address to Faculty and Administrative Force." April 23, 1942. Southwestern Baptist Theological Seminary. Typescript.

This also includes an "Address to Student Body, April 24, 1942"; and "Address to Graduating Class and Exercises at Unveiling of Portrait of President Scarborough, Thirty-fifth Commencement, Friday, May 8, 1942"; and "A Brief Review of the Seminary and My Resignation." After the death of B. H. Carroll, L. R. Scarborough was President from 1915 to 1942.

105.   Schwalm, Vernon F. "Bethany Seminary and the Church." *Brethren Life and Thought*, Winter 1978, pp. 22-30.

Written on the occasion of the Seminary's fiftieth anniversary and reflecting upon the personalities of the early leaders who shaped Bethany and the ways in which Bethany has influenced the Church of the Brethren. Looks briefly at the religious atmosphere of America at the time of the anniversary celebration.

106.   *The Seminarian*, "Fortieth Anniversary, 1947-1987: 'A glorious past -- a brilliant future.'" September, 1987. Hispanic Baptist Theological Seminary.

107.   *Significant Events in the History of Southwestern Baptist Theological Seminary.* Southern Baptist Convention, Executive Committee, Nashville, TN: 1963. Mimeo.

This compilation of events is largely taken from reports of the Seminary in the Southern Baptist Convention Annuals and includes the years 1901 to 1960.

108.   Snyder, Graydon F. "Present Trends in Theological Education."

Brethren Life and Thought, Summer 1978, pp. 165-68.

A comparison of then-current trends in theological education in general with trends at Bethany Theological Seminary.

109.   "Southeastern Seminary Reflects on 10 Years Work." *Charity and Children,* December 1960, pp. 1-3.

Several feature articles and contemporary pictures accompany the lead story highlighting events of the founding and first ten years of the Seminary.

110.   Southwestern Baptist Theological Seminary. *Newspaper Clippings, Programs, Brochures about the Seminary.* 16 vols. Fort Worth, TX: 1932-1960. Scrapbooks.

L. R. Elliott, Southwestern Librarian for thirty-eight years, began these scrapbooks in the 1930s to preserve articles and programs. The sixteen volumes serve as the nucleus of the Seminary's historical materials.

111.   *Southwestern Evangel.* Fort Worth, TX: Southwestern Baptist Theological Seminary, 1924-1931.

This monthly publication was a merger of the earlier Southwestern Journal of Theology and the Seminary "Clip Sheet." It contained scholarly articles by the faculty as well as general news items about the seminary family. It became a victim of the depression in 1931.

112.   *Southwestern Journal of Theology.* Fort Worth, TX: Southwestern Baptist Theological Seminary, 1917-1924 and since 1958.

Articles by and about Southwestern faculty as well as other writers are included in this journal.

113.   *Ten Men from Baylor.* Kansas City, KS: Central Seminary Press, 1945.

Biographical essays about Benajah Harvey Carroll and Lee Rutland Scarborough, men who were prominent in the history of Southwestern Seminary, are included in this collection.

114.   Tull, James E. "Southeastern Seminary -- Whence? What? Whither? Founder's Day Address, March 10, 1981." Wake Forest, NC: Southeastern Baptist Theological Seminary. Typescript.

Summarizing briefly the facts about its early founding, Theology Professor Dr. Tull then describes the "Southeastern Dream," which he feels gives the school its unique character. He enlarges upon his understanding of what a theological seminary is and how he thinks Southeastern has endeavored to be such a school. A closing section deals with the ominous threat of radical inerrancy.

115.   Von Berge, Herman. "Our School of the Prophets." In *Those Glorious Years*, 64-69. By Charles F. Zumach. Cleveland, OH: Roger Williams Press, 1942.

        Deals with the North American Baptist General Conference. Contains chapters or parts covering North American Seminary history.

116.   Wagner, Murray L., Jr., ed. *Brethren Life and Thought*, Winter 1980.

        A collection of essays by faculty members prepared on the occasion of the Seminary's seventy-fifth anniversary. Rather than accounts of the history and achievements, the essays reflect on the anniversary theme, "For the Work of Ministry."

117.   Walker, Arthur L., ed. *Directory of Southern Baptist Colleges and Schools, 1987-88*. Nashville, TN: Education Commission of the Southern Baptist Convention, 1987.

        Includes a short history, a description of the school facts, which would be of interest to prospective students.

118.   Wayland, John T. "True to the Dream: Founder's Day Address, March 15, 1988." Wake Forest, NC: Southeastern Baptist Theological Seminary, 1988.

        Emeritus Professor of Christian Education, Dr. Wayland recognizes the importance of the seedbed of conditions and ideas extending back to the formation of the Southern Baptist Convention in 1845. He then traces the line of "apostolic succession" in spirit and scholarship of Southern Seminary's presidents and professors and how this influence was felt by Southeastern's future leaders. Dr. Wayland taught under each of Southeastern's presidents and portrays how their special abilities suited them for the tasks necessary for leading the seminary at that period of time.

119.   Williams, Charles B. *B. H. Carroll: The Titanic Interpreter and Teacher of Truth*. Lakeland, FL: n.d. Typescript.

        C. B. Williams was one of the original faculty members of Southwestern when it was established in Waco. He taught from 1908-1919. Though he left Southwestern, his admiration for its founder never diminished.

120.   Williams, Lucinda Beckley. *Golden Years: An Autobiography*. Edited by J. B. Cranfill. Dallas, TX: Baptist Standard Publishing Company, 1921.

        In her later years, Mrs. Williams helped raise $50,000 to

build the Woman's Missionary Training School building at Southwestern Seminary with the girls to be in charge of campus beautification and social graces.

121.   Woyke, Frank H. *Heritage and Ministry of the North American Baptist Conference.* Oakbrook Terrace, IL: North American Baptist Conference, 1979 (pp. 247-248; 330-350; 411-427).

The North American Seminary began under the aegis of the America Baptist Convention as a German Ethnic department in 1852, emerged a separate entity in 1874 and moved into the American pluralistic, cultural stream in the mid-1950s; its documentary history in bibliographical context is bilingual. This book deals in part with the Seminary's history.

122.   Young, Warren C. *Commit What You Have Heard: A History of Northern Baptist Theological Seminary, 1913-1988.* Wheaton, IL: Harold Shaw Publications, 1988.

Showing the comprehensive history of the Seminary published in its seventy-fifth year.

CHAPTER 3
CATHOLIC SEMINARIES
Mary A. Grant

123.   Arbuckle, Gerald A. "Seminary Formation as a Pilgrimage." *Human Development* 7 (Spring 1986): 27-33.

Describes a model of formation called the "pilgrimage" model explaining it in the light of two types of culture, societas in which there is role differentiation and liminal which is undifferentiated. Points out that the Second Vatican Council challenged the Church to enter into a dialogue with the world, and that theological education is growth in Christian living and ministry which is best achieved through action and reflection on Church and society.

124.   Baars, Conrad W. "Your Seminary Right or Wrong?" *Homiletic and Pastoral Review* 82 (January 1982): 57-61.

Relates the decline in priestly vocations to the abandonment of philosophical anthropology within the seminary curricula, and its replacement with psychologies of the secular humanists. Looks at the vocation overflow in Poland and cites Father Francis Lescoe (*Philosophy Serving Contemporary Needs of the Church: The Experience of Poland*) who believes that American seminaries must begin with a re-organization of the philosophical components of the seminarian's education, if theological training is to improve.

125.   Bauer, Francis C. "Admission to Diaconate, Seminary, or Consecrated Life After Annulment." *The Jurist* 44 (No. 2, 1984): 441-44.

Explains the principle that the degree of maturity and psychological competence required for the sacrament of holy orders is no less required for the sacrament of matrimony. Describes the psychological grounds on which an annulment is usually granted but cautions that an individual whose marriage was declared null and void by the Church on such grounds, should not be ruled out automatically from becoming a candidate for the priesthood. Exhorts special care be taken in the psychological screening process of a prospective candidate for the seminary who has received a Church annulment.

126.   Baum, William W. "The State of U.S. Free-Standing Seminaries." *Origins*, October 16, 1986, pp. 313-25.

Report to the United States Bishops by Cardinal Baum on each of the thirty-eight "free-standing" post-college seminaries examined in the first phase of study of United States seminaries mandated by Pope John Paul II in June 1981. Discusses seminary leadership, admission and evaluation of seminaries, older vocations, spiritual and liturgical formation, theological dissent, celibacy, non-seminarians in seminary classes, and pastoral formation.

127.   Baumer, Fred. "Communication in Seminary Education." *Seminary News*, December 1982, pp. 3-6.

Attempts to bring about an awareness of the teaching of communication theory and process in seminary education. Expresses concern for the lack of media literacy, the need to clarify philosophy of communication, and the need to develop the knowledge and skills necessary for expressing the theological content learned in the classroom.

128.   Bernardin, Joseph L. "Challenges and Changes: The Education and Formation of Priests." *The Priest*, March 1985, pp. 11-14.

Exhorts those at St. John's Seminary in Boston, as they celebrate the Seminary's centennial, to meet the changing needs of the Church at the end of this century. Reflects on specific challenges -- priests as teachers, shepherds, healers and reconcilers, and as men of prayer.

129.   Burghardt, Walter J. "Priestly Preparation and Academic Excellence." *Seminaries in Dialogue*, September 1987, pp. 1-9.

Addresses the assertion that unless the majority of Catholic seminarians cultivate intelligence in depth and with seriousness, there is risk of losing the educated Catholic laity who comprise the masses. Explains the kind of cultural climate and human situation the newly ordained priest will encounter, the intellectual life of the seminarian and priest, and the specific contribution the Catholic priest can offer.

130.   Carbine, Francis A. "The College Seminary: Creative Response to a Pastoral Need." *Dimension*, Winter 1977, pp. 164-69.

Finds that too many Catholic college seminarians enter the seminary lacking an awareness of the Church's tradition in doctrine and devotion. Describes the development of courses at St. Charles Seminary to foster an appreciation for Catholic tradition in matters of faith, conscience and morality, loyalty to authentic teaching authority, and liturgy and worship.

131.   Center for Applied Research in the Apostolate (CARA). "A Commentary on Seminary Priesthood Enrollment Statistics for 1988 -- Part I." *Seminary Forum*, Autumn and Winter 1987, pp. 1-16.

Provides the 1988 enrollment statistics of priesthood students in Roman Catholic high school, college, and theological seminaries in the United States. Notes the pattern of decline, presents reasons for the decline and cites the effect on specific schools. Sees concern but not pessimism on the part of seminary college rectors.

132.   Center for Applied Research in the Apostolate (CARA). "The Future of the Seminary College -- Part I." *Seminary Forum*, Summer 1983, pp. 1-8.

"The Future of the Seminary College -- Part II." *Seminary Forum*, Autumn 1983, pp. 1-8.

Presents the results of a study on the future of the seminary college in the United States. Gives in Part I, the responses and comments of college seminary and theologate rectors concerning a six year preparation period for the priesthood with non-seminary college education. Indicates that they do not see a shift to a six year theology program as either probable or desirable. Gives responses to the questions: Can the seminary colleges survive? What will be their role in the future? Provides no definite answer to the first question; however, the rectors of collaborative seminary colleges believe the collaborative type has a definite future. Predicts the role of the seminary college in the future will remain the same.

133.   Center for Applied Research in the Apostolate (CARA). "A Success Story: Seminary College Cooperative Venture." *Seminary Forum*, Autumn and Winter 1984, pp. 1-2.

Researches the collaboration between the Capuchin Province of St. Augustine and Diocese of Cleveland to close the Capuchin seminary college of St. Fidelis in Herman, Pennsylvania, and transfer the Capuchin students and faculty members to the Borromeo College of Ohio. Explains the origin, work and results of the Capuchin Select Committee, the basic philosophy and contractual terms, the advantages, areas of concern, and the reasons for the success of the collaboration.

134.   Ciuba, Edward J. "The Impact of Changing Ecclesiological and Christological Models on Roman Catholic Seminary Education." *Theological Education* 24 (Autumn 1987): 57-72.

Explains how the ecclesiological model of the Church flows out of the underlying image of Jesus Christ and gives an historical development of the Christological and Ecclesiological models of the Church before Vatican II. Provides insight into the implications for Catholic seminary education today because of the underlying models of the Church and different images of Jesus Christ since Vatican II.

135.   Coleman, John A. "Critical Evaluation of American Culture and

Its Consequences for Theological Education." *Seminaries in Dialogue*, October 1986, pp. 8-13.

Defines theology of culture and a methodology for listening to a culture in order to hear Christ already present. Demonstrates three key elements in a theology of culture as the gospel, the church and culture with the gospel and church interacting within the culture. Notes that the mission of the Church is to preach the gospel in the language the hearer will hear and that a genuine Christian identity grows out of a theology of culture. Asks where in the seminary curriculum are the sociological and anthropological tools, as well as the pastoral tools for understanding a theology of culture, and for identifying the key elements of American culture.

136.   Congregation for Catholic Education. "Circular Letter Concerning Some of the More Urgent Aspects of Spiritual Formation in Seminaries." *Origins*, March 6, 1980, pp. 610-19.

Reflects on the spiritual formation of seminarians set forth in a Vatican Circular Letter of January 6, 1980, distributed to the bishops of the world. Discusses priests and self-denial and obedience; and the seminary as a school of devotion to the Mother of God.

137.   Conners, Quinn R.   "Seminary to Parish Transition: Role Adjustment in the Early Years." *Human Development* 6 (Summer 1985): 37-39.

Discusses the results of a study conducted in 1982 to determine if the seminary training of young clergy relates to their future work, if seminary performance predicts performance in the full-time role of minister, and if the presence of a supervisor in the early years reduces the conflict of those years. Recommends supervision for the young priest as a source of support and continuing development, the evaluation of placement procedures, and continuing education and skills development programs.

138.   Costello, Timothy J.   "Psychological Evaluation of Vocations: Human Rights and Responsibilities Evoke Ethical Conflicts." *Human Development* 6 (Winter 1985): 37-42.

Addresses the moral questions encompassing the use of psychology within the context of seminary and religious formation. Explains how psychological assessment can help to focus on personality dimensions: religious and personal ideals, actual attitudes and behaviors, and underlying motivations. Discusses guidelines to help respect candidate's right to privacy within the context of seminary or religious formation.

139.   Cox, Joseph Godfrey.   "The Administration of Seminaries: Historical Synopsis and Commentary." J.C.D. dissertation. The Catholic University of America, 1931.

Surveys clerical education from the first centuries of the
Church to the Council of Trent in 1563 when the Tridentine decree
ordaining the establishment of seminaries and outlining their
organization was drafted. Gives the full text of the decree which
marked the beginning of a new era in clerical education. Discusses
legislation on seminary education after the Council, and the new
Code of Canon Law legislation based on the Tridentine decree
including aspects of episcopal jurisdiction and seminary officials.

140.   D'Arcy, Paul F. and Eugene C. Kennedy. *The Genius of the
         Apostolate: Personal Growth in the Candidate, the Seminarian and
         the Priest.* New York: Sheed and Ward, 1965.

         Applies the insights of the priest-psychologist to the different
phases of religious vocational development. Underlines the concept
that full personal growth comes from within and discusses the
process of growth and maturity at each level of a vocation to the
priesthood emphasizing the person and life as a process.

141.   Deck, Allan Figueroa. "Hispanic Vocations: 'What Happens Once
         You Have Them'?" *Seminaries in Dialogue*, April 1986, pp. 11-15.

         Discusses some of the issues impacting on vocations to the
diocesan priesthood, particularly on Hispanic-American vocations.
Addresses the areas of recruitment and processing, personal and
spiritual formation, and recognizes the acculturation dynamic
working both ways.

142.   Dudziak, Paul M. "The Marginalization of Associate Pastors: Some
         Implications for Seminaries." *The Jurist* 43 (No. 1, 1983): 199-213.

         Studies the effects of the emergence of ministries in many
parishes on the structure of ministry, the place of the associate
pastor, and the training of seminarians. Demonstrates the forms
of organization within a parish and the changing system of ministry.
Suggests that seminary education include new pastor training
programs developed in communication with experienced pastors
and with a new emphasis on working within groups.

143.   Eddy, William A. "Value Systems and the High School Seminary."
         Seminary News, February 1985, pp. 3-6.

         Emphasizes the importance of the minor seminary in today's
society as an "oasis" in which young men can perceive and discern
a call from God in their lives. Focuses on the need to encourage
and sustain minority vocations since an increasing number of
students are coming from minority families. Discusses the open
value system of today's youth and the necessity to assess and
understand the strengths and weaknesses of both closed and open
value systems.

144.   Ellis, John Tracy. *Essays in Seminary Education*. Notre Dame, IN: Fides Publishers, 1967.

Brings together in one volume the author's writings which appeared in other forms. Includes: The Apostolic Age of Trent; From Trent to the 1960s; Diocesan Theological Seminaries in the Middle West, 1811-1889; The Seminary in the Shadow of Vatican Council II; The Seminary Today; and The Priest as Intellectual.

145.   Fischer, James, ed. "Lay and Ordained Ministry Training and Today's Seminaries." *Seminaries in Dialogue*, February 1985, pp. 1-8.

Reflects on Church and ministry according to the ecclesiology expressed by the Second Vatican Council discussing the role of the local church and lay ministry, and the local church and priestly ministry. Maintains that the seminary should work in collaboration with the local church and be willing to lend its resources.

146.   Fisher, Eugene J. *Seminary Education and Christian-Jewish Relations: a Curriculum and Resource Handbook*. Washington DC: The National Catholic Educational Association, 1983.

Advocates the integration of insights, attitudes and understandings of Jewish-Christian relations derived from dialogue and scholarship, into the existing Catholic seminary curriculum. Suggests means of achieving this integration within the academic areas, as well as spiritual formation and field education.

147.   Golden, Paul L., ed. "Formation in Priestly Celibacy for Today's Church." *Seminaries in Dialogue*, April 1983, pp. 2-8.

Discusses in Part I celibacy in the Church today and shares reflections that are considered effective and helpful. Sets forth in Part II the principles for formation in celibacy indicating the seminary must be a supportive environment, the students must have information on the intellectual and affective level, and the Church has the responsibility to determine the candidates who evidence the ability to live a celibate life.

148.   Grace, James P. "The College Seminary, An Anachronism: A Rector's Response." *Seminaries in Dialogue*, February 1985, pp. 19-21.

Believes there is a strong case to be made for the college seminary and discusses the contemporary scene of the 1980s. Expresses the need for todays' seminarian to have a strong philosophical background in the tradition, as well as in contemporary thought. Recognizes the need for a well-developed formation program to foster personal growth and formation in Catholic ideals and values.

149.   Gray, Howard J. "Sexual Education for Celibacy: Policy as Direction and Decision." *Seminaries in Dialogue*, November 1983, pp. 4-7.

States that celibacy is a discipline, that it is important theologically and sociologically to give better justification and communication of this discipline in the Catholic seminary formation program. Makes observations concerning the educational environment, the direction of a public policy and the making of a policy decision to promote sound education in celibacy.

150.   Grindel, John. "Different Expectations of Priests, Different Kinds of Training." *Origins*, August 18, 1983, pp. 187-94.

Summarizes the *Program of Priestly Formation*, and raises questions and challenges concerning present-day seminary programs. Analyzes the ways different models of the Church influence the seminary in the conception of the priesthood, and recognizes the pressures resulting from preparing men for the priesthood based on the traditional model while responding to the demands of different models of the Church since Vatican II.

151.   Gurrieri, John A. "Liturgy as the Integrating Force in the Seminary Program." *Seminaries in Dialogue*, April 1984, pp. 1-5.

Explains that liturgy integrates Christian life and spirituality, that a priest is ordained primarily to preside over the community through sacramental rites, and that there can not be a real understanding of the Church's faith without relating it to the Church's prayer. Discusses the rite of ordination, the function of the presbyter and instruction on liturgical formation.

152.   Halligan, Nicholas. "Statement on Education in Canon Law For Future Ministers of the Church in the United States." *The Jurist* 42 (No. 1, 1982): 196-99.

Gives the text of a statement adopted by the Annual Convention of the Canon Law Society of America on October 15, 1981 in Chicago, Illinois. Expresses concern about the inadequacy of education in Canon Law provided in Catholic seminaries and theologates in the United States. Makes recommendations for a more adequate preparation for future priests in Canon Law.

153.   Hemrick, Eugene F. "The American Catholic Culture and Its Challenge to Priesthood." *Seminary News*, September 1987, pp. 7-11.

Explores the culture of today's more independent and assertive American Catholic and discusses the type of priest needed to challenge the laity with thoughts of renewal and improvement. Reiterates the meaning of the priesthood and its ministry as defined by the third Synod of Bishops in Rome in 1971. Urges an emphasis in seminary education on philosophy that challenges thinking powers, philosophy in concert with social sciences.

154.   Hemrick, Eugene F. and Dean R. Hoge. *Seminarians in Theology: A National Profile.* Washington DC: United States Catholic Conference, 1986.

Provides the results of a survey prepared by the Office of Research of the U.S. Catholic Conference and conducted by E. Hemrick and D. Hoge. Gathered data from a questionnaire sent to fifty-three United States seminaries which consisted of three parts: 1) the profile of seminarians; 2) various influences on the decision to choose priesthood; 3) a seminarian's vision about ministry and about himself as a priest. Includes commentaries by Thomas J. Murphy, John A. Grindel, and John E. Haag.

155.   Hines, Mary, and Mary Irving. "Women, A Significant Contribution to the Seminary Theological Program." *Seminary News*, February 1984, pp. 2-4.

Presents two topics on women in the seminary program: 1) The Perspective of the Woman as Teacher by Sister Mary Hines and 2) Women in Seminary Formation Programs by Sister Mary Irving. Explains the positive effects of women on formation teams and women as spiritual directors. Notes the powerful sign to seminarians of the value of women in the Church.

156.   Hoge, Dean R. *Future of Catholic Leadership: Responses to the Priest Shortage.* New York: Sheed and Ward, 1987.

Summarizes three years of research on the priest shortage and reviews related work by other researchers and observers. Discusses the reasonableness of six assumptions derived from previous research and on which the present research is based. Includes in these assumptions: 1) the vocation shortage is long term; 2) the American Church is moving rapidly from an immigrant to mainstream middle class culture; 3) the shortage of priests is an institutional, not a spiritual problem. Concludes that there are eleven options for response to the priest shortage, two of which are rated as having a high impact: ordaining married as well as celibate men and expanding and developing lay ministries.

157.   Hoge, Dean R., Raymond H. Potvin and Kathleen M. Ferry. *Research on Men's Vocations to the Priesthood and the Religious Life.* Washington DC: United States Catholic Conference, 1984.

Summarizes all the studies conducted in the United States on vocations to the priesthood and finds that there is a lack of scientific research concerning the present status of priestly vocations. Identifies the questions that have been asked: What are the trends in vocations? Are there trends in the characteristics of seminarians? What factors facilitate vocations? Evaluates research needs and includes commentaries by three Catholic theologians, Joseph A. Komonchak, Richard P. McBrien, and Philip J. Murnion.

158.   Kavanagh, Charles M. "The High School Seminarian -- Different Understandings, Different Needs, Different Development." *Seminaries in Dialogue*, April 1982, pp. 9-12.

Discusses how today's Catholic high school students have a different attitude and understanding of the Church than those who grew up in the Church prior to Vatican II. Notes the different understandings of vocation and priesthood, and therefore, of seminary. Reaffirms the importance of the high school seminary today, not as a seminary, but seen by students as "...preparing someone for the seminary."

159.   Keller, James and Richard Armstrong, eds. *Apostolic Renewal in the Seminary In the Light of Vatican Council II.* New York: The Christophers, 1965.

Comprises the papers of twenty-one Catholic scholars such as Avery Dulles, Bernard Haering, and Bernard J. Cooke, given at the second Christopher Study Week of July 20-24, 1964. Includes the conclusions of the first and second Christopher weeks which related to the formation of seminarians.

160.   Kennedy, Leonard A. "The Seminarian and Thomist Philosophy." *Homiletic and Pastoral Review* 87 (January 1987): 20-26.

Comments on four points: 1) A seminarian needs philosophy; 2) The argument for philosophy is for sound philosophy; 3) The argument for sound philosophy is for Christian philosophy; and 4) The argument for Christian philosophy is for Thomist philosophy. Believes that more time than is recommended by the American Bishops must be devoted to philosophy in the seminary. Deplores the state of philosophy in most Catholic colleges and universities in the United States and comments that many seminarians study in these institutions.

161.   Krosnicki, Thomas A. and John A. Gurrieri. "Seminary Liturgy Revisited." *Worship* 54 (March 1980): 158-69.

Interprets the instruction on Liturgical Formation in Seminaries from the Congregation on Education underscoring the relationship between liturgy and the doctrine of faith and the special importance this has in the correct liturgical formation of future priests. Sees the Document as a directive of highest importance shaping worship in the life of the seminarians according to the norms of the Church; they then will be ready to help shape the worship life of the parishes to which they will be assigned.

162.   Lee, James Michael and Louis J. Putz, eds. *Seminary Education in*

a Time of Change. Notre Dame, IN: Fides Publishers, 1965.

Comprises a volume of seventeen scholarly essays in which nationally recognized authorities in their fields consider the basic elements of seminary education in the light of the new spirit of *aggiornamento* infused by Vatican Council II. Looks at the preparation of young men for the pastoral ministry in the modern world.

163.   Mackin, Kevin E. "The Seminary College, An Anachronism? Are Theologates Really Concerned For Seminary Colleges or Will the Former Go It Alone?" *Seminaries in Dialogue*, Feburary 1985, pp. 14-18.

Raises questions about the idea of a seminary in general, and about seminary college enrollments and finances. Speaks of the free-standing seminary college, the collaborative seminary college and pre-theology programs. Concludes that free-standing seminary colleges are in danger of becoming extinct, but believes that young men should have the option of a college seminary. Says that the college seminaries serve as "feeder schools" to the theologates and they must convince bishops and others of the purpose for their existence.

164.   Mahoney, Gerard M. "The Academic Curriculum in Minor Seminaries." J.C.D. dissertation. The Catholic University of America, 1965.

Explains and interprets according to canon law the content and methodology of academic studies in the Catholic minor seminary just after Vatican Council II. Gives an historical summation of the clerical training of young men from Apostolic origins to the American minor seminary legislation of the Councils of Baltimore in 1868 and 1884. Provides a commentary on canonical law, religious discipline, the study of Latin, Greek, and modern languages, as well as on the modern standards of minor seminary education.

165.   Marshall, John A. "The American Seminary Today: Its Present State and Its Future Hopes." *Seminaries in Dialogue*, March 1988, pp. 1-11.

Addresses the question of how to make the priesthood and message of Christ relevant in a rapidly changing technological world. Discusses what was accomplished by the visitations of the Catholic seminaries in the United States during the present papal study. Treats of areas which need study and improvement: teaching of theology, pastoral programs of field education, non-ordained faculty, non-seminarians in the classroom, community life, Ordinaries and seminary direction.

166.   McDonnell, James. "The Integration of Communication in Priestly

34   Religious Seminaries in America

Formation." *Seminary News*, December 1985, pp. 3-7.

Claims that the area of communication in the seminary consists mainly of carefully designed courses in skills and techniques that will be used in preparing and delivering homilies. Contends that communication is broader in scope, and as a process of sharing and dialogue within the seminary community, plays an important role in integrating academic and spiritual education with pastoral practice.

167.   Mexican-American Cultural Center and The Saint Meinrad School of Theology. *Ministry Among Hispanic Americans: Report of a Cooperative Program in Preparing Seminarians for Ministry.* St. Meinrad, IN: Saint Meinrad School of Theology, 1980.

Explains the origin and development of the MACC-Saint Meinrad program which was a response to meet the needs of the Hispanic-American population. Gives a description and evaluation of this experimental project designed to educate seminarians for ministry in the Hispanic-American community. Includes an analytical overview of the Hispanic socio-human situation in the United States and presents reflections on a survey of Hispanic priests in the United States.

168.   Midwest Seminary Rectors. "Reflections on Current Research in Theological Education." *Seminaries in Dialogue*, March 1987, pp. 1-9.

Reflects on the research studies of Potvin, *Seminarians of the Eighties: A National Survey*; and Hemrick, *Seminarians in Theology; A National Profile.* Discusses the concern regarding the experience of transition from seminary to priestly life, the implications for formation programs and admissions, and the concern for an active recruitment program that identifies and nurtures quality candidates for the priesthood.

169.   Mitchell, Nathan. "Liturgical Education in Roman Catholic Seminaries: A Report and an Appraisal." *Worship* 54 (March 1980): 129-57.

Reviews issues that were raised about liturgy in seminaries as a result of the *The CARA Report 1974*, a survey about the teaching and celebration of liturgy in Catholic seminaries. Concludes that the quality of liturgical instruction is improving steadily, that contemporary students are cautious in matters of piety and doctrine, and psychological and cultural environment factors affect their ability to engage fully in liturgical worship.

170.   Morris, William Stephen. "The Seminary Movement in the United States: Projects, Foundations, and Early Development 1833-1866." Ph.D. dissertation. The Catholic University of America, 1932.

Describes the seminary movement in the United States
between 1833 and the Civil War and the efforts of the Catholic
Bishops to establish seminaries that would lay the foundations of a
native clergy.

171.   Murnion, Philip J. "Demands and Styles of Parish Ministry:
        Implications for Seminary Programs." *Seminaries in Dialogue*,
        November 1983, pp. 10-14.

        Asserts that the demands of parish ministry have to be
turned into objectives of seminary formation. Discusses the factors
that are related to the people's satisfaction with parish life, and the
styles of parish leadership. Points out the common elements to each
style and draws the implications for active ministry as well as for
the kinds of programs implemented in Catholic seminaries.

172.   Murphy, Charles M. "What Excellence in Seminary Education
        Requires Today." *Seminaries in Dialogue*, March 1988, pp. 20-23.

        Explains the nature of the ministerial priesthood and urges
a sound theological education as a requirement for formation of
excellence. Points out that sound theology strengthens spirituality,
and that pastoral practice requires constant theological reflection if
it is not to become mindless activism.

173.   Murphy, Thomas J. "College Seminaries: Do They Have a Future?"
        Seminary News, May 1987, pp. 3-8.

        Reflects on the issues facing college seminaries: the purpose
and mission of a college seminary, the importance of challenging
young men to consider a vocation to the priesthood, and the
obligation of the Christian community to foster vocations to the
priesthood and religious life. Believes that college seminaries have
a future and every means possible must be used to realize that
future.

174.   Murphy, Thomas J. "Forces Shaping the Future of Seminaries."
        Origins, February 25, 1988, pp. 637-40.

        Analyzes present realities within the Church and the
seminary and within the Church and society. States the need for
seminaries to articulate a theology of priesthood and discusses three
trends that will impact on seminary programs: a) the changing
profile of the parish; b) the changing resources for parish staffing;
and c) the change in parish status and leadership structures.

175.   Murphy, Thomas J. "The Quality of Candidates for the
        Priesthood." *Origins*, August 18, 1983, pp. 131, 183-86.

        Describes the societal influences on young men who
contemplate entering the priesthood, as well as personal factors and
those in the life of the Church that have a bearing on the quality

of candidates for the priesthood.   Explains that the quality of candidates is a priority for the Church of today and tomorrow, and that there is a need to bridge the ideal and the reality of the variables and questions raised.

176.   National Catholic Educational Association.   "The Black Seminarian." *Seminary News*, September 1983, pp. 3-6.

Contains four papers that were presented at the NCEA Annual Convention, April 7, 1983.   Includes: Some Expectations of the Church Concerning the Seminary and Seminarians by Most Rev. E.A. Marino; Commitment for the Black Seminarian by C. Harvin; Attracting and Educating Black Seminarians: A Personal Perspective by Bro. W. Bonnam; and The Black Seminarian: Culture and Person, a Key to the Formation Program by Rev. E. Branch.

177.   National Catholic Educational Association.   *Seminaries and Psychology*. Washington DC: NCEA, 1978.

Gives the six major presentations of a workshop presented in July 1977 by the Seminary Department of NCEA.   Includes: Psychological Testing by K. J. Pierre; How to Use a Consulting Psychologist by P. D. Cristantiello; Use of Testing and Evaluation for Religious Communities by W. C. Wester II and E. R. Miller; Confidentiality: A Dual Responsibility by W. C. Wester II; Seminary Counseling: Five Dilemmas to Consider by P. D. Cristantiello; and The Seminary As a Psychologically Healthy Atmosphere by K. J. Pierre.

178.   National Conference of Catholic Bishops. *Liturgical Formation in Seminaries: A Commentary*.   Washington DC: United States Catholic Conference, 1984.

Explains the scope and significance of the document from the Congregation for Catholic Education, *Instruction on Liturgical Formation in Seminaries*.   Delineates the liturgical life and the teaching of the sacred liturgy in Catholic seminaries in the United States.

179.   National Conference of Catholic Bishops. *Pastoral Formation and Pastoral Field Education in the Catholic Seminary*.   Washington DC: United States Catholic Conference, 1985.

Offers guidelines for the pastoral activity entered into by the seminarian with emphasis on pastoral field education.   Discusses how pastoral field education is developed in tandem with spiritual-theological development.   Explains the standards for the position of director and recognizes the need of pastoral formation for nonpriesthood students at schools of theology who are preparing for a pastoral mission within the Church.

180.   National Conference of Catholic Bishops. *The Program of Priestly Formation*. 3rd ed. Washington DC: United States Catholic Conference, 1982.

Contains the official guidelines for all types of Catholic Seminaries in the United States. Directs priestly formation in relationship to all the documents of the Second Vatican Council, the *Ratio Fundamentalis Institutionis Sacerdotalis*, and documents published by the Sacred Congregation for Catholic Education during the previous ten years.

181.   National Conference of Catholic Bishops. *Spiritual Formation in the Catholic Seminary*. Washington DC: United States Catholic Conference, 1984.

Explores the development of a theological-spiritual vision for the diocesan priestly ministry reflecting on assumptions concerning the growth of individuals, the formation program, the seminary and its sense of connections with the Church and world. Discusses the program of formation at St. Mary of the Lake Seminary in Mundelein, Illinois.

182.   O'Donnell, George E. *St Charles Seminary Philadelphia: A History of the Theological Seminary of Saint Charles Borromeo, Overbrook, Philadelphia, Pennsylvania, 1832-1964, With a Chronological Record of Ordination and Pictures of the Living Alumni*. Philadelphia, PA: The American Catholic Historical Society, St. Charles Seminary, 1964.

Narrates the development of Saint Charles Seminary under the direction of the different Ordinaries of Philadelphia including St. John Nepomucene Neumann, fourth Bishop of Philadelphia. Features the paintings, statues and the shrines at Overbrook.

183.   Perrault, Joseph. "What Do We Mean When We Use the Term 'Formation'?" *The Priest*, January 1982, pp. 18-20.

Understands the concept of priestly formation as a journey of formation involving primary and secondary levels. Sees the candidate for the priesthood as primarily responsible for his own formation and the role of the formator in the seminary as being co-present with God in the development of the life of the seminarian.

184.   Potvin, Raymond H. *Seminarians of the Eighties: A National Survey*. Washington DC: National Catholic Educational Association, 1985.

Researches the questions: Why is there a shortage of young men entering Catholic seminaries or theologates? and Why do some seminarians leave the seminary? Presents data received from a questionnaire survey of 916 seminarians from fifty-three Catholic seminaries in the United States. Compares the data with the findings of a 1966-67 study (Potvin and Suziedelis. *Seminarians of the Sixties*).

185. Ramirez, Ricardo. "The Challenge for Seminaries of the U.S. Bishops' Pastoral Letter on Hispanic Ministry." *Seminaries in Dialogue*, November 1984, pp. 2-5.

Reflects on the Vatican II principles in the pastoral letter on Hispanic ministry and discusses ideas and recommendations for meeting the challenge of Hispanic candidates and culture in American seminaries.

186. Ryan, John Henry. "The Teaching of Oral Interpretation in Roman Catholic Seminaries in the United States," Ph.D. dissertation. University of Missouri-Columbia, 1973.

Analyzes the data obtained from a questionnaire study of 128 seminaries concerning the extent of the training of candidates to the Catholic priesthood in the art of oral interpretation, the nature of the training, and any recommendations for improvement of the training. Indicates a strong orientation to the development of speech skills. Presents data obtained from a survey of priests who advise seminarians to prepare well in attitude and behavior for interpretative responsibilities at liturgical functions.

187. Scanlon, Arthur J. *St Joseph's Seminary Dunwoodie, New York 1896-1921; With an Account of the Other Seminaries of New York.* New York: The United States Catholic Historical Society, 1922.

Chronicles the history of the attempts to establish a seminary in the diocese of New York beginning in 1836 and commemorates the twenty-fifth anniversary of the final foundation of St. Joseph's Seminary at Dunwoodie.

188. Schoenherr, Richard A. and Annemette Sorensen. "Social Change in Religious Organizations: Consequences of Clergy Decline in the U.S. Catholic Church." *Sociological Analysis* 43 (Spring 1982): 23-52.

Focuses on the structural changes occurring in the Catholic Church following Vatican II. Demonstrates the demographic transition of the Catholic Church and the altering of the age and normative structures of the Church because of the decline of the priest population. Concludes that some elements in the political economy of the dioceses will change but others will be reproduced, as will the traditional structures of power as the demographic transition of U.S. dioceses "runs its course."

189. Schreiter, Robert J. "Fragmentation and Unity in Theological Education: A Roman Catholic Response to Edward Farley's *Theologia*." *Seminaries in Dialogue*, May 1985, pp. 2-11.

Identifies some of the distinctive historical causes that have
shaped Roman Catholic theological education in the United States
and demonstrates how these factors contributed to Farley's critique
of theological education. Comments on Farley's thesis that the
causes of ills of contemporary theological education are rooted in
history, that theological study has moved from sapiential knowledge
to a dispersal into independent disciplines related to the practice of
ministry. Discusses the implications for theological education of the
meaning of professionalism, the multiplication of courses directed
by a social science methodology, and the integration of field
education and practical disciplines into the curricula.

190.   Schuler, Richard J. "Gregorian Chant and Latin in the
        Seminaries." *Sacred Music* 107 (Spring 1980): 3-5.

        Decries the decline of use of Latin in the Church and
explains the negative effects to Christian culture, theological
development and liturgical growth. Emphasizes the norms for
liturgical formation for seminaries as issued by the Sacred
Congregation for Catholic Education.

191.   Shelton, Charles. "The Impact of American Culture on the Young
        Person Trying to Discern a Priestly Vocation." *Seminaries in
        Dialogue*, March 1987, pp. 10-16.

        Explores how young people form their values. Describes
these values and the social factors in American culture which
influence the discernment of a priestly vocation. Discusses the
different types of candidates for the priesthood and suggests
possible ways to assist young people in exploring existing tensions
as they discern their call to the priesthood.

192.   Smith, John Talbot. *The Training of a Priest; An Essay on Clerical
        Education With a Reply to the Critics.* New York: Longmans,
        Green and Co., 1908.

        Advocates and defends at the turn of the century, new
methods and standards for clerical education in Catholic American
Seminaries. Introduces the work with an essay by Bishop Bernard
McQuaid who founded St. Bernard Seminary in 1893, "a
well-ordered American seminary."

193.   Sweeney, Richard J. "The R.C.I.A. As a Model For Seminary
        Formation." *Seminaries in Dialogue*, November 1984, pp. 11-15.

        Reviews the components of the *Rite of Christian Initiation
of Adults* promulgated by the Sacred Congregation for Divine
Worship in 1972, and explains how the underlying principles of
Christian formation of RCIA have been applied to the formation
program at Mt. St. Mary's Seminary of the West.

194.   Vanasse, Roman R. "Educating Seminarians for Ministry in an
        Emerging World Church." *Seminary News*, September 1985, pp.
        5-8.

        Describes the development of the Church into a "global
        village." Suggests that a global theology is appropriate for the
        post-industrial society in which most of today's seminarians will
        function and advocates the pursuance of studies with a global or
        world perspective.

195.   Weisgerber, Charles A. *Testing the Seminarian: A Review of
        Research.* Washington DC: Center for Applied Research in the
        Apostolate (CARA), 1977.

        Reports the research finding of tests used for screening
        Catholic minor seminarians and applicants to male religious orders
        beginning in 1931. Discusses the data for different psychological
        instruments which are designed to establish the level of adjustment,
        maturity and motivation of the candidate.

196.   White, Joseph M. "American Diocesan Seminaries, 1791 to the
        1980's." *Seminaries in Dialogue*, April 1986, pp. 16-19.

        Narrates a brief history of the American Catholic diocesan
        seminary from the first foundation at St. Mary's Seminary in
        Baltimore in 1791 under the direction of the Sulpician priests who
        left France during the French Revolution, to the period after
        Vatican II. Demonstrates the change in priestly formation from the
        clerical state to preparation for ministry.

197.   White, Joseph M. "St. John's Seminary and the Transition of
        American Catholic Seminaries, 1884-1910." *Seminaries in
        Dialogue*, November 1984, pp. 6-10.

        Contains a brief history of the formation years of St. John's
        Seminary in Boston and reflects on the development of American
        Diocesan seminaries during this time as a period of transition
        bridging the missionary phase of the American Catholic Church
        and the Catholicism of the decades prior to the second Vatican
        Council.

198.   Wuerl, Donald W. "Academic Freedom and Priestly Formation."
        Seminaries in Dialogue, March 1988, pp. 12-19.

        Discusses academic freedom according to secular terms and
        as defined in the traditional models of academic freedom which
        underline the distinction between philosophy and theology.
        Explains the roles of Revelation and Magisterium and the role of
        scholarship and the theologian in the Church. Affirms that there
        is no inherent conflict between the exercise of freedom in
        scholarship and priestly formation.

CHAPTER 4
CHRISTIAN CHURCH (DISCIPLES OF CHRIST) SEMINARIES
John M. Imbler

Seminaries and Divinity Schools

199.   Barron, Jack. "The Early Years of Phillips University: 1906-1912." M.A. thesis. Phillips University, 1943.

200.   Bennett, Anita Cole. "Phillips University: A Survey of the Aims and Purposes." M.A. thesis. Phillips University, 1949.

201.   Fey, Harold Edward. *Ministerial Education at Christian Theological Seminary.* Indianapolis, IN: Christian Theological Seminary, 1964.

202.   Fowler, Newton, B. "LTS as a Graduate Professional School." *Lexington Theological Quarterly* 13 (October 1978): 125-28.

203.   Hale, Evelyn Faye. "The Formation of Christian Theological Seminary." Unpublished typescript, Christian Theological Seminary, 1962.

204.   Hall, Colby D. *A History of Texas Christian University.* Fort Worth, TX: Texas Christian University Press, 1947.

205.   Marshall, Frank and Martin Powell. *Phillips University's First Fifty Years.* 3 vols. Enid, OK: Phillips University Press, 1957-67.

206.   Moore, Jerome A. *Texas Christian University: A Hundred Years of History.* Fort Worth, TX: Texas Christian University Press, 1974.

207.   Osborn, Ronald E. "Education for Ministry: Heritage and Contribution." *CTS Bulletin* 14 (November 1973): 3-13.

208.   Pope, R. M. "College of the Bible." *College of the Bible Quarterly* 38 (April 1961): 4-27.

209.   Powell, Wilfred Evans. "The Mystic Harmony: The Story of the Windows in the Marshall Building, Phillips University." Enid, OK: Phillips University, 1978. (Pamphlet).

210.   Shaw, Henry King. "The Founding of Butler University, 1847-1855." N.p. 1962. (Reprinted from *Indiana Magazine of History*, September 1962.)

211.   Stevenson, Dwight E. "College of the Bible Idea." *College of the Bible Quarterly* 40 (January 1963): 5-9.

212.   Stevenson, Dwight E. *Lexington Theological Seminary: 1865-1965*. St. Louis, MO: Bethany Press, 1974.

ESSAY

The current network of Disciples theological schools began as departments of religion, then evolved into graduate divisions of Disciples colleges. Disciples seminaries and divinity schools did not actually realize autonomy until the 1950s, even though they encouraged the recognition of professional ministerial credentials in the 1920s and were instrumental in the formation of the American Association of Theological Schools in the late 1930s which established a process for standardized accreditation. As a result the histories of most seminaries are contained in the histories of the colleges with which they were affiliated. The exception is Dwight Stevenson's outstanding book on Lexington Theological Seminary written for that school's centennial. It is noteworthy, however, that Colby Hall's analysis of Texas Christian University and Frank Marshall's three volumes on Phillips University explain in detail the interrelatedness of the liberal arts colleges and the Bible colleges.

Toward the fulfillment of degree requirements, a few graduate students at Phillips University have written enlightening theses on specific aspects of their school. Additional contributions to the body of literature have accrued through faculty lectures, particularly at Lexington and Christian Theological Seminary, which were later published in local journals. Catalogs, minutes of board of trustees, and newsletters offer the best information on growth and academic trends but are often difficult to obtain apart from school archives.

Divinity Houses and Seminary Foundations

213.   Arnold, Charles Harvey. "A Religion that Walks the Earth: Edward Scribner Ames and the Chicago School of Theology." *Encounter* 30 (Fall 1969): 314-39.

214.   Blakemore, William Barnett. *Quest for Intelligence in Ministry: The Story of the First Seventy-Five Years of the Disciples Divinity House of the University of Chicago*. Chicago: The Disciples Divinity House of the University of Chicago, 1970.

215.   Browning, Don S. "The Disciples Divinity House and the University." *Criterion* 17 (Autumn 1978): 4-7.

216.   Conkin, Paul Keith. *Gone with the Ivy: A Biography of Vanderbilt University*. Knoxville, TN: University of Tennessee Press, 1985.

217.   Cummins, D. Duane. "From Buffalo to Claremont." *Impact: Disciples of Christ on the Pacific Slope* 11 (1983): 5-13.

218.   McGraw, Robert A. *A Brief History of Vanderbilt University: 1972-1982*. Nashville: Vanderbilt University, 1983.

219.   Reisinger, Donald D. and Ronald E. Osborn. "20th Anniversary
         Celebration." *Impact: Disciples of Christ on the Pacific Slope* 5
         (Special edition, 1980): 1-37.

220.   Storr, Richard J. *Harper's University: the Beginning. A History of
         the University of Chicago*. Chicago, IL: University of Chicago
         Press, 1966.

221.   Thompson, Bard. *Vanderbilt Divinity School: A History*.
         Nashville, TN: Vanderbilt University, 1958.

ESSAY

The Christian Church (Disciples of Christ) pioneered in the
establishment of divinity houses. In cooperation with the divinity schools at
the University of Chicago (1894), Vanderbilt University (1941), and the
School of Theology at Claremont (1960), these denominational houses on
ecumenical campuses offer Disciples students residential facilities, field
education assistance, collegial support groups, and financial aid in addition to
providing polity orientation. Because the houses are so well integrated into
the divinity schools, their importance is best reflected through the broader
institutional histories. Few individual histories have been published, the most
notable being *Quest for Intelligence in Ministry* by William Barnett Blakemore
and "The Disciples Divinity House and the University" by Don S. Browning,
both former deans of the house at the University of Chicago. Duane
Cummins' published lecture on the Disciples Seminary Foundation and the
special anniversary edition of *Impact* edited by Donald Reisinger and Ronald
Osborn offer special insights into the nature of Disciples theological education
on the Pacific Slope.

Denominational Resources

222.   Boren, Carter E. *Religion on the Texas Frontier*. San Antonio, TX:
         The Naylor Company, 1968.

223.   Cotten, Carroll C. *The Imperative is Leadership*. St. Louis, MO:
         The Bethany Press, 1973.

224.   England, Stephen J. *Oklahoma Christians*. St. Louis, MO:
         Bethany Press, 1975. (Printed for the Christian Church in
         Oklahoma.)

225.   Fortune, Alonzo Willard. *The Disciples of Kentucky*. Lexington,
         KY: The Convention of the Christian Churches in Kentucky, 1932.

226.   Garrison, Winfred E. and Alfred T. DeGroot. *The Disciples of
         Christ: A History*. St. Louis, MO: Christian Board of Publication,
         1948.

227.   Hall, Colby D. *Texas Disciples*. Fort Worth, TX: TCU Press,
         1953.

228.   Haynes, Nathaniel S. *History of the Disciples of Christ in Illinois:
         1819-1914*. Cincinnati, OH: The Standard Publishing Company,

1915 (especially pp. 57-58).

229.   Imbler, John M. "By Degrees: The Development of Theological
        Education Within the Christian Church (Disciples of Christ)."
        STM thesis. Christian Theological Seminary, 1981.

230.   Montgomery, Riley B. *The Education of Ministers of Disciples of
        Christ.* St. Louis, MO: The Bethany Press, 1931.

231.   Norton, Herman A. *Tennessee Christians: A History of the
        Christian Church (Disciples of Christ) in Tennessee.* Nashville, TN:
        Reed, 1971.

232.   Osborn, Ronald E. *The Education of Ministers for the Coming
        Age.* St. Louis, MO: CBP Press, 1987.

233.   Schroeder, Oliver C., Jr., et al. "Seminary Study Group Report to
        the General Board of the Christian Church (Disciples of Christ)."
        Indianapolis, IN: Task Group report, 1978. Typescript.

234.   Shaw, Henry King. *Hoosier Disciples.* St. Louis, MO: Bethany
        Press, 1966.

235.   Tucker, William E. and Lester G. McAllister. *Journey in Faith: A
        History of the Christian Church (Disciples of Christ).* St. Louis,
        MO: The Bethany Press, 1975.

ESSAY

Denominational resources often provide the best descriptions of
theological education because of the unique covenantal relationship between
the Christian Church (Disciples of Christ) and its seminaries.   Most
prominent are regional histories which detail the histories of the schools in
relation to the ethos of the Christian Church in specific geographic areas.
Herman Norton, retired dean of the Disciples Divinity House at Vanderbilt;
Colby Hall, dean of Brite College of the Bible then dean of Texas Christian
University for twenty years; Henry Shaw, former librarian at Christian
Theological Seminary; and Stephen England, dean emeritus at Phillips College
of the Bible, carefully integrate the growth of the educational institutions with
the progress of the regional churches.
    General denominational studies have focused on theological education
in the context of the ministry for the total church. Riley Montgomery's *The
Education of Ministers* assesses pre-seminary days when theological studies
were under the aegis of the colleges and prescribes courses desirable for
graduate study.   Carroll Cotten's more recent *The Imperative is Leadership*,
commissioned by the General Board of the Christian Church (Disciplines of
Christ) in 1969, contains numerous demographic charts and tables plus
recommendations on ministerial preparation to which the church is still
responding.   The 1978 "Seminary Study Group Report to the General Board
of the Christian Church (Disciples of Christ)" follows Cotten's work with an
in depth analysis of the seven institutions affiliated with the Christian Church
particularly addressing student recruitment, church relations, curricular
offerings, and financial support.   In his 1987 volume, *The Education of*

Ministers for the Coming Age, Ronald Osborn reviews the changing nature of Christian ministry in a changing social order and suggests models for the education of Disciples ministers, lay and ordained, into the year 2000. John Imbler's thesis on the development of Disciples theological education, from 1865 to 1945, is the only comparative history of that network to date.

Biographies

236. Ames, Van Meter, ed. *Beyond Theology: The Autobiography of Edward Scribner Ames.* Chicago, IL: University of Chicago Press, 1959.

237. Bower, William Clayton. *Through the Years: Personal Memoirs.* Lexington, KY: Transylvania College Press, 1957.

238. Fortune, Alonzo Willard. *Thinking Things Through with E. E. Snoddy.* St. Louis, MO: Bethany Press, 1940.

239. Goodspeed, Thomas Wakefield. *William Rainey Harper, First President of the University of Chicago.* Chicago, IL: University of Chicago Press, 1928.

240. McAllister, Lester G. *Z. T. Sweeney: Preacher and Peacemaker.* St. Louis, MO: Christian Board of Publication, 1968.

241. McGarvey, John W. *The Autobiography of J. W. McGarvey.* Lexington, KY: The College of the Bible, 1960.

242. Morro, W. C. *Brother McGarvey: The Life of President J. W. McGarvey of the College of the Bible, Lexington, Kentucky.* St. Louis, MO: The Bethany Press, 1940.

243. Osborn, Ronald E. *Ely Vaughn Zollars: Teacher of Preachers, Builder of Colleges.* St. Louis, MO: Christian Board of Publications, 1947.

244. Pierson, Roscoe M., ed. *To Do and To Teach: Essays in Honor of Charles Lynn Pyatt.* Lexington, KY: The College of the Bible, 1953.

245. Reisinger, Donald D., ed. *A Living Witness to Oikodome: Essays in Honor of Ronald E. Osborn.* Claremont, CA: Disciples Seminary Foundation, 1982.

246. Tucker, William E. *J. H. Garrison and Disciples of Christ.* St. Louis, MO: The Bethany Press, 1964.

247. Williamson, Clark M., ed. "The Mind of a Faculty: Essays Presented to Beauford A. Norris." *Encounter* 34 (Autumn 1973): 271-386.

248. Williamson, Clark M., ed. "The Witness of a Faculty: Essays Presented to T. J. Liggett." *Encounter* 48 (Winter 1987): 1-161.

ESSAY

The most interesting and readable institutional stories are found in the biographies of people who brought those institutions into being and maintained them. The divinity house at the University of Chicago is well served by the biographical accounts of house dean (1927-1945) Edward Scribner Ames, first university president William Rainey Harper, and editorial advocate J. H. Garrison. Christian Theological Seminary is depicted in the life story of prime mover and benefactor Z. T. Sweeney, as is Lexington Theological Seminary through E. E. Snoddy, professor of Christian doctrine and practical theology, and J. W. McGarvey, first a professor then president. Ronald Osborn's excellent study of Ely Vaughn Zollars captures his educational philosophy and influence on the College of the Bible as founder and president of Phillips University as well as his brief service as president of Texas Christian University.

Festschrifts introduce a different cast of characters acquainting readers with schools' faculties and friends. While neither precisely biography nor history, they reflect feelings and add dimensions which cannot be detected in other types of writings.

CHAPTER 5
CHURCH OF THE BRETHREN SEMINARIES
Kenneth M. Shaffer, Jr.

The Brethren are a group of Protestant denominations which trace their origins back to eight people in Schwarzenau, Germany, in 1708. The eight people, three women and five men, sought to live according to the principles of the New Testament, both in their individual lives and in their community life. In their search they were greatly influenced by Pietism and Anabaptism. By 1750 most of the early Brethren had moved from Europe to colonial America. Over the next one hundred fifty years, the Brethren spread across America as far as the West Coast. During the 1880s major divisions occurred with a more conservative group and a more liberal group each leaving the main body. Today there are five major groups of Brethren -- Brethren Church, Church of the Brethren, Dunkard Brethren, Fellowship of Grace Brethren Churches, and Old German Baptist Brethren.

Three of the Brethren groups have seminaries. These include Ashland Theological Seminary, related to the Brethren Church; Bethany Theological Seminary, supported by the Church of the Brethren; and Grace Theological Seminary, related to the Fellowship of Grace Brethren Churches. The following bibliography of Brethren seminaries is representative, not comprehensive.

249.   Beher, Linda. "The Bethany That Eludes the Catalog." *Messenger*, June 1972, pp. 15-17.

        Summarizes conversations with twenty-five Bethany students concerning their experiences at Bethany. The areas covered include directions, diversities, disappointments, and challenges.

250.   Bowman, Robert C. "Bible Teachers at Bethany -- Mentors and Models." *Brethren Life and Thought*, Winter 1983, pp. 49-56.

        Provides vignettes, as well as background information, about the men and women who have taught Bible courses at Bethany. In conclusion, the author notes the similarities and differences of these teachers over the years.

251.   *The Brethren Encyclopedia*, 1983. S.v. "Ashland Theological Seminary," by Joseph R. Schultz.

        Summaries briefly the history of the seminary from its beginnings as a seminary department of Ashland College in 1906 to 1982, by which time it had developed into a graduate-level seminary with 436 students on a separate campus in Ashland, Ohio, with extensions in Akron, Canton, and Cleveland.

252.   *The Brethren Encyclopedia*, 1983. S.v. "Bethany Theological Seminary," by Murray L. Wagner, Jr.

Summarizes the history of the seminary from its beginning in Chicago as a Bible school in 1905 to 1980, by which time it was located on a suburban campus near Oak Brook, Illinois. Special attention is given to each of Bethany's six presidents.

253.   *The Brethren Encyclopedia*, 1983. S.v. "Grace Schools (Grace Theological Seminary, Grace College)," by Homer A. Kent.

Outlines the history of Grace from the time of its establishment as a seminary separate from Ashland Theological Seminary in 1937 up to 1980 when the student body totaled 429. Included also in the entry is a brief history of Grace College (1948), which has the same president and board of trustees as the seminary.

254.   Emrick, Ernestine Hoff. "The Bethany They Remember." *Brethren Life and Thought*, Summer 1966, pp. 4-36.

Presents personal recollections about life at Bethany during the first twenty years of its existence. These recollections are taken from questionnaires which were sent to one hundred thirty-three persons connected with the seminary during its early years.

255.   Emrick, Ernestine Hoff. "Bethany's Beginnings: A Sixtieth Anniversary Recollection of Bethany Seminary's Exciting First Twenty Years." *Messenger*, September 30, 1965, pp. 2-9.

Examines events leading up to the founding of Bethany and the problems faced by the school during its first twenty years. Several photographs are included.

256.   Garber, Merlin E. "The Clergy Crisis." *Brethren Life and Thought*, Winter 1970, pp. 33-42.

Presents the theory that the problem with pastors in the Church of the Brethren is the training they receive in seminary. In particular, pastors are being trained to defend the faith intellectually, instead of being trained to proclaim it.

257.   Groff, Warren F. "Bethany: Place of Learning, Center of Mission." *Messenger*, June 1972, pp. 11-14.

Answers questions posed to Warren Groff, the Bethany dean, concerning Bethany's objectives, its relationship to the church, and recent developments in its approach to theological education.

258.   Hanle, Robert V. "Bethany Bible School." In "A History of Higher

Education Among the German Baptist Brethren: 1708-1908," pp. 273-80. Ph.D dissertation. University of of Pennsylvania, 1974.

Reviews the developments in the church that led to the founding of Bethany. This author gives particular attention to the reactions among Brethren to the new school, especially their objectives.

259. Hoff, Ernest G. *Emmanuel B. Hoff: Bible Teacher.* Elgin, IL: Brethren Publishing House, 1943.

Biography of one of Bethany's founders. This biography was written by Hoff's eldest son.

260. Hoyt, Herman A. "The Academic History of Grace Theological Seminary." In *Charis* (1951 Yearbook of Grace Theological Seminary), 40-47.

Outlines the development of theological education beginning at Ashland in 1930 and continuing at Grace up through the early 1950s. Special attention is given to those who taught at Grace over the years.

261. Hoyt, Herman A. "The Collegiate Divisions and the New Th.B. Degree." *The Brethren Missionary Hearld*, August 28, 1948, pp. 753-54.

Presents the reasons for the creation of the two-year collegiate division at Grace Theological Seminary in 1948. This collegiate division eventually developed into Grace College.

262. Hoyt, Herman A. "Dr. L. S. Bauman and Brethren Theological Education." *The Brethren Missionary Herald*, January 6, 1951, pp. 21-22.

Describes Bauman's involvement at Ashland College and the seminary and the part he played in the founding of Grace Theological Seminary. This article is part of the Louis S. Bauman memorial number of *The Brethren Missionary Herald*, which was published shortly after his death. Included in the memorial number are articles about his life and memorial tributes.

263. "Jubilee Year, Ashland Theological Seminary, 1930-1980." *The Brethren Evangelist*, January 1981, pp. 12-17.

Presents several short articles commemorating the first fifty years of the seminary. Included are articles by Joseph R. Shultz, the president, and Charles R. Munson, the acting dean.

264. Kent, Homer A. "Grace Theological Seminary Is Born 1937." In *Conquering Frontiers: A History of the Brethren Church (The National Fellowship of Brethren Churches)*, rev. ed., pp. 150-59. Winona Lake, IN: BMH Books, 1972.

Presents the events surrounding the founding of Grace Theological Seminary in 1937. Initially the seminary was located in the Ellet Brethren Church of Akron, Ohio, but in 1939 it moved to Winona Lake, Indiana.

265.   Kieffaber, Alan. "Peace Studies at Bethany Theological Seminary." *Brethren Life and Thought*, Winter 1978, pp. 45-46.

Describes briefly Bethany's participation in a peace studies graduate program in cooperation with Associated Mennonite Bible Seminaries and Earlham School of Religion.

266.   Lehman, James H. "Bethany: Equipping the Saints... and Others." *Messenger*, July 1980, pp. 18-21.

Reviews briefly the history of Bethany. The article is based on the script of a slide/tape production which was prepared by the author for Bethany.

267.   Lehman, James H. "For the Training of Christian Workers." In *Beyond Anything Foreseen: A Study of the History of Higher Education in the Church of the Brethren*, 50-54. Richmond, IN: Prepared for the Conference on Higher Education and the Church of the Brethren, 1976.

Places the founding of Bethany within the larger context of the development in institutions of higher education among the Brethren. Particularly interesting is the conclusion that because of the Brethren concern for right practice, Bethany stressed clinical experience before it was popular in theological education.

268.   Martin, Dennis. "Ashland College Versus Ashland Seminary (1921-1937): Prelude to Schism." *Brethren Life and Thought*, Winter 1976, pp. 37-50.

Traces the events at Ashland College over a twenty-year period that sparked the division within the Brethren Church which led to the formation of Grace Theological Seminary (1940). In 1976 the National Fellowship of Brethren Churches changed its official name to Fellowship of Grace Brethren Churches.

269.   Martin-Adkins, Ron. "The Peace Witness of Bethany Bible School During World War I." *Brethren Life and Thought*, Spring 1980, pp. 83-90.

Discusses how Bethany represented the Brethren peace position after the war began in 1914. While the school had not prepared in advance for such witness, it managed to present the peace tradition to its students, the church, and government officials.

270.   McClain, Alva J. "The Background and Origin of Grace Theological Seminary." In *Charis* (1951 Yearbook of Grace

Theological Seminary), 9-39.

Reviews the events leading up to the location of Grace at Winona Lake in 1939. Of particular interest is the discussion of the proposal to form a seminary in southern California in 1929.

271.   Reber, Daniel Herbert. "The Religious Practical Work of Bethany Biblical Seminary." B.S.L. thesis. Bethany Biblical Seminary, 1937.

Presents opportunities for and value of practical work done by Bethany students in the city of Chicago. It is the writer's understanding that that A.C. Wieand wanted to locate the school in a large city because of the possibilities for practical work.

272.   Ronk, Albert T. "College and Seminary." In *History of the Brethren Church*, pp. 484-90. Ashland, OH: Brethren Publishing Company, 1968.

Outlines developments at Ashland Theological Seminary (and college) from 1940 through 1968. Of particular note is the fact that in the 1950s the seminary moved from the college campus to the John C. Myers estate in Ashland, Ohio.

273.   Schwalm, Vernon F. *Albert Cassell Wieand*. Elgin, IL: Brethren Publishing House, 1960.

Biography of one of Bethany's founders. Wieand was also the first president of the school.

274.   Schwalm, Vernon F. "Bethany Seminary and the Church." *Brethren Life and Thought*, Spring 1956, pp. 22-30.

Presents four ideas which gave shape to Bethany and contrasts these ideas with religious developments in the United States during the 1950s. The author also comments on various Bethany leaders and how they contributed to the seminary during its first fifty years.

275.   Sharp, S. Z. "History of Bethany Bible School." In *Education History of the Church of the Brethren*, pp. 274-302. Elgin, IL: Brethren Publishing House, 1923.

Includes details about the founding of the seminary and information about the curriculum during the first fifteen years. Particular attention is given to the relationship of the Bethany to the Church of the Brethren.

276.   Snyder, Graydon F. "Present Trends in Theological Education." *Brethren Life and Thought*, Summer 1978, pp. 165-68.

Reviews developments in theological education during the 1970s and describes how these have been expressed at Bethany.

The developments included are theological education as ecclesiology, parish-based education, women in theological education, and extension and continuing education.

277.   Stoffer, Dale Rupert. "The Background and Course of the Brethren-Fundamentalist Controversy (1920-1939)." In "The Background and Development of Thought and Practice in the German Baptist Brethren (Dunker) and the Brethren (Progressive) Churches (c. 1650-1979)," pp. 680-739. Ph.D. dissertation. Fuller Theological Seminary, 1980.

Analyzes in depth the events and theological debate leading up to the schism in the Brethren Church and the founding of Grace Theological Seminary.

278.   Wagner, Murray L., Jr., ed. *Brethren Life and Thought*, Winter 1980.

Presents a collection of essays prepared on the occasion of the seminary's seventy-fifth anniversary. The essays are reflections by faculty members on the anniversary theme, "for the work of ministry."

CHAPTER 6
EPISCOPAL SEMINARIES
David S. Armentrout

Introduction

During the colonial period one had to return to England for theological education or read for orders with a clergyman. At different times in the Eighteenth Century, the College of William and Mary had professors of divinity, but never really developed a theological school. Around 1813 the Fairfield Academy in Herkimer County, New York, operated as a "Divinity School."

In 1804 the eighth General Convention adopted a "Course of Ecclesiastical Studies," which was a list of books for those reading for orders. This "Course" remained unchanged until 1892, and was the backbone of most of the curricula for Episcopal theological seminaries during most of the nineteenth century.

As a national entity, the Episcopal Church has started only one theological seminary, the General Theological Seminary in New York City. The twelfth General Convention, May 20-27, 1817, meeting at New York adopted a resolution creating the General Theological Seminary. It was named General because it was created by the General Convention. The 1820 General Convention voted to move it to New Haven where it opened on September 13, 1820. The first special General Convention of 1821 voted to move it back to New York and it opened there on February 13, 1822.

After the establishment of General Seminary, numerous seminaries were established by dioceses, bishops and clergy. The eleven accredited seminaries today are: General (1817), Virginia Theological Seminary, Alexandria (1823), Bexley Hall, Rochester, New York (1824), Nashotah House, Nashotah, Wisconsin (1842), Berkeley Divinity School, New Haven (1854), Seabury-Western Theological Seminary, Evanston, Illinois (1858), Episcopal Divinity School, Cambridge (1867), School of Theology, University of the South, Sewanee, Tennessee (1878), Church Divinity School of the Pacific, Berkeley, California (1893), Episcopal Theological Seminary of the Southwest, Austin (1951), and Trinity Episcopal School for Ministry, Ambridge, Pennsylvania (1976).

Throughout most of its history the Episcopal church did not have a national program of theological education and had no board or commission to coordinate programs and planning. In 1940 the General Convention established the Standing Joint Commission on Theological Education to study the needs and trends of theological education in the Church. The 1967 General Convention established the Board for Theological Education with a full-time director. The directors have been the Rev. Almus Thorp, Sr. (1969-1977), Dr. Fredrica Thompsett (1977-1984), and the Rev. Preston T.

Kelsey, II (1984-).

Sources

The three primary sources for the history of theological education in the Episcopal Church are the catalogues and papers of the individual seminaries, the annual journals of the diocesan conventions, and the journals of General Convention. The most important periodical sources are the *Historical Magazine of the Protestant Episcopal Church* (quarterly, 1932-), which with the March 1987 issue changed its title to *Anglican and Episcopal History, Forth* (1940-1960), *The Episcopalian* (1960-), *The Living Church* (1978-), and *The Witness* (1922-).

Acknowledgements

Two individuals assisted greatly in the preparation of this bibliography. Sue Armentrout, head of the Interlibrary Loan Department of the Du Pont Library, University of the South, secured numerous documents not available at the Du Pont Library. Mr. Robert Furniss, senior seminarian at the School of Theology and a candidate from the Diocese of Chicago, has been my research assistant for three years, and helped to locate much of the material. To both I express my deepest appreciation. Finally, I wish to thank the Reverend Professor John Booty for reading the bibliography and making helpful suggestions.

Outline

The bibliography is divided into five parts. The first part treats the journals of the General Convention. Part two contains general articles on theological education and Episcopal seminaries. The third part treats the eleven accredited Episcopal seminaries. Part four treats the seminaries that are no longer in existence. Part five treats the diocesan training schools.

Part I. Journals of the General Convention of the Protestant Episcopal Church, 1785-1985.

These are the primary documents for theological education in the Episcopal Church. Each year with a reference to theological education will be noted and annotated. *1789* (July-August), Canon 8, pp. 59-60 in the volume for 1785-1814, states that persons to be ordained must know Greek and Latin; *1789* (September-October), Canon VII, p. 96, "Of the learning of those who are to be ordained", grants exemptions from Greek and Latin; *1792*, Canon VII, pp. 129-30, states areas of study; *1795*, Canon IV, pp. 154-55, states that bishops may grant exemption from Greek and Latin; *1799*, Canon IV, p. 187, repealed any exemptions from Greek and Latin; *1801*, Canon II, p. 208, restored the bishop's right to grant exemptions from Greek and Latin; *1804*, pp. 230-33, "Course of Ecclesiastical Studies," lists books to be used by those reading for orders; *1808*, Canon IX, X and XI, pp. 331-32, names four areas of examination and acquaintance with the Hebrew language; *1814*, pp. 294, 303, Christopher Gadsden of South Carolina moved that a theological seminary be established; *1817* p. 33, committee on a

Theological seminary moved that "The Theological Seminary of the Protestant Episcopal Church in the United States of America" be established (this is General Seminary, New York City); *1820*, pp. 41-42, 64-85, voted to move General Seminary to New Haven; *1821*, pp. 11-14, 23-32, approved constitution of General Seminary and voted to return it to New York; *1823*, pp. 84-101, reports on General Seminary; *1826*, p. 85, canon passed requiring that a person seeking ordination must be candidate for three years before ordination; pp. 86-90, "Report of the Trustees of the General Theological Seminary of the Protestant Episcopal Church in the United States" (hereafter "RTGS"); *1829*, pp. 93-98, "RTGS"; *1832*, pp. 124-28, "RTGS"; *1835*, pp. 114-21, "RTGS"; *1838*, pp. 125-31, "RTGS"; *1841*, pp. 137-42, "RTGS"; pp. 142-43, report urging that course of study at General be extended to four years; *1844*, pp. 227-30, "RTGS"; pp. 230-31, report which raises concern about the Oxford Movement at General; pp. 232-50, questions and answers of professors about the Oxford Movement at General; *1847*, pp. 98-99, revised canon on candidates for orders; 219-22, "RTGS"; *1850*, pp. 211-16, "RTGS"; *1853*, pp. 310-315, "RTGS"; *1856*, p. 206, committee appointed to revise the "Course on Ecclesiastical Studies"; pp. 292-301, "RTGS"; *1859*, pp. 347-52, "RTGS"; *1862*, pp. 274-80, "RTGS"; *1865*, pp. 278-302, "RTGS"; *1868*, pp. 132, 133, 164, 175, 248, 259, 272, Joint Committee on Theological Education created; 354-67, "RTGS"; *1871*, pp. 501-09, "RTGS"; *1874*, pp. 494-96, "RTGS"; *1877*, pp. 473-82, "RTGS"; *1880*, pp. 396-405, "RTGS"; *1883*, pp. 523-35, "RTGS"; *1886*, pp. 624-32, "RTGS"; *1889*, pp. 595-601, "RTGS", pp. 747-62; "Report on the Revision of the Course of Theological Study"; *1892*, pp. 511-15, "RTGS"; *1895*, pp. 479-90, "RTGS"; *1898*, pp. 479-92, "RTGS"; *1901* pp. iii, 44, 61-63, "Committee on a Central Board of Examiners for Holy Orders"; pp. 437-49, "RTGS"; *1904*, pp. 452-59, "RTGS"; *1907*, pp. 459-68, "RTGS"; *1910*, pp. v, 80, 89, 116, 158, 262, 298, 355, Joint Commission on the Status of Theological Education in this Church created; pp. 475-83, "RTGS"; *1913*, pp. 38, 55, 56, 95, 115, 116, 529-32, "Report of the Commission on the Status of Theological Education"; pp. 434-35, "RTGS"; *1916*, pp. 438-41, "RTGS"; *1919*, pp. 524-26, "RTGS"; *1925*, pp. 520-21, "RTGS"; *1928*, pp. 393-94, "RTGS"; *1931*, pp. 414-17, "RTGS"; *1934*, pp. XIV, 371, "Joint Commission to Consider the Present Facilities for Theological Education in the Church"; *1937*, 369-75, 554-60, "Theological Education - Report of Joint Commission on - Joint Commission on the Ministry Appointed - National Board of Examiners Approved - Study of Work of Theological Seminaries Requested"; pp. 463-65, "RTGS"; *1940*, pp. xv, 180-84, 232-33, 377-79, 382, 658-71, "Report of the Joint Commission on Theological Education - 1940", this is the first detailed report on the seminaries presented to the General Convention; pp. 462-65, "RTGS"; *1943*, pp. xvi, 322, 331, 551, 575-95, "Report of the Joint Commission on Theological Education", another detailed report on the twelve seminaries; pp. 391-94, "RTGS"; *1946*, pp. xvii, 312, 314, 635-50, "Report of the Joint Standing Commission on Theological Education"; pp. 426-29, "RTGS"; *1949*, pp. xvii, 335-42, 639-51, "Report of the Standing Joint Commission on Theological Education"; pp. 421-24, "RTGS"; *1952*, pp. xiv, 25, 117, 267-68, 293-95, 637-57, "Report of the Joint Standing Commission on Theological Education"; pp. 359-62, "RTGS"; *1955*, pp. xv, 239, 275, 276, 278, 279, 283, 625-59, "Report of Joint Standing Commission on Theological Education"; pp. 348-50, "RTGS"; *1958*, pp. xiv, 26, 37, 40, 69, 330-31, 682-707, "Report of the Joint Standing Committee on Theological

Education"; pp. 461-65, "RTGS"; *1961*, pp. 36, 59, 60, 92, 116, 177, 212, 246, 445, 455, 457, 712-29, "Report of the Joint Standing Commission on Theological Education"; pp. 540-43, "RTGS"; *1964*, pp. xviii, 62, 364, 376, 630-50, "Report of the Joint Standing Commission on Education for Holy Orders"; pp. 546-48, "RTGS"; *1967*, pp. xiii, xviii, 18, 29, 44, 46, 69, 170, 193, 219, 435, 502, 505, Appendix 20: 1-12, "Report of the Special Committee on Theological Education in the Episcopal Church"; Appendix 21: 1-16, "Report on the Joint Commission on Education for Holy Orders", action of this Convention created the Board for Theological Education; Appendix 17: 1-3, "RTGS"; *1969*, pp. 381-90, "Interim Report of the Board of Theological Education"; *1970*, pp. 7, 341, 342, 734-66, 794-96, "Report of Board for Theological Education; *1973*, pp. 21, 112, 116, 213, 215, 286, 447-49, 452-53, 1010-1042, 1108, "Report of Board for Theological Education"; pp. 561-66, "RTGS"; *1976*, pp. A-24, B-33, B-136, B-159, C-116, D-153; AA-162-93, AA-182, "Report of Board for Theological Education"; *1979*, pp. A-30, B-53, B-55, B-56, B-69, B-103, B-105, B-135, B-144, C-78, C-80, C-93-96, D-53, D-58, D-59, D-65, D-69, D-81, D-121, D-154-55, AA-309-39, "Report of Board for Theological Education"; AA 102-03, "RTGS"; *1982*, pp. A-36, C-90, C-114, Supplement - 350-86, "Report of Board for Theological Education" and Resolution A-125, the 1 Percent Resolution, which stated: "Each parish and mission... shall give annually at least 1 percent of its net disposable budgeted income... to one or more seminaries"; pp.   97-98, "RTGS"; *1985*, pp. 239-40, 254, 483, 603-04, Supplement - 308-24, "Report of Board for Theological Education" and "Guidelines for Theological Education"; pp. 104-05, "RTGS".

Part II. General Articles on Episcopal Seminaries and Theological Education

279.   Addison, James T. *The Episcopal Church in the United States, 1789-1931.* New York: Charles Scribner's Sons, 1951.

          Treats the founding of the major Episcopal seminaries until 1931.

280.   Albright, Raymond W. *A History of the Protestant Episcopal Church.*   New York: Macmillan   Company;   London: Collier-Macmillan Limited, 1964.

          Treats the founding of the major Episcopal seminaries.

281.   Bigham, Thomas J., Jr. "Seminary Study and Practical Training." *Anglican Theological Review* 23 (October 1941): 315-28.

          Urges practical training for seminarians.

282.   Board for Theological Education.   *Selection, Screening and Evaluation of Applicants for Holy Orders.* New York: Seabury Professional Services, 1979.

          Discusses the screening and evaluation procedure of the ten accredited Episcopal seminaries.

283.   Booty, John E. "The Problem of Theological Education and the Seminaries." *The Living Church*, January 22, 1967, pp. 8-10.

Argues for a servant ministry and for seminaries to have contact with universities and involvement with the world.

284.   Bosher, Robert S. "Curriculum for Competence." *Forth* 123 (January 1958): 20-21, 30-31.

Traces briefly the advances made in theological education.

285.   Bowdoin, James L. "Some American Theological Seminaries." *The Sunday Magazine* 10 (November 1881): 465-74.

Notes that in 1879 there were 131 theological seminaries in the United States and discusses a few of the representative ones. The two Episcopal schools discussed are General and Bexley Hall.

286.   Brewer, Clifton H. *A History of Religious Education in the Episcopal Church to 1835.* New Haven: Yale University Press 1924; reprint, New York: Arno Press & The New York Times, 1969.

The chapters on "Provisions for Educating a Native Clergy, 1789-1815," and "The Development of Theological Seminaries, 1815-1835" treat the beginning of theological education in the Episcopal Church. Most of the early efforts are traced in detail.

287.   Brickley, Charles Newton. "The Episcopal Church in Protestant America, 1800-1860: A Study in Thought and Action." Ph.D. dissertation. Clark University, Worcester, MA, 1949.

Discusses theological education, 1800-1860, in the chapter "The Episcopal Church and an Educated Clergy."

288.   Brown, William Adams. "A Century of Theological Education and After." *The Journal of Religion* 6 (July 1926): 363-83.

Treats the development of American theological education from the founding of the Theological Seminary of the Reformed Church at New Brunswick (1774) to 1926, including Episcopal seminaries.

289.   Brown, William Adams. *Ministerial Education in America: Summary and Interpretation.* Vol. 1 of *The Education of American Ministers.* New York: Institute of Social and Religious Research, 1934.

The second major study of American theological education, this one by the Conference of Theological Seminaries in the United States and Canada and the Institute of Social and Religious Research. It surveys the status of theological education in 1934.

290.   Carper, Wood B., Jr. "The Church and Theological Education."

In *The Episcopal Church and Education*, pp. 138-49. Edited by Kendig Brubaker Cully. New York: Morehouse-Barlow Co., 1966.

The professor of pastoral theology at the General Theological Seminary discusses the reform of theological education around four terms used by Bishop John Henry Hobart -- learned, orthodox, pious and practical.

291. *Changing Patterns of the Church's Ministry in the 1970's: Report to the 1976 General Convention of the Episcopal Church by the Study Committee on Preparation for the Ordained Ministry.* Dolores, CO: Episcopal Study Committee on Preparation for the Ordained Ministry, 1976.

Known as "the Krumm Report" since the committee was chaired by Bishop John M. Krumm of Southern Ohio, this is a thorough report on the ten accredited seminaries, the non-accredited programs and diocesan school of theology, as well as most other aspects of theological education. It is the most significant report since *Ministry for Tomorrow*, 1967.

292. Chorley, E. Clowes. *Men and Movements in the American Episcopal Church.* New York: Charles Scribner's Sons, 1946.

Notes the churchmanship of some of the seminaries.

293. Clark, Kenneth E. "Clinical Approaches to Learning." *St. Luke's Journal of Theology* 13 (January 1970): 32-44.

Urges Episcopal seminaries to have supervised training in working in helping relationships.

294. Coburn, John B. "Anglican Theological Education: Some Reflections Following a Visit to England and Their Implications for the Episcopal Church." *Anglican Theological Review* 48 (April 1966): 131-56.

Argues that theological education must be more open to social studies, contemporary cultural and political issues, and the structures of modern society.

295. Coburn, John B. "We Are Neglecting the Preparation of Our Clergy." *The Episcopalian* 125 (October 1960): 57-60.

Argues that the Episcopalian Church has no national policy on theological education and that there is no "mind" of the Church with regard to the support and direction of its seminaries.

296. Coleman, Leighton. *The Church in America.* London: Wells Gardner, Darton & Co., 1895.

Treats founding of major Episcopal seminaries.

297.   Dell, Edward T., Jr. "After Pusey What?" *The Episcopalian* 133 (January 1968): 22-25.

Urges the Church to take action on the report, *Ministry for Tomorrow*, which criticized Episcopal theological seminaries.

298.   Dell, Edward T., Jr. "Sam Brown's Question." *The Episcopalian* 129 (January 1964): 12-15.

Continues to argue that theological education is a stepchild in the Episcopal Church.

299.   Dell, Edward T., Jr. "The Seminaries: Help Needed." *The Episcopalian* 136 (January 1971): 23, 42.

Calls for seminaries not to compete but to cooperate.

300.   Dell, Edward T., Jr. "The Seminaries: Planning for Change." *The Episcopalian* 135 (April 1970): 19.

Discusses the creation of the Board for Theological Education and the need for cooperation by the twelve seminaries.

301.   Dell, Edward T., Jr. "Still A Stepchild." *The Episcopalian* 128 (January 1963): 10-12.

Describes the lack of funds and students for the seminaries.

302.   Dell, Edward T., Jr. "Your Stake in the Seminaries." *The Episcopalian* 132 (January 1967): 8-10.

Urges support of Theological Education Sunday Offering.

303.   DeMille, George E. "One Man Seminary." *Historical Magazine of the Protestant Episcopal Church* 38 (December 1969): 373-79.

Discusses role of Samuel Johnson (1696-1772) at Stratford, Connecticut, as theological educator. Henry Caner, John Beach, Thomas Bradbury Chandler, Abraham Jarvis, second Bishop of Connecticut, and others studied with Johnson for ordination before Johnson became president of King's College, New York, in 1754.

304.   Dunphy, William H. "Candid Reflection on Our Theological Seminaries." *The Living Church*, June 21, 1942, pp. 9-11.

Calls for a thorough overhaul of Episcopal theological seminaries and for a reduction in their number.

305.   Edwards, O. C., Jr. "The Strange Case of the Diocesan Training Schools." *The Christian Century*, February 6-13, 1980, pp. 131-33.

Argues that Diocesan Training Schools (the Episcopal Church had thirty-three in 1974) are unnecessary and that lay education should be emphasized.

306.   Ehrich, Thomas L., ed. *New Perspectives on Episcopal Seminaries.*
          Cambridge, MA: Episcopal Divinity School, 1986.

               The papers presented at a meeting of representatives of
          Episcopal Church agencies and the eleven Episcopal seminaries at
          the Episcopal Divinity School, January 20-22, 1985. The papers
          focus on the responsibilities of the seminaries to the future of the
          Church.

307.   "Episcopal Seminaries: Training Ministers for Tomorrow." *The
          Episcopalian* 140 (January 1975): 8-9.

               Reflections by deans and students about life at the
          seminaries.

308.   Evans, Allen. "Concerning the Situation of Seminaries in
          Wartime." *The Southern Churchman*, January 23, 1943, p. 6.

               Discusses the negative impact of World War II on the
          seminaries.

309.   Evans, H. Barry. *Continuing Education in Episcopal Dioceses: A
          Creative Ferment.* New York: Board for Theological Education,
          1962.

               Discusses the variety of continuing education programs
          including the theological seminaries.

310.   "Financial Aid for Theological Students." *The Church Militant* 5
          (April 1902): 3-4.

               Urges support for all Episcopal Theological Seminaries.

311.   Fletcher, John C. *The Futures of Protestant Seminaries.*
          Washington: Alban Institute, 1983.

               Explains the difficult future faced by American seminaries
          including the Episcopal ones.

312.   Foster, W. Roland. *Episcopal Seminaries, What Are They?*
          Cincinnati, OH: Forward Movement Publications, n.d.

               Briefly describes the ten accredited Episcopal seminaries at
          the time of writing.

313.   Frey, Wallace A. "BTE Annual Seminary Survey 1985-1986." *The
          Episcopalian* 151 (November 1986): 18-19.

               Lists statistics of the eleven Episcopal seminaries and their
          distinctive features.

314.   Gambrell, Mary Latimer. *Ministerial Training in Eighteenth-Century New England.* New York: Columbia University Press, 1937; reprint, New York: AMS Press, Inc., 1967.

         Deals mainly with Congregationalism, but treats Anglican efforts like candidates studying with Samuel Johnson at Stratford.

315.   Gessell, John M. "Are Seminaries in Touch?" *The Episcopalian* 133 (November 1968): 34-35.

         Calls for changes in theological seminaries such as student participation in continuous curriculum revision.

316.   Gessell, John M. "Crisis in Theological Education." *The Witness,* March 3, 1960, pp. 12-14.

         Urges the Church to develop an adequate field work training program and to provide a substantial theological base for courses in education and pastoral care.

317.   Gessell, John M. "Isn't It Time to Stop the Talk and Start the Action." *The Living Church,* January 26, 1969, pp. 8-9, 12.

         Urges consolidation and re-development of present resources and calls for interdisciplinary studies.

318.   Gessell, John M. "Pusey Report Don't Offer Much." *The Witness,* September 28, 1967, pp. 11-13.

         Claims that the "Pusey Report" did not go far enough and calls for strong, quasi-independent, regional seminaries.

319.   Gessell, John M. "The Pusey Report: What Next?" *The Living Church,* October 29, 1967, pp. 19-29.

         Urges that the Episcopal Church move forward on the recommendations of the Pusey Report (*Ministry for Tomorrow*).

320.   Gessell, John M. "The Renewal of Theological Education." *The Witness,* March 16, 1967, pp. 8-11.

         Calls for the creation of structures which would promote regional autonomy and development.

321.   Gonzalez, Justo L. *The Theological Education of Hispanics.* New York: Fund for Theological Education, 1988.

         Treats theological education of Hispanics and notes the work of the Episcopal Seminary of the Southwest at Austin.

322.   Grant, Frederick C. "The Idea of a Theological College." *Kenyon College, Bexley Hall Bulletin* (June 1944): 1-21.

Argues for a return of Episcopal seminaries to the classical Anglican model of a theological college.

323.   Guerry, Moultrie. "Are Examining Chaplains and Canonicals Outmoded?" *St. Luke's Journal of Theology* 13 (January 1970): 3-9.

Argues for the retention of examining chaplains and canonical examinations for candidates for the ministry of the Episcopal Church.

324.   Harris, Charles U. "The Ministry, the Seminaries, and Church Renewal." *The Living Church*, January 27, 1974, pp. 8-10.

Argues that ministerial preparation should take place in a seminary devoted primarily to the education of persons for the sacred ministry.

325.   Harris, Edward G. "Theological Education Challenge Presented by Dean E. G. Harris." *The Witness*, January 19, 1967, pp. 3-6, 14-15.

Urges that the seminaries be made resourceful enough and strong enough to forge a new excellence for Christ's sake.

326.   Higgins, John S. "The Church's Seminaries." *The Living Church*, November 7, 1965, pp. 14, 20.

Argues for fewer seminaries, reducing time from thirty-three to twenty-seven months, and that the seminaries be governed by the provinces.

327.   Holder, Ray. "Central U.S. Theological College -- A Plan for Our Time?" *The Living Church*, April 23, 1961, pp. 14-15, 22.

Argues that the eleven seminaries should be liquidated and one centrally located theological college established.

328.   Holmes, Urban T. "The Strangeness of the Seminary." *Anglican Theological Review, Supplementary Series* 6 (June 1976): 135-49.

Argues that formation is the purpose of theological education.

329.   Hopkins, John Henry, Jr. *The Life of the Late Right Reverend John Henry Hopkins, First Bishop of Vermont, and Seventh Presiding Bishop.* New York: F. J. Huntington and Co., 1873.

Discusses Hopkin's efforts in 1836 to establish a seminary at Burlington.

330.   Hubbell, William K. "Henry Caswall (1810-1870) and the Backwoods Church." *Historical Magazine of the Protestant Episcopal Church* 29 (September 1960): 219-39.

Traces Caswall's years as a student at Kenyon College/Bexley Hall, his time as professor of Sacred Literature at seminary in Lexington, Kentucky, and his time as professor of divinity at Kemper College, St. Louis.

331. Insko, W. Robert. "Conservative Sensitivity Training in Clinical Pastoral Education." *St. Luke's Journal of Theology* 15 (January 1972): 19-32.

The some-time dean of the Kentucky Theological Seminary urges a balanced use of sensitivity training.

332. Joint Commission on Education for Holy Orders. *Theological Studies and Examinations: A Syllabus.* New York: National Council, Episcopal Church, 1964.

Suggests the standards of intellectual achievement the Episcopal Church seeks to uphold in its clergy.

333. Joint Commission on Theological Education. *Theological Studies and Examinations: A Bibliography.* New York: National Council, Episcopal Church, 1960.

Lists books for use in Episcopal seminaries in 1960.

334. Keizer, Lewis S. "Ministers: The New Breed." *The Episcopalian* 133 (November 1968): 20-22.

Discusses the new breed of seminarian who is a socially involved activist.

335. Kelly, Alden Drew. "A Dean Looks at Clinical Training." *Journal of Pastoral Care* 5 (Spring 1951): 61-65.

A former dean of Seabury-Western Theological Seminary argues that clinical pastoral training contributes to a person's ministry and to the minister as a whole person.

336. Kelly, Alden Drew. "The Laity and the Seminaries." *The Living Church*, January 19, 1947, p. 11.

Discusses the laity's role in recruitment and financial support.

337. Kelly, Alden Drew. "Theological Education." *Theology* 53 (August 1950): 289-95.

Discusses the confusion in Episcopal theological seminaries and calls for a carefully planned strategy for coordination and cooperation.

338. Kelly, Robert L. *Theological Education in America: A Study of One*

Hundred Sixty-One Theological Schools in the United States and Canada. New York: George H. Doran Company, 1924.

The first major study of American seminaries done by the Institute of Social and Religious Education, this study focuses on every aspect of theological education. Episcopal seminaries included are College of St. John the Evangelist, Greeley, Colorado; Berkeley Divinity School, Middletown, Connecticut; Western Theological Seminary, Chicago; Episcopal Theological School, Cambridge; DeLancey Divinity School, Buffalo; General Theological Seminary, New York; Divinity School of the Protestant Episcopal Church in Philadelphia; and Protestant Episcopal Theological Seminary in Alexandria, Virginia. Notes that School of Theology of the University of the South, Sewanee, Tennessee; Nashotah House, Nashotah, Wisconsin; and Church Divinity School of the Pacific, Berkeley, California, did not respond to survey. No mention is made of Bexley Hall, Kenyon College, Gambier, Ohio, and Seabury Divinity School, Fiarbault, Minnesota.

339.   Kirk, Richard J. *Paths to Ministry: Some Alternatives in Theological Education.* New York: Seabury Professional Services, 1979.

Analyzes diocesan schools and other training programs which focus on pre-ordination and lay training, and discusses the debate between the seminaries and the diocesan schools.

340.   Lawrence, W. Appleton. "Our Church and Her Ministry." *The Witness,* September 17, 1959, pp. 11-14; September 24, 1959, pp. 10-13.

Urges review and revision of theological education.

341.   Lichtenberger, Arthur. "The Seminary's Obligation." *Forth* 124 (April 1959): 6-7, 27.

Maintains that seminaries should develop in their students "the love of learning, the love of people, the love of God."

342.   Lowery, James L., Jr. "The Clergy, the Professional, and Preparation for Ordained Ministry." *St. Luke's Journal of Theology* 14 (September 1971): 47-75; and 15 (January 1972): 58-75.

Treats the clergy as professionals and the need for adequate preparation. Argues that preparation never ends.

343.   Lowery, James L., Jr. "The Many Academic Roads to Ordination." *The Episcopalian* 143 (August 1978): B.

Discusses four educational tracks towards ordination: 1) a theological seminary; 2) reading privately with a mentor; 3) diocesan night and weekend school; and 4) theological education by extension.

344.   Lowery, James L., Jr. "Many Roads Lead to Ordination." *The Episcopalian* 144 (June 1979): B-C.

         Defends earlier article about many educational programs for ordained priests apart from accredited Episcopal seminaries.

345.   Manross, William W. *The Episcopal Church in the United States, 1800-1840. A Study in Church Life.* New York: Columbia University Press, 1938. Reprint. New York: AMS Press, Inc., 1967.

         Treats fully theological education in this period.

346.   Manross, William W. *A History of the American Episcopal Church.* New York & Milwaukee, WI: Morehouse Publishing Co., 1935.

         Treats founding of major Episcopal seminaries.

347.   May, Mark A., and Frank K. Shuttleworth. *Appendices.* Vol. 4 of *The Education of American Ministers.* New York: Institute of Social and Religious Research, 1934.

         Contains numerous appendices to volume two, *The Profession of the Ministry.* This is the information gathered in this five-year research project.

348.   May, Mark A., et al. *The Institutions That Train Ministers.* Vol. 3 of *The Education of American Ministers.* New York: Institute of Social and Religious Research, 1934.

         Analyzes the faculties, students, teaching methods and religious life of American seminaries.

349.   May, Mark A., et al. *The Profession of the Ministry: Its Status and Problems.* Vol 2 of *The Education of American Ministers.* New York: Institute of Social and Religious Research, 1934.

         Analyzes the education of American ministers in the early 1930s.

350.   McConnell, S. D. *History of the American Episcopal Church, 1600-1915.* 11th ed. Milwaukee: Morehouse Publishing Co.; London: A. R. Mowbray & Co., 1934.

         Notes founding of major Episcopal seminaries.

351.   Moore, H. Randolph. "A Unified Program of Theological Education." *Anglican Theological Review* 24 (October 1942): 355-63.

Analyzes distribution of courses in some of the seminaries and calls for a unified program.

352.   Moreau, Jules L. "More About Theological Education." *The Witness*, January 19, 1961, pp. 13-15.

Urges that seminaries train men for a ministry and not just prepare them to "get into the ministry." Also criticizes diocesan training school.

353.   Moreau, Jules L. "What Should the Church Be Doing in Theological Education?" *The Witness*, November 3, 1960, pp. 7-10; November 10, 1960, pp. 7-11.

Urges a complete review and restructuring of theological education in the light of H. Richard Niebuhr's *The Advancement of Theological Education* (1957).

354.   Morgan, Carl H. *The Status of Field Work in the Protestant Theological Seminaries.* Philadelphia, PA: By the Author, 1942.

One of the first studies of field education. The Episcopal schools included are Church Divinity School of the Pacific, Virginia Theological Seminary, Episcopal Theological School, Philadelphia Divinity School, General Theological Seminary and Bexley Hall.

355.   Moulton, Janis. "Seminaries in Motion." *The Episcopalian* 134 (January 1969): 14-15, 18.

Discusses mergers of seminaries and the creation of clusters of theological schools.

356.   Myers, C. Kilmer. "The Church and the Seminary." *The Living Church*, January 20, 1946, p. 9.

Insists the seminaries must be brought from the periphery to the very center of the Church's life.

357.   Nes, William H. "Theological Education." *The Living Church*, January 16, 1949, p. 13.

Dean of Nashotah House argues that the destiny of the Episcopal Church is dependent upon support of the seminaries.

358.   Niebuhr, H. Richard, Daniel Day Williams and James M. Gustafson. *The Advancement of Theological Education.* New York: Harper & Brothers, 1957.

Major study of main line theological education by the American Association of Theological Schools and the Carnegie Corporation of America.

359.   Norris, Richard A., Jr. "The Episcopal Church and Theological
         Education." *Anglican Theological Review, Supplementary Series* 2
         (September 1973): 88-95.

         Argues that the attitude of the Episcopal Church to
         theological education has been benign neglect, and calls for
         coordination of resources among the seminaries.

360.   O'Neill, Joseph P. "Seminary Mergers in the Protestant Episcopal
         Church, 1933-1983." Princeton, NJ: November, 1984. Mimeo.

         Traces the mergers from that of Western and Seabury in
         1933 to that of Philadelphia and ETS in 1971.

361.   Peat, Marwick, Mitchell & Co. *A Financial Assessment of the
         Accredited Seminaries and Highlights from the PMM & Co. Report,
         "Theological Education in Accredited Episcopal Seminaries."* New
         York: Board for Theological Education, 1982.

         Analyzes the *laissez faire* funding policy of seminaries by the
         Episcopal Church, and recommends more coordinated financial
         management.

362.   Peat, Marwick, Mitchell & Co. *Theological Education in Accredited
         Episcopal Seminaries: The Data to Support the Case for
         Strengthening the Partnership Between Episcopal Seminaries and the
         Episcopal Church.* New York: Board for Theological Education,
         1982.

         An in-depth study of the financial and educational resources
         of the ten accredited Episcopal seminaries.

363.   Phelps, Rose. "Theological Education Conference." *The Witness*,
         April 30, 1942, p. 12.

         Discusses conference at Princeton, April 14-15, 1942, which
         focused on pre-seminary training, seminary education and
         post-seminary education.

364.   Pierce, Janette. "Report Raises Issues in Theological Education."
         The Episcopalian 141 (February 1976): 11.

         Reflects on the Report of the Episcopal Study Committee on
         the Preparation for the Ordained Ministry, "the Krumm Report,"
         and notes the proliferation of diocesan training centers and the
         growth of non-stipendary ministry.

365.   Pittenger, W. Norman. "Theological Education in the American
         Church." *Pan-Anglican* 8 (Fall 1957): 30-36.

         Surveys the status of theological education at the time.

366.   Powell, Noble C. "Post-Ordination Training in the Episcopal

Church." *Anglican Theological Review* 24 (July 1942): 210-16.

Argues that seminary begins a priest's education and that post-ordination training is essential.

367.   Pregnall, William. "The Episcopal Seminary System and the Mission of the Church During the Decline of the American Empire." 1987. Photocopy.

Argues that radical changes must be made in Episcopal theological education.

368.   Pregnall, William. "Is '1 Percent Resolution' Batting Little League or Big League?" *The Episcopalian* 152 (September 1987): L.

Notes that about fifty percent of the Episcopal Churches and missions give annually at least one percent of their net disposable budgeted income to one or more seminaries.

369.   "A Proposal for Episcopal Seminaries." *The Episcopalian* 138 (April 1973): 47-48.

Reports on proposal to consolidate the eleven Episcopal seminaries into four regional centers: Berkeley, California, Chicago, Alexandria, Virginia, and the Northeast.

370.   Pusey, Nathan M. "Let's Get on with the Job." *The Episcopalian* 130 (January 1965): 10-13.

Asks how much longer must theological study and teaching remain one of the depressed areas of the Episcopal Church.

371.   Pusey, Nathan M. "Statement on Theological Education." *The Witness*, October 5, 1967, pp. 10-13.

Comments on the study later published as *Ministry for Tomorrow* and notes the challenges facing theological education.

372.   "The Report of the Committee on the Church's Overseas Mission." *The Living Church*, February 12, 1961, pp. 14-15, 19-21.

Discusses the training needed for missionaries.

373.   "Report of the Joint Commission on Theological Education." *The Living Church*, June 25, 1961, pp. 13, 17.

Notes that seminary enrollment was well below capacity.

374.   Richards, David E. "Assessing Spiritual Formation and Spirituality in Applicants for Admission to Ministry." *St. Luke's Journal of Theology* 18 (March 1975): 189-95.

Argues that the spirituality of applicants for seminary can

be measured.

375. Rodenmayer, Robert N. "Remember the Quiet Need." *The Episcopalian* 131 (January 1966): 8-12.

Urges support of Episcopal seminaries.

376. Roozen, David A. and Adair T. Lummis. *Leadership and Theological Education in the Episcopal Church.* Hartford, CT: Hartford Seminary Center for Social and Religious Research, 1987.

This study, commissioned by the Board for Theological Education, analyzes the differences among the seminaries, the criteria for evaluating the quality of a seminary, and the current state of Episcopal seminaries.

377. Ross, Bob. "On Building a Broader Data Base for Planning Theological Education." *St. Luke's Journal of Theology* 16 (December 1972): 68-71.

Urges the inclusion of the Church at large in designing theological education.

378. Scott, David A. "Anglican and Episcopal Theologians: A Usable Past for Postliberal Theology." *Anglican and Episcopal History* 56 (March 1987): 7-26.

Traces the theological contributions of Francis J. Hall (1857-1932), professor of theology at Western Seminary, Chicago, and the General Theological Seminary, New York, and W. Norman Pittenger, professor of apologetics at the General Theological Seminary.

379. "The Seminary, the City." *The Episcopalian* 129 (January 1964): 32-36.

Discusses inner-city work of seminarians in West Philadephia.

380. Sherman, Arthur M. "Theological Education." *The Living Church*, May 10, 1964, pp. 12-15.

Urges that Canon 29, "Of the Normal Standard of Learning and Examination of Candidates for Holy Orders" be revised and up-dated.

381. Shewmaker, William O. "The Training of the Protestant Ministry in the United States of America Before the Establishment of Theological Seminaries." In *Papers of the American Society of Church History, Second Series*, Vol. 6, pp. 71-202. Edited by Frederick W. Loetcher. New York and London: G. P. Putnam's Sons, 1921.

Treats early Anglican efforts such as the College of William and Mary, Thomas Bray's *Bibliotheca Parochials*; and reading for orders.

382.   Strategic Planning Committee. "The Future of Theological Education in the Episcopal Church." 1987. Mimeo.

Written by John E. Booty, this report urges cooperation among the eleven accredited seminaries.

383.   Strider, Robert E. L. "On Theological Education." *The Witness*, May 14, 1942, pp. 7-8.

Discusses the role of the standing commission on theological education created by the General Convention of 1940.

384.   Sumner, David E. *The Episcopal Church's History: 1945-1985*. Wilton, CT: Morehouse-Barlow, 1987.

In the chapter on "The Clergy and the Seminaries," the author discusses seminary enrollment trends, finances, new degrees, the Board for Theological Education (1969), seminary mergers, new seminaries and diocesan seminaries.

385.   "Survey of Seminarians Shows Financial Help Needed." *The Episcopalian* 152 (July 1987): E.

Notes that costs of seminaries greatly exceed scholarships and grants.

386.   Sweet, William Warren. "The Rise of Theological Schools in America." *Church History* 6 (September 1937): 260-73.

Mentions General and Virginia Seminaries as earliest Episcopal Schools.

387.   Swing, William E. "Where Have All the Young Men Gone?" *The Living Church*, December 2, 1984, p. 9.

The Bishop of California argues that more younger men should go to seminary and that the Church must be creative in placing ordained persons.

388.   Taylor, Charles L., Jr. *Ministry for Tomorrow: Report of the Special Committee on Theological Education*. New York: Seabury Press, 1967.

Analyzes the status of theological education in the Episcopal Church and reports that it has been "remiss" in its concerns for theological education.

389.   Taylor, Charles L., Jr. "Seminaries in the Postwar World." *Forth* 112 (January 1947): 14, 25.

Discusses the problems facing the seminaries after World War II including the numerous applications from veterans.

390.   Taylor, Charles L., Jr. The Task of the Theological School in 1945." *The Southern Churchman*, April 7, 1945, pp. 5-7, 10.

A dean of the Episcopal Theological School, Cambridge, argues that seminaries must produce consecrated, authentic Men of God who are indomitable champions of the right, interpreters of the good news of Christ, indefatigable helpers of men in their time of need, and alert messengers to win the world.

391.   "Theological Education Board Proposes Five New Centers." *The Witness*, I, February 1970, pp. 3-4.

Reports on the Board for Theological Education's recommendation to restructure the eleven seminaries into five theological centers.

392.   "Theological Education Suddenly Becomes Headline News." *The Witness*, November 4, 1965, pp. 3-5.

Discusses the plans for a study of theological education, which results in the "Pusey Report."

393.   Thompsett, Frederica Harris. "To Strengthen and to Coordinate: A Decade of Partnership in Theological Education. The Episcopal Church Foundation and the Board for Theological Education, 1970-1980," May 8, 1980. Photocopy.

Discusses how the Board for Theological, which was created in 1967, has used funds given by the Episcopal Church Foundation.

394.   Thorp, Almus M. "Cold Facts, Hard Thought, Wild Dreams." *The Episcopalian* 135 (March 1970): 21-22.

Argues that the Episcopal Church needs only five centers for theological education.

395.   Tiffany, Charles C. *A History of the Protestant Episcopal Church in the United States of America*. New York: Christian Literature Co., 1895.

Treats the founding of Episcopal seminaries and lists fifteen in operation as of 1895.

396.   Turner, Franklin D. and Adair T. Lummis. *Black Clergy in the Episcopal Church: Recruitment, Training, and Deployment*. New York: Office for Black Ministries, 1979.

A full discussion of the education of blacks for ministry in the Episcopal Church. The report is preceded by an essay by J.

Carleton Hayden, "The Black Ministry of the Episcopal Church: A Historical Overview," which discusses the Bishop Payne Divinity School (1878-1949) at Petersburg, Virginia, and King Hall (1899-1908) at Howard University, Washington, D.C.

397.   Walsh, Chad. "Where Do the Seminaries Fit In?" *The Living Church*, January 22, 1950, pp. 7-9.

Claims that the Episcopal Church does not support theological education.

398.   Walters, Sumner, Jr. "The Development of Education in the Theological Colleges and Seminaries of the Church of England and the Protestant Episcopal Church in America, 1900-1950." Ph.D. dissertation. Oxford University, 1955.

Describes in great detail theological education in the first half of the twentieth century.

399.   Walters-Bugbee, Christopher. "Going Public: Seminaries in Search of Support." *The Christian Century*, May 13, 1981, pp. 538-43.

Argues that Episcopal Seminaries need much greater financial support and that the Episcopal Church is indifferent to the financial needs of the seminaries.

400.   Wedel, Theodore O. "Theological Education." *The Living Church* 119 (October 30, 1949): 17-18.

Urges support of the ten seminaries.

401.   Westerhoff, John H., III. "Theological Education and Models for Ministry." *St. Luke's Journal of Theology* 25 (March 1982): 153-69.

Argues against professional model for theological education and urges a catechetical model which stresses formation and nurture.

402.   Wilberforce, Samuel. *A History of the Protestant Episcopal Church in America.* New York: Stanford and Swords, 1849.

Treats the founding of the earliest seminaries.

403.   Younger, George D. *From New Creation to Urban Crisis: A History of Action Training Ministries, 1962-1975.* Chicago: Center for the Scientific Study of Religion, 1987.

Along with other denominations, treats the role of the Episcopal Church and some of its seminaries in action training ministries.

Part III. The Eleven Accredited Episcopal Theological Seminaries.

Berkeley Divinity School, 1854, Middletown, Connecticut, 1854-1928, New Haven, Connecticut, 1928 -

404.   Allen, Michael. "Making Men Out of Priests." *The Witness*, I, February 1971, pp. 7-10.

Discusses the proposed merger of Berkeley with Yale Divinity School.

405.   Beardsley, E. Edwards. *The History of the Episcopal Church in Connecticut*. Vol. 2. *From the Death of Bishop Seabury to the Present Time*. 4th ed.   Boston, MA: Houghton, Mifflin and Company, 1883.

Traces briefly the establishment of a theological department at Trinity College and the founding of the Berkeley Divinity School in 1854.

406.   Beardsley, William A. "John Williams, Bishop of Connecticut, 1865-1899." *Historical Magazine of the Protestant Episcopal Church* 14 (June 1943): 119-50.

Traces briefly the theological department at Trinity College, Hartford and the establishment of the Berkeley Divinity School at Middletown, in Jarvis House which opened on October 2, 1854.

407.   "Berkeley Celebrates Centennial." *The Churchman* 168 (June 1954): 9.

Briefly describes Berkeley's 100 years.

408.   *Berkeley Quarterly Bulletin* (April 1909-June 1966), *Building Churches, Berkeley Divinity School at Yale* (May 1972-October 1974), *Berkeley Serves* (Fall 1975-Winter 1985); *Berkeley Newsletter* (January 1978-   ).

These provide information about students, faculty and alumni/ae.

409.   Burr, Nelson R. *The Story of the Diocese of Connecticut: A New Branch of the Vine*. Hartford, CT: Church Missions Publishing Co., 1962.

Briefly traces the establishment of a theological course at Trinity College, Hartford, in 1849, and the history of the Berkeley Divinity School which opened on October 2, 1854, under the direction of Bishop John Williams, who served as dean until his death in 1899. In 1928 it moved to New Haven.

410.   Hardy, Edward R., Jr. "The Berkeley Divinity School, One Hundred Years, 1854-1954." *Historical Magazine of the Protestant*

Episcopal Church 24 (March 1955): 15-38.

> The only full history of Berkeley that has been written.

411.   Raftery, Elizabeth B. "Berkeley Divinity School Founder's Day Address, May 3, 1966: Berkeley's Three Founders." *Berkeley Divinity School Bulletin* (Summer 1966): 1-31.

> Traces the history of Berkeley from the idea of Bishop George Berkeley, through its founding at Middleton, Connecticut, by Bishop John Williams in 1854, to its removal to New Haven under Dean William Palmer Ladd in 1928.

412.   Steiner, Bernard C. *The History of Education in Connecticut.* Washington, DC: Government Printing Office, 1893.

> Discusses the theological department at Trinity College and the founding of Berkeley.

413.   Weaver, Glenn. *The History of Trinity College.* Hartford, CT: Trinity College Press, 1967.

> Traces the theological department at Trinity College from its establishment in 1849 until the opening of the Berkeley Divinity School at Middletown in 1854 "which was merely the former Theological Department of Trinity College."

Bexley Hall, 1824, Worthington, Ohio, 1824-1828, Gambier, Ohio, 1828-1968, Rochester, Ohio, 1968-

414.   "Bexley Students Open Rural Church." *Forth* 113 (June 1948): 8-9.

> Treats the mission work of Bexley students and briefly treats its history.

415.   *Bulletin from the Hill* (1928-).

> Contains information about Bexley after the merger in 1968.

416.   Carus, William, ed. *Memorials of the Right Reverend Charles Petit McIlvaine, D.D., D.C.L., Late Bishop of Ohio.* New York: Thomas Whittaker, 1882.

> Notes that McIlwaine organized and built Bexley Hall as a seminary and building. It was founded by Bishop Philander Chase.

417.   Chase, Philander. *Bishop Chases's Reminiscences: An Autobiography.* 2d ed. 2 vols. Boston, MA: James B. Dow, 1848.

> Treats the founding of Kenyon College and Bexley Hall Seminary.

418.   Dyer, Heman. *Records of an Active Life.* New York: Thomas

Whittaker, 1886.

Provides reflections on Kenyon College and Bexley Hall.

419.   Hughes, John D. "Student Life at Bexley Hall." *The Southern Churchman*, January 24, 1948, pp. 5-6.

Briefly describes student life in 1947-1948.

420.   "A New Frontier in Theological Education." *The Southern Churchman*, January 24, 1948, pp. 7-8.

Unsigned article discusses Bexley Hall's commitment to the practical application of the historic disciplines to the work of the actual ministry.

421.   Roach, Corwin C. "Bexley Hall, The Divinity School of Kenyon College -- Its Past History and Present Purpose." *The Southern Churchman*, January 24, 1948, pp. 3-4.

Briefly traces the history of Bexley Hall from its founding in 1824, and notes its commitment to thorough scholarship.

422.   Smith, Laura Chase. *The Life Of Philander Chase, First Bishop of Ohio and Illinois, Founder of Kenyon and Jubilee Colleges.* New York: E. P. Dutton & Company, 1903.

Discusses the founding and history of Kenyon College and Bexley Hall.

423.   Smythe, George F. *A History of the Diocese of Ohio Until the Year 1918.* Cleveland, OH: By the Diocese, 1931.

On November 4, 1824, Bishop Philander Chase, first Bishop of Ohio, founded The Theological Seminary of the Protestant Episcopal Church in the Diocese of Ohio at Worthington. This volume traces the founding of this seminary, later called Bexley Hall; the college associated with it, Kenyon College; its move to Gambier in 1828, and its subsequent history under Bishops Charles McIlvaine (1832-1873), Gregory T. Bedell (1873-1889) and William A. Leonard (1889-1930).

424.   Smythe, George F. *Kenyon College -- Its First Century.* New Haven: Yale University Press, 1924.

Discusses fully the founding of the Theological Seminary of the Protestant Episcopal Church in the Diocese of Ohio in 1824 at Worthington, the college associated with it, Kenyon College, its move to Gambier in 1828, and its history to 1924.

425.   Spielmann, Richard M. *Bexley Hall: 150 Years. A Brief History.* Rochester, NY: Colgate Rochester Divinity School/Bexley Hall/Crozer Theological Seminary, 1974.

The only complete history of Bexley Hall which was founded in 1824 by Bishop Philander Chase and which moved to Rochester in 1968.

426.   Tucker, Beverly D. "A Vital Seminary." *The Southern Churchman*, January 24, 1948, pp. 6-7.

The Bishop of Ohio, 1938-1952, describes Bexley Hall in 1947-1948.

Church Divinity School of the Pacific, 1893, San Mateo, California, 1893-1930, Berkeley, California, 1930-

427.   Breck, Charles, comp. *The Life of the Reverend James Lloyd Breck, D.D., Chiefly from Letters Written by Himself.* New York: E. & J. B. Young & Co., 1883.

Discusses the founding of the Missionary College of St. Augustine at Bernicia, California in 1868.

428.   *CDSP Bulletin* (November 1935 - May 1951), *CDSP Times* (April 1952 - Spring 1977), *Crossings* (Fall 1977-   ).

Contains information about students, faculty and alumni/ae.

429.   Gillies, Donald A. "Introduction of Massey H. Shepherd, Jr." *Criterion* 17 (Autumn 1978): 21-22.

Treats Shepherd's naming as alumnus of the year by the Divinity School of the University of Chicago.

430.   Glens, Ronald V. "A Select Bibliography of the Works of Massey Hamilton Shepherd, Jr." In *Worship Points the Way: A Celebration of the Life and Work of Massey Hamilton Shepherd, Jr.*, pp. 273-83. Edited by Malcolm C. Burson. New York: Seabury Press, 1981.

Lists the works of a major liturgics scholar and teacher in the Episcopal Church.

431.   Glens, Ronald V. "The Writings of Samuel McCray Garrett: A Select Bibliography." *Historical Magazine of the Protestant Episcopal Church* 53 (September 1984): 257-58.

Lists the publications of the retired professor of church history at the Church Divinity School of the Pacific (1950-1984).

432.   Holcombe, Theodore I. *An Apostle of the Wilderness: James Lloyd Breck, D.D. His Missions and His Schools.* New York: Thomas Whittaker, 1903.

Treats briefly the Missionary College of St. Augustine founded by Breck in 1868.

433.   Johnson, Sherman E. "Massey Shepherd and the Episcopal
        Church: A Reminiscence." In *Worship Points the Way: A
        Celebration of the Life and Work of Massey Hamilton Shepherd,
        Jr.*, pp. 5-17. Edited by Malcolm C. Burson. New York: Seabury
        Press, 1981.

        Treats the life and contributions of a professor of Church
        History at the Episcopal Theological School (1940-54), professor of
        Liturgics at the Church Divinity School of the Pacific (1954-81).

434.   Kelley, Douglas O. *History of the Diocese of California from 1849
        to 1914*. San Francisco, CA: Bureau of Information and Supply,
        1915.

        Traces the founding of the Missionary College of St.
        Augustine at Bernicia by James Lloyd Breck on January 20, 1868,
        to closing in 1870, and the founding of the Church Divinity School
        of the Pacific in October, 1893.

435.   Sanford, Louis S. *The Province of the Pacific*. Philadelphia:
        Church Historical Society, 1949.

        Traces the founding of the Church Divinity School of the
        Pacific at San Mateo in 1893 by Bishop William Ford Nichols and
        its move to Berkeley in 1930.

436.   Shepherd, Massey H., Jr. "In Tribute: Sherman Elbridge Johnson."
        Anglican Theological Review, Supplementary Series, 3 (March
        1974): 5-14.

        Discusses the many contributions of the dean of CDSP.

437.   Shepherd, Massey H., Jr. "Response." *Criterion* 17 (Autumn
        1978): 23-27.

        Reflections by Shepherd on his education at the Divinity
        School of the University of Chicago when he was named its
        alumnus of the year.

438.   Shires, Henry H. "History of the Church Divinity School of the
        Pacific." *Historical Magazine of the Protestant Episcopal Church*
        11 (June 1942): 179-88.

        Describes the Missionary College of St. Augustine at Bernica
        founded by James Lloyd Breck, which operated from 1868 to 1870,
        and the history of the Church Divinity School from its founding in
        1893 to 1942.

Episcopal Divinity School, 1867, Cambridge, Massachusetts (Philadelphia Divinity School, 1857, Merged with Episcopal Theological School on June 6, 1974)

439.   Addison, Charles M. "Professor P. H. Steenstra." *The Church Militant* 5 (April 1902): 6.

           Describes the many contributions of Peter Henry Steenstra, professor of Bible, 1867-1907.

440.   Addison, Daniel D. "George Hodges -- Twenty-Five Years Dean." *The Church Militant* 22 (February 1919): 10.

           Describes Hodges' deanship (1894-1919), and contributions to the school.

441.   Allen, Alexander V. G. "The Early Days of the Cambridge School." *The Church Militant* 7 (April 1904): 6, 8.

           Describes the founding and early history of the school.

442.   Allen, Alexander V. G. "William Lawrence as Dean of the Cambridge School." *The Church Militant* 6 (October 1903): 6-7.

443.   Berry, Joseph B. *History of the Diocese of Massachusetts, 1810-1872.* Boston, MA: Diocesan Library, 1959.

           Treats the effort to establish the Episcopal Theological Seminary in Massachusetts in 1836 and the founding of ETS in 1867.

444.   Blackman, George L. *Faith and Freedom: A Study of Theological Education and the Episcopal Theological School.* New York: Seabury Press, 1967.

           A full discussion of Episcopal theological education prior to 1867 and the definitive history of the seminary at Cambridge.

445.   "Charles L. Taylor: Biographical Sketch." *Theological Education* 2 (Summer 1966): xi-xii.

           Brief sketch of Charles L. Taylor, dean of the Episcopal Theological School, 1944-1957, and first executive secretary of the American Association of Theological Schools.

446.   Clark, Davis W. "One Very Good Dean: George Hodges." *The Methodist Review* 69 (October 1920): 633-40.

           Describes the work and personality of the fifth dean of ETS.

447.   Dun, Angus. "E.T.S. -- Seventy-five Years Old." *The Church Militant* 45 (May 1942): 12-13.

Traces the school briefly from 1867 to 1942.

448.   *EDS News* (Fall, 1974-   ). (From Fall, 1974 to Spring, 1977 it was called *EDS Newsletter*.)

Contains information about students, faculty, and alumni/ae.

449.   Fletcher, Joseph F. "A Quarter-Century of Christian Ethics at ETS: A Rear-View Mirror." *The Witness*, II, November 1970, pp. 6-9; I, December 1970, pp. 7-9.

Reflects on teaching ethics at ETS in the 1940s, 1950s and 1960s.

450.   Garfield, James. "Charles Taylor as Dean." *Theological Education* 2 (Summer 1966): 5-5 to 5-8.

Discusses Taylor's tenure as dean of the Episcopal Theological School, 1944-1957.

451.   Gray, George Zabiskie. "The Episcopal Theological School in Cambridge, Mass." In *The History of the American Episcopal Church, 1587-1883*. Vol. 2: *The Organization and Progress of the American Church, 1783-1883*, pp. 535-38. Edited by William S. Perry. Boston: James R. Osgood, 1885.

Describes the founding and early history of the school.

452.   Hiatt, Suzanne R., David Siegenthaler and John H. Snow. "The Episcopal Divinity School, Cambridge." In *The Episcopal Dioceses of Massachusetts, 1784-1984: A Mission to Remember, Proclaim, and Fulfill* pp. 684-87. Edited by Mark J. Duffy. Boston, MA: Episcopal Diocese of Massachusetts, 1984.

Brief description of the Episcopal Divinity School, which resulted from merger of the Episcopal Theological School, Cambridge (1867) and the Philadelphia Divinity School (1857) in 1974.

453.   Hodges, George. "The Purpose of the Cambridge School." *The Church Militant* 5 (April 1902): 5.

States that the purpose of the school is to train men to be scholarly and effective Christian ministers.

454.   Hodges, George. "Some Needs of the School." *The Church Militant* 7 (April 1904): 8.

Lists need for scholarships and books.

455.   Hodges, Julia Shelley. *George Hodges: A Biography*. New York and London: Century Co., 1926.

Treats fully the life and work of the fifth dean of the Episcopal Theological School, 1894-1919.

456.   Lawrence, William. "The Cambridge School -- Fifty Years Ago." *The Church Militant* 22 (November 1919): 2-5.

Describes the founding and history of the school.

457.   Lawrence, William. "The Episcopal Theological School." *The Church Militant* 23 (May 1920): 8-11.

Describes the school and urges financial support of it.

458.   Lawrence, William. *Memories of a Happy Life.* Boston and New York: Houghton Mifflin Company, 1926.

Reflections on the Episcopal Theological School by its fourth dean, 1889-1893.

459.   Lawrence, William. *Seventy-Three Years of the Episcopal Theological School, Cambridge: A Narrative. 1867-1940.* N.p. 1940.

Briefly describes the founding and history of ETS.

460.   Muller, James Arthur. *The Episcopal Theological School, 1867-1943.* Cambridge, MA: Episcopal Theological School, 1943.

Traces the history of this school beginning with the efforts to establish the "Massachusetts Episcopal Theological School." Includes lists of faculty members, part-time instructors, and faculty bibliography.

461.   Nash, Henry S. "The Episcopal Theological School, Cambridge, Mass." *The Churchman*, June 26, 1886, pp. 722-23.

Brief description of the seminary by the professor of New Testament.

462.   Rockwell, Hays H. "John B. Coburn: An Appreciation." *Anglican Theological Review, Supplementary Service* 4 (June 1976): 7-16.

Discusses the contributions of the eighth dean of ETS.

463.   Rogers, Arthur. "Professor Alexander V. G. Allen." *The Church Militant* 5 (April 1902): 7, 10.

Describes the contributions of Allen, professor of church history, 1867-1908.

464.   Slattery, Charles Lewis. *Certain American Faces: Sketches from Life.* New York: E. P. Dutton & Company, 1918.

Provides sketches of Alexander Viets Griswold Allen and Henry Sylvester Nash, two professors at the Episcopal Theological School.

465.   Well, Charles L.   "Memoir of Alexander Viets Griswold Allen, D.D." *Proceedings of the Massachusetts Historical Society* (January 1911): 355-62.

Briefly describes the life of the professor of ecclesiastical history, 1867-1908, at the Episcopal Theological School.

466.   Wharton, Helen. *Francis Wharton: A Memoir.* Philadelphia, PA: n.p. 1891.

Reflections by A.V.G. Allen on Wharton's years as a professor at the Episcopal Theological School, 1867-1881. Wharton was dean from April to July, 1867.

467.   Willard, Pitt S. "Charles Taylor as Pastor's Teacher." *Theological Education* 2 (Summer 1966): S-1 to S-4.

Describes Taylor's work as professor of Old Testament at the Episcopal Theological School.

468.   Wolf, William J.   "Curriculum Revision at the Episcopal Theological School and Some Dynamics of Its Acceptance. *Theological Education* 4 (Summer 1966): S104 - S115.

Treats the curriculum revision at ETS and its new emphasis.

Philadelphia Divinity School, Philadelphia, Pennsylvania, 1857-1974

469.   "Changes at Philadelphia." *The Living Church*, June 21, 1942, pp. 18-21.

Treats non-reappointment of two tutors at the Philadelphia Divinity School.

470.   Howe, M. A. DeWolfe. *Memoirs of the Life and Services of the Rt. Rev. Alonzo Potter, D.D., LL.D., Bishop of the Protestant Episcopal Church in the Diocese of Pennsylvania.* Philadelphia, PA: J. P. Lippincott & Co., 1871.

Traces briefly the founding of the Philadelphia Divinity School.

471.   Manross, William W. "A Great Evangelical: Alonzo Potter, the Third Bishop of Pennsylvania." *Historical Magazine of the Protestant Episcopal Church* 9 (June 1940): 97-130.

Briefly describes the founding of the Philadelphia Divinity School in 1857 by Bishop Potter.

472.   "Seminarians Study in Cloister and Clinics." *Forth* 108 (June 1943):
            14-15.

                        Treats Philadelphia's field education program in hospitals.

473.   Taylor, Raymond R.   "A Century of the Philadelphia Divinity
            School, 1857-1957."   *Historical Magazine of the Protestant
            Episcopal Church* 26 (September 1957): 204-23.

                        Briefly describes the history of the seminary in Philadelphia
            which merged with the Episcopal Theological School at Cambridge
            on June 6, 1974 to create the Episcopal Divinity School.

474.   Taylor, Raymond R.   "A History of the Divinity School in
            Philadelphia." Th. D. thesis. Philadelphia Divinity School, 1958.

                        Traces the history of this seminary from 1857 to 1958, with
            numerous appendices.

475.   West, Stanley R. *Centennial History of the Philadelphia Divinity
            School: The Divinity School of the Protestant Episcopal Church in
            Philadelphia, 1857-1957.* Philadelphia, PA: By the Author, 1971.

                        The most complete history of the Philadelphia Divinity
            School.

Episcopal Theological Seminary of the Southwest, 1951, Austin, Texas

476.   Blandy, Gray M., and Lawrence L. Brown. *The Story of the First
            Twenty-five Years of the Episcopal Theological Seminary of the
            Southwest.* Austin, TX: Episcopal Theological Seminary of the
            Southwest, 1976.

                        Traces the history from its beginning in 1951 to 1976.
            Includes listing of all faculty members and their publications.

477.   Clebsch, William A. "The Founding of the Episcopal Theological
            Seminary of the Southwest." *Historical Magazine of the Protestant
            Episcopal Church* 28 (September 1958): 247-52.

                        Traces the founding of this seminary at Austin, Texas.

478.   *Newsletter: Episcopal Theological Seminary of the Southwest.*
            (1965-1986).

                        Contains information about the students, faculty and
            alumni/ae of the school.

479.   *Ratherview: Episcopal Theological Seminary of the Southwest*
            (Spring 1986-   ).

                        Contains information about the students, faculty and
            alumni/ae of the school.

General Theological Seminary, 1817, New York, 1817-1820, New Haven, Connecticut, 1820-1821, New York, 1822-

480.   "Alumni List." *Bulletin of the General Theological Seminary*, 54 (February 1958): 3-122.

         Lists alumni from 1822 to December 1957.

481.   "Alumni List." *Bulletin of the General Theological Seminary*, 59 (February 1963): 3-132.

         Lists alumni from 1822 to December 1962.

482.   Beardsley, William A. "Thomas Church Brownell -- Third Bishop of Connecticut." *Historical Magazine of the Protestant Episcopal Church* 6 (December 1937): 350-69.

         Treats Brownell's desire to establish a seminary at Schenectady, New York, his support of the General Theological Seminary while at New Haven, 1820-1821, where he taught pastoral theology, and his disappointment when General was moved back to New York in 1821.

483.   Bloodgood, Francis J. "Profile of Frank Gavin (1890-1938), Priest and Scholar." *Historical Magazine of the Protestant Episcopal Church* 29 (March 1960): 51-55.

         Briefly describes the life and work of the ninth professor of Ecclesiastical History at the General Theological Seminary (1923-1938), and a leader of the Liberal Catholic party of the Episcopal Church.

484.   Carpenter, James A. "An Appreciation of Powell Mills Dawley." *Anglican and Episcopal History* 56 (September 1987): 233-35.

         Discusses the contributions of the tenth professor of church history at the General Theological Seminary.

485.   *Catalogue of the Associate Alumni of the General Theological Seminary, with an Index, Also a List of the Sermonizers, Essayists, McVikar and Seymour Prizeman.* New York: Executive Committee, Associate Alumni, 1887.

         Contains many helpful listings.

486.   Chorley, E. Clowes. "The Oxford Movement and the Seminary." *Historical Magazine of the Protestant Episcopal Church* 5 (September 1936): 177-201.

         Treats the impact of the Oxford Movement on the General Seminary, an impact that earned General the nickname "Little Oxford," as well as the investigation of the seminary by the House of Bishops and the suspension of Bishop Benjamin T. Onderslank of New York from the episcopate.

487.   "Church Tradition Centers Around 'General'." *Forth* 106 (March 1941): 18-19, 29.

         Treats General's many years of service to the Church.

488.   Dawley, Powell Mills. "In Memoriam: The Rev. Robert Semple Bosher, Ph.D., S.T.D., Priest and Professor, 1911-1976, the General Theological Seminary." *Historical Magazine of the Protestant Episcopal Church* 46 (September 1977): 273-74.

         Briefly describes the work of the eleventh professor of Ecclesiastical History at General Seminary.

489.   Dawley, Powell Mills. *The Story of the General Theological Seminary: A Sesquicentennial History, 1817-1967.* New York: Oxford University Press, 1969.

         The definitive history of the General Theological Seminary, New York City, from its founding on May 27, 1817, by the General Convention of the Episcopal Church to 1967. Dawley traces its founding, its move to New Haven in 1820-21, its return to New York and its subsequent history. He treats faculty members, curriculum changes, buildings and renovations and student life. Special emphasis is placed upon Deans Eugene Augustus Hoffman (1879-1902) and Hughell Edgar Woodall Fosbroke (1917-1947).

490.   Gates, Miko H. "Deans and Professors." *Historical Magazine of the Protestant Episcopal Church* 5 (September 1936): 238-64.

         Discusses personalities and has bibliography of the major works of the deans and professors of the General Theological Seminary, as well as a list of all faculty members by departments.

491.   Gillespie, Stephen W. "John Murray Forbes, 1807-1885; First Permanent Dean of General Theological Seminary." *Historical Magazine of the Protestant Episcopal Church* 24 (December 1955): 332-65.

         Traces the career of Forbes, who was rector of St. Luke's Church, New York City, joined the Roman Cathoic Church in 1849, returned to the Episcopal Church in 1859, was elected dean of General Seminary on October 12, 1869, and resigned on November 1, 1872.

492.   Hardy, Edward R., Jr. "The Organization and Early Years of the General Theological Seminary." *Historical Magazine of the Protestant Episcopal Church* 5 (September 1936): 147-76.

         Fully treats the founding of the seminary from its proposal in 1814 by Bishop Theodore Dehon of South Carolina through its establishment in 1819 to the year 1836.

493.   Hoffman, Eugene A. "Historical Sketch of the General Theological
         Seminary." In *The History of the American Episcopal Church,
         1587-1883*. Vol. II: *The Organization and Progress of the American
         Church, 1783-1883*, pp. 507-34. Edited by William S. Perry.
         Boston, MA: James R. Osgood, 1885.

         The first detailed account of the founding and development
         of the seminary by its third dean.

494.   Howe, Gregory. "On Being a Seminarian." *The Witness*, January
         24, 1963, pp. 9-11.

         Describes life at General in 1963.

495.   Keyes, C. Don. "Human Transcendence: Clue to Julian Casserley's
         Hope for the Twenty-first Century." *St. Luke's Journal of Theology*
         27 (March 1984): 101-12.

         Discusses the theology of Julian Victor Langmead Casserley
         (1909-1978), professor of Dogmatic Theology at the General
         Theological Seminary, 1951-1959.

496.   Mampoteng, Charles. "The Library and the American Church."
         Historical Magazine of the Protestant Episcopal Church 5
         (September 1936): 225-37.

         Lists the Episcopal Church periodicals available at the
         General Theological Seminary library.

497.   Manross, William W. "Growth and Progress Since 1860."
         Historical Magazine of the Protestant Episcopal Church 5
         (September 1936): 202-24.

         Traces the General Theological Seminary from the lowest
         point in its history, 1860, through its revival under Dean Eugene
         Augustus Hoffman and Hughell Edgar Woodall Fosbrooke.

498.   *Proceedings of the Board of Trustees of the General Theological
         Seminary of the Protestant Episcopal Church in the United States.*
         7 vols. New York: Numerous publishers, 1821-1901.

         Contains the minutes of the board.

499.   Riley, Theodore M. *A Memorial Biography of the Very Reverend
         Eugene Augustus Hoffman, Late Dean of the General Theological
         Seminary.* 2 vols. Jamaica, NY: Privately printed, 1904.

         Discusses fully the life and work of the third dean of the
         General Theological Seminary (1879-1902).

500.   *Seminary News*, I, 1 (March 1975-   ).

         Contains much information about students, faculty,

alumni/ae and seminary events.

501.   Turner, Samuel Hulbeart. *Autobiography.* New York: A. D. F. Randolph, 1864.

A primary source for the founding and development of the General Theological Seminary by the professor of historic theology (1819-1921) and professor of biblical learning and the interpretation of scripture (1821-1861).

502.   Walworth, Clarence E. *The Oxford Movement in America; or, Glimpses of Life in an Anglican Seminary.* New York: Catholic Book Exchange, 1895.

Traces the Oxford Movement at General Seminary.

503.   White, William. *Memoirs of the Protestant Episcopal Church in the United States of America.* 3rd ed. Edited by B. F. DeCosta. New York: E. P. Dutton, 1880.

Contains Bishop White's reflections on the establishment of the General Theological Seminary.

504.   Wilson, Bird. *Memoirs of the Life of the Right Reverend William White, D.D., Bishop of the Protestant Episcopal Church in the State of Pennsylvania.* Philadelphia, PA: James Kay, Jun. & Brother, 1839.

Provide White's thoughts about the founding of the General Theological Seminary.

505.   Wilson, James G., ed. *The Centennial History of the Protestant Episcopal Church in the Diocese of New York, 1785-1885.* New York: D. Appleton and Company, 1886.

Traces the founding and history of the General Theological Seminary.

506.   Wright, J. Robert. "Guest Editorial [Powell Mills Dawley]." *Anglican and Episcopal History* 56 (September 1987): 229-31.

Brief biography of the tenth professor of church history at the General Theological Seminary.

507.   Wright, J. Robert. "Provisional Bibliography: The Published Writings of Powell Mills Dawley." *Anglican and Episcopal History* 56 (September 1987): 331-35.

Lists the writings of the tenth professor of church history at the General Theological Seminary.

Nashotah House, 1842, Nashotah, Wisconsin

508. Anderson, Harry H., ed. "Remembrances of Nashotah Days: Two Letters of Gustaf Unonius." *Swedish Pioneer Historical Quarterly* 27 (1976): 111-15.

    Reflections by Nashotah's first graduate who worked among Scandinavian Lutherans and Episcopalians.

509. Blackburn, Imri M. "A Chronology: Some Events in the History of Nashotah House." *Nashotah House Quarterly Review* 1 (Summer 1961): 51-54.

    Lists significant events from 1834 to 1959.

510. Blackburn, Imri M. *Nashotah House: A History of Seventy-five Years.* 2 vols. Nashotah, WI: Nashotah House, 1966.

    Fully tells the story of Nashotah House until the first World War.

511. Breck, Charles, comp. *The Life of the Reverend James Lloyd Breck, D.D., Chiefly from Letters Written by Himself.* New York: E. & J. B. Young & Co., 1883.

    Treats fully the founding of the Nashotah mission and Nashotah House in 1842.

512. "Buffalo Robes to Gray Cloisters - Nashotah Epic." *Forth* 107 (May 1942): 20-21.

    Reflects on Nashotah's history at the time of its centennial.

513. Carroon, Robert G. "Nashotah House During the Civil War." *Nashotah Quarterly Review* 2 (Fall 1961): 24-34.

    Describes Nashotah's difficulties during this period.

514. Chorley, E. Clowes. "The Missionary March of the Episcopal Church: IX: Jackson Kemper and the Northwest." *Historical Magazine of the Protestant Episcopal Church* 17 (March 1948): 3-17.

    Notes briefly the founding of Nashotah.

515. Cooper, Frank M. "An Annotated Calendar of Papers for the Study of the History of Nashotah House," 1972. Library, Nashotah House, Nashotah, Wisconsin.

    Lists the documents related to the history of Nashotah House.

516. Crumb, Lawrence N. "A Statistical and Biographical Study of

Students Entering Nashotah House Seminary in the Year 1842-1970, Inclusive." STM thesis, Nashotah House Seminary, 1973.

Contains information on students at Nashotah House.

517.   Doane, Gilbert. "The Roots of Nashotah." *The Living Church*, May 17, 1942, pp. 11-12.

Describes Nashotah's founding.

518.   Egar, John H. *The Story of Nashotah*. Milwaukee, WI: Burdick & Armitage, 1874.

Describes the founding and early history of Nashotah.

519.   Estlund, Ann. "Dean Reuf Reflects on Challenges and Changes at Nashotah." *The Episcopalian* 144 (October 1979): A-B.

Notes changes such as Nashotah House changing from a "male enclave" to a family community.

520.   Golder, James T. "Nashotah Today." *The Living Church*, May 17, 1942, pp. 18-19.

Describes Nashotah at the time of its centennial.

521.   Grant, Frederick C. "Nashotah House's Legacy." *The Living Church*, November 12, 1967, pp. 17-18.

Notes the great teachers and scholars in Nashotah's history.

522.   Greene, Howard. *The Reverend Richard Fisk Cadle: A Missionary of the Protestant Episcopal Church in the Territories of Michigan and Wisconsin in the Early Nineteenth Century. A Biographical Study*. Waukesha, WI: Privately printed, 1936.

Briefly mentions the founding of Nashotah House.

523.   Hallock, Donald H. V. "Nashotah House's Heritage." *The Living Church*, November 12, 1967, pp. 16, 19.

Briefly traces the history of Nashotah House and its college department.

524.   Hallock, Donald H. V. "Nashotah's Hundred Years." *The Living Church*, May 17, 1942, pp. 13-14.

Traces Nashotah's history.

525.   Hallock, Donald H. V. "The Story of Nashotah." *Historical Magazine of the Protestant Episcopal Church* 11 (March 1942): 1-17.

A brief centennial history of Nashotah House.

526.   Hardy, Edward R., Jr. "Kemper's Missionary Episcopate: 1835-1859." *Historical Magazine of the Protestant Episcopal Church* 3 (September 1935): 195-218.

Briefly describes founding of Nashotah House.

527.   Holcombe, Theodore I. *An Apostle of the Wilderness: James Lloyd Breck, D.D. His Missions and Schools.* New York: Thomas Whittaker, 1903.

Treats fully Breck's establishment of the Nashotah mission and Nashotah House in 1842.

528.   Hunt, Joseph I. "Nashotah House Theological Seminary." 1979 Nashotah House, Nashotah, WI. Photocopy.

Briefly discusses Nashotah House from 1842 to about 1979.

529.   *In Memoriam: Joseph Morison Clarke, D.D., 1827-1899.* Burlington, VT: Free Press Association, 1901.

Notes briefly Clarke's years, 1886-1891, as dean and professor of Exegesis, Biblical Literature and Hebrew at Nashotah.

530.   Ivins, Benjamin F. P. "The Influence of Nashotah." *The Living Church*, May 17, 1942, p. 16.

Describes Nashotah as a mission.

531.   Ivins, Sarah S. *The Founding of Nashotah Mission.* N.p. 1924.

Traces the founding of the Associate Mission and Brotherhood.

532.   Kip, William Ingraham. *Few Days at Nashotah.* Albany, NY: J. Munsell, 1849.

Describes Nashotah in August 1847 after a visit. The writer was later Bishop of California.

533.   Lacher, J. H. A. "Nashotah House, Wisconsin's Oldest School of Higher Education." *Wisconsin Magazine of History* 16 (December 1932): 123-62.

Treats fully the founding of Nashotah House.

534.   *Nashotah House*, first called *Nashotah* (March 1983-   ).

Contains information about students and faculty.

535.   "Nashotah House and the Future." *The Living Church*, September

7, 1947, pp. 10-11, 23.

Discusses Nashotah's future as the seminary most definitely and unequivocally identified with the Catholic movement.

536.   "The Nashotah Liturgy." *Historical Magazine of the Protestant Episcopal Church* 29 (December 1960): 287-301.

Presents for the first time in print the liturgy used by the founders of Nashotah House in 1842.

537.   *Nashotah Quarterly Review*, later changed to *Nashotah Review*, I, 1 (Fall 1960) - XVI, 3 (Fall 1976).

This *Review*, which ceased publication in 1976, has information about students, faculty and alumni.

538.   *The Nashotah News*, began as *Nashotah Alumni Bulletin*, later called *The Nashotah News and Alumni Bulletin* (September 1926 - May 1960).

Carried news about "The House."

539.   *Nashotah Scholiast*, later named *Church Scholiast* (December 1883 - July 1888).

Carries information about Nashotah House.

540.   Nutter, E. J. M. "Nashotah's Aim." *The Living Church*, May 17, 1942, pp. 15, 20.

Describes Nashotah's aim to revive and maintain traditional and historical principles.

541.   Orth, William H. "Materials for the History of Nashotah House." Nashotah House, Nashotah, WI. 1974.

A collection of documents on the history of Nashotah.

542.   Parsons, Donald J. "Nashotah: Today and Tomorrow." *The Living Church*, November 12, 1967, pp. 11-14.

Reflects on Nashotah's history and opportunities.

543.   Simpson, James. "The Uncloistered Life of Nashotah." *The Milwaukee Journal*, 19 March 1967.

Tells the story of Nashotah in a popular way.

544.   *This is Nashotah* (October 1969 - December 1982).

Provides news and information about the school.

545.   Wagner, Harold E. *The Episcopal Church in Wisconsin, 1847-1947:*

A History of the Diocese of Milwaukee. Milwaukee, WI: Diocese of Milwaukee, 1947.

Traces the founding and early history of Nashotah House.

546.   Walworth, Clarence E. *The Oxford Movement in America; or, Glimpses of Life in an Anglican Seminary.* New York: Catholic Book Exchange, 1895.

Briefly discusses the founding of Nashotah.

547.   Webb, William Walter. "Nashotah: The First Attempt to Found a Religious House in the American Catholic Church." *The Living Church*, April 11, 1903, pp. 845-47.

Briefly discusses the founding of the Nashotah Mission in 1842.

School of Theology, University of the South, 1879, Sewanee, Tennessee

548.   Alexander, George M. "Some Reflections on Theological Education." *St. Luke's Journal of Theology* 10 (June 1967): 4-9.

The Dean of the School of Theology, 1956-1972, discusses the complexities of theological education in the late 1960s.

549.   Armentrout, Donald S. "The Beginnings of Theological Education at the University of the South: The Role of John Austion Merrick." *Historical Magazine of the Protestant Episcopal Church* 51 (September 1982): 253-67.

Discusses Merrick's role in establishing the Sewanee Training and Divinity School.

550.   Armentrout, Donald S. *Bibliography of the Faculty Members of the School of Theology, University of the South, 1871-1978.* Sewanee, TN: *St. Luke's Journal of Theology*, 1979.

A complete listing of all faculty publications.

551.   Armentrout, Donald S. "John Howard Winslow Rhys: Professor of New Testament, 1953-1983." *St. Luke's Journal of Theology* 26 (September 1983): 279-83.

Articulates the contributions of the ninth professor of New Testament at the School of Theology and lists his publications.

552.   Armentrout, Donald S. *The Quest for the Informed Priest: A History of the School of Theology.* Sewanee, TN: School of Theology, University of the South, 1979.

The definitive history of the School of Theology at Sewanee, Tennessee, from its founding in 1878 to 1979. He treats faculty members, curriculum changes, liturgical life and student life. The thirty appendices provide much information.

553.   Armentrout, Donald S. "The School of Theology of the University of the South Celebrates 100 Years." *The Living Church*, May 13, 1979, pp. 12-13, 18.

A brief account of the founding of the School of Theology.

554.   Armentrout, Donald S.   "Some Conclusions about the First One-Hundred Years of the School of Theology." *St. Luke's Journal of Theology* 23 (December 1979): 33-42.

Articulates the contributions of the School of Theology to Episcopal theological education.

555.   Booty, John E. "The 1982 Matriculation Sermon." *St. Luke's Journal of Theology* 26 (December 1982): 5-9.

Argues against bifurcation of *theoria* and *praxis*, and urges a theological education model of sacrificial service.

556.   Chitty, Arthur B. "Heir of Hopes: Historical Summary of the University of the South." *Historical Magazine of the Protestant Episcopal Church* 23 (September 1954): 258-65.

Summary of the contributions of the University of the South, including the School of Theology.

557.   Chitty, Arthur B. *Reconstruction at Sewanee: The Founding of the University of the South and Its First Administration, 1857-1872.* Sewanee, TN: University Press, 1954.

Traces the founding, refounding and first administration of Vice-Chancellor Charles Todd Quintard of the University of the South. Treats beginnings of theological education before there was a Theological Department.

558.   Chitty, Arthur B.   *Sewanee Sampler.*   Sewanee, TN: Historiographer, University of the South, 1978.

A collection of stories about persons associated with the University of the South, including the school of Theology.

559.   DuBose, William P. "The Romance and Genius of a University." *Sewanee Review* 13 (October 1905): 496-502.

Reflects on the meaning of the University of the South and its School of Theology.

560.   DuBose, William P. *Turning Points in My Life.* New York: Longman's, Green and Co., 1912.

Discusses his role in founding the School of Theology.

561. DuBose, William P. "The University of the South." In *The History of the American Episcopal Church, 1587-1883.* Vol. 2. *The Organization and Progress of the American Church, 1783-1883*, pp. 557-60. Edited by William S. Perry. Boston: James R. Osgood, 1885.

The second dean of the School of Theology describes the school as "a university under the distinct sanction of the Christian faith."

562. Dudney, Rainsford F. G., Helen A. Petry, and Elizabeth N. Chitty, eds. *Centennial Report of the Registrar of the University of the South.* Sewanee, TN: University of the South, 1959.

Lists administrators, trustees and many other persons at the University of the South, including the School of Theology.

563. Fairbanks, George F. *History of the University of the South, at Sewanee, Tennessee, from Its Founding by the Southern Bishops, Clergy and Laity of the Episcopal Church in 1857 to the year 1905.* Jacksonville, FL: H. & W. B. Drew, 1905.

The first history of the University of the South, including the School of Theology, by one of its founders and trustees.

564. "Gospel Wagon Roams Over Mountains." *Forth* 108 (August 1943): 26-27.

Discusses how seminaries serve in rural missions around Sewanee.

565. Griffin, William A. "The Bible as the Basis of Theological Education." *St. Luke's Journal of Theology* (Fall 1963): 9-13.

Urges greater study of the Bible in theological education.

566. Guerry, Moultrie. *Men Who Made Sewanee.* Sewanee, TN: University Press, 1932; expanded by Arthur B. and Elizabeth N. Chitty, 1981.

Biographical essays on outstanding leaders of the University of the South, including the School of Theology.

567. Holmes, Urban T. "The Seminary as Method." *St. Luke's Journal of Theology* 16 (September 1973): 5-12.

The tenth Dean of the School of Theology argues that the seminary should be a method for professional training, graduate education, and formation.

568. "The Parson's Wife Goes to School." *Forth* 113 (November 1948):

16-17.

Treats the "miniature theological education" program, instituted by Dean Robert F. Gibson, Jr., for wives of seminarians after World War II.

569.   Petry, Helen A., Elizabeth N. Chitty and Mary C. Hunt, eds. *Centennial Alumni Directory.* Sewanee, TN: *Sewanee Alumni News,* 1954-1962.

Lists alumni of the University of the South, including the School of Theology.

570.   Trent, William P. "The University of the South." In *Higher Education in Tennessee,* pp. 202-13. Edited by Lucius S. Merriam. Washington: Government Printing Office, 1893.

A brief history of the University of the South, including the School of Theology.

571.   "University of the South." *The Church Review* 50 (December, 1887): 641-80.

An unsigned, early account of the founding and history of the University of the South and its School of Theology.

572.   Yerkes, Royden Keith. "The Beginnings of the Graduate School of Theology of the University of the South." *Historical Magazine of the Protestant Episcopal Church* 29 (December 1960): 315-24.

Traces the beginnings of the Graduate School of Theology which was founded in 1937.

Seabury-Western Theological Seminary, 1858, Evanston, Indiana (Seabury Divinity School, 1858, Fiarbault, Minnesota, and Western Theological Seminary, 1885, Chicago, Illinois, Merged on July 1, 1933.)

573.   Breck, Charles, comp. *The Life of the Reverend James Lloyd Breck, D.D., Chiefly from Letters Written by Himself.* New York: E. & J. B. Young & Co., 1883.

Treats fully the founding of Seabury Divinity Hall at Fiarbault, Minnesota in 1858.

574.   Elmen, Paul. "Seabury-Western Is More Than the Total of Two Parts." *Advance* (January 1959): 4, 6-7.

Briefly traces the history and contributions of Seabury-Western.

575.   Holcombe, Theodore I. *An Apostle of the Wilderness: James Lloyd Breck, D.D. His Missions and His Schools.* New York: Thomas Whittaker, 1903.

Treats Breck's establishment of Seabury Divinity Hall at Faribault, Minnesota in 1858.

576.   Johnson, Sherman E.   "Frederick Clifton Grant (1891-1974)." *Anglican Theological Review* 57 (January 1975): 3-15; and *Nashotah Review* 15 (Spring 1975): 4-18.

Discusses the contributions of the dean of Western Theological Seminary and his work in merging Seabury and Western in 1933.

577.   McElwain, Frank A. "Seabury-Western Theological Seminary: A History. Part I: Seabury Divinity School." *Historical Magazine of the Protestant Episcopal Church* 5 (December 1936): 286-301.

Traces the founding of Seabury in 1858 and its subsequent history to 1933.

578.   Norwood, Percy V. "Seabury-Western Theological Seminary: A History. Part II: Western Theological Seminary." *Historical Magazine of the Protestant Episcopal Church* 5 (December 1936): 301-11.

Traces the founding of Western at Chicago in 1885 and its subsequent history to July 1, 1933 when Seabury merged with it.

579.   "Seventy Years of Seabury Divinity School, 1858-1928, Faribault, Minnesota." *Seabury Divinity School Bulletin* 10 (December 1927): 1-23.

Traces the founding and history of Seabury.

580.   Sheppard, E. L. *The Second Fifty Years: The Diocese of Minnesota and the Diocese of Duluth from 1907 to 1957.* Minneapolis: Diocese of Minnesota, 1972.

Traces briefly the merger of Seabury and Western in 1933.

581.   Tanner, George C. *Fifty Years of Church Work in the Diocese of Minnesota, 1857-1907.* St. Paul, MN: Published by the Committee, 1909.

Traces the founding of the Bishop Seabury University at Faribault and its becoming the Seabury Divinity School.

582.   Whipple, Henry B. *Lights and Shadows of a Long Episcopate.* New York: Macmillan Company, 1899.

Briefly mentions Seabury Divinity School.

Trinity Episcopal School for Ministry, 1976, Ambridge, Pennsylvania

583.   Duin, Julia. "Steel Town Seminary." *Acts 29: Newsletter of the Episcopal Renewal Ministries* (December 1987): 1-2.

Briefly describes Trinity's evangelical and renewal mission.

584.   Fairfield, Leslie P. "A Listening People: Biblical Training at Trinity School for Ministry." *Kerygam* (January 1980): 4-7.

Discusses Trinity's commitment to the authority of Scripture as the basis of its evangelical emphasis.

585.   Fairfield, Leslie P. "Living in God's Providence: Trinity Episcopal Church for Ministry Grows and Moves." *Kerygma* (June 1978): 6-9.

Notes growth of Trinity and move from Robert Morris College, Sewickly to Ambridge, Pennsylvania.

586.   Fairfield, Leslie P. "The New Evangelical Seminary." *The Living Church*, February 11, 1979, pp. 10-11.

Explains why Trinity Episcopal School for Ministry at Ambridge, Pennsylvania, was founded and opened on September 25, 1976.

587.   Fairfield, Leslie P. "Why Trinity Episcopal School for Ministry?" *Kerygma* (October 1976): 3.

Notes that Trinity is to be Evangelical, Anglican, open to the Holy Spirit and dedicated to the ministry of all God's people.

588.   Leighton, Christopher and Robert Richard. "Trinity's First Year: Two Student Responses." *Kerygma* (October 1976): 12-13.

Describes life at Trinity School.

589.   Nagiel, Esther-Marie. "A Look at Trinity Episcopal School for Ministry." *The Anglican Digest* 28 (Lent 1986): 4-9.

Describes the mission and ministry of Trinity as an Evangelical school.

590.   Rodgers, John H. "Education for Ministry in the Anglican Evangelical Perspective." *Kerygma* (October 1976): 9-11.

Notes the theme of Anglican Evangelicalism to be stressed at Trinity.

591.   *Seed & Harvest*, Vol. I, 1 (July 1980-   ).

Carries news about the seminary.

592.   "Trinity Episcopal School for Ministry Opens." *Kerygma* (October 1976): 4-8.

          Explains the purpose of Trinity School.

Virginia Theological Seminary, 1823, Alexandria, Virginia

593.   Glenn, C. Leslie. "Virginia Has Great Missionary Heritage." *Forth* 111 (April 1946): 16-17, 34-35.

          Treats Virginia's great commitment to foreign missions.

594.   Goodwin, Edward L. *The Colonial Church in Virginia with Biographical Sketches of the First Six Bishops of the Diocese of Virginia.* Milwaukee, WI: Morehouse Publishing Co.; London: A. R. Mowbray & Co., 1927.

          Treats the Protestant Episcopal Theological Seminary at Alexandria under Bishops Richard C. Moore, 1814-41, William Meade, 1841-62, John Johns, 1862-76, Francis Whittle, 1876-1902, and Robert Gibson, 1902-19.

595.   Goodwin, William A. R., ed. *History of the Theological Seminary in Virginia and Its Historical Background.* 2 vols. New York: Edwin S. Gorham, 1923.

          Traces in detail the first hundred years of the Protestant Episcopal Theological Seminary in Virginia at Alexandria. It treats every facet of the seminary's life, as well as the Bishop Payne Divinity School at Petersburg.

596.   Johns, John. *A Memoir of the Life of the Right Rev. William Meade, D.D., Bishop of the Protestant Episcopal Church in the Diocese of Virginia.* Baltimore: Innes & Company, Publishers, 1867.

          Treats Meade's role in the organization and development of the Virginia Theological Seminary.

597.   Kevin, Robert O. "Seminary Deans, 1823-1916." *The Virginia Seminary Journal* 21 (March 1969): 40-44.

          Treats briefly the tenures of Reuel Keith, William Sparrow, Joseph Packard, Cornelius Walker, and Angus Crawford.

598.   Krumm, John M. "Albert T. Mollegen: An Appreciation." *Anglican Theological Review, Supplementary Series* 7 (November 1876): 9-18.

          Discusses the many contributions of this professor at VTS and lists his publications.

599.   Miller, J. Barnett. "The Theology of William Sparrow." *Historical*

Magazine of the Protestant Episcopal Church 46 (December 1977):
443-54.

> Traces Sparrow's understanding of justification by grace
> through faith and its place within the teaching at the Protestant
> Episcopal Seminary in Virginia and the Evangelical party of the
> Episcopal Church. Sparrow taught at Kenyon College from 1825
> to 1840, and from 1841 to 1874 was professor of theology at
> Virginia Seminary.

600.   Packard, Joseph. *Recollections of a Long Life.* Edited by Thomas
        J. Packard. Washington, DC: Byron S. Adams, Publishers, 1902.

> Reflections on the Virginia Theological Seminary by a man
> who was professor, dean and professor emeritus for sixty-six years,
> 1836-1902.

601.   Pisani, Frank. "The Trotter Years." *The Virginia Seminary Journal*
        21 (March 1969): 5-20.

> Discusses the tenure of Jesse Trotter, eleventh dean of VTS,
> 1956-1968.

602.   Price, Charles P. "Clifford Leland Stanley: Teacher and
        Theologian." *Anglican Theological Review, Supplementary Series*, 7
        (November 1976): 19-30.

> Discusses the contributions of this professor of Systematic
> Theology at VTS and lists his publications.

603.   Prichard, Robert W. "Virginia Seminary Since World War II."
        Virginia Seminary Journal 38 (June 1985): 33-43.

> Tells the story of VTS under Deans Alexander Zabriskie
> (1940-1950), Stanley Brown-Sherman (1951-1952), E. Felix Kloman
> (1953-1956), Jesse M. Trotter (1956-1969), and Granville Cecil
> Woods, Jr. (1969-1985).

604.   Stanley, Clifford L. "Seminary Deans, 1916-1956: Personal
        Recollections." *The Virginia Seminary Journal* 21 (March 1961):
        45-48.

> Reflects on the tenures of Berryman Green, Wallace Eugene
> Rollins, Alexander Zabriskie, Stanley Brown-Sherman, and E. Felix
> Kloman.

605.   *The Theological Repository*, I, 1 (August 1819-1830).

> Contains news about Virginia Seminary.

606.   Trotter, Jesse M. "The Pusey-Taylor Report and the Virginia
        Seminary." *The Seminary Journal* 19 (December 1967): 1-3.

Maintains that VTS is "ahead of the report," *Ministry for Tomorrow* (1967).

607. *The Virginia Seminary Journal* I, 1 (September 1954 -). Originally called *The Seminary Journal.*

Reports news about students, faculty and alumni/ae.

608. *Virginia Seminary Magazine*, I, 1 (December 1887 - November 1892), became the *Protestant Episcopal Review*, and ceased publication in 1900.

Contains news about students, faculty and alumni.

609. Walker, Cornelius. *The Life and Correspondence of Rev. William Sparrow, D.D.* Philadelphia, PA: James Hammond, 1876.

Describes the life and contributions of Sparrow, professor of systematic divinity at VTS.

Part IV. Theological Seminaries No Longer in Existence

Absalom Jones Theological Institute, Atlanta, Georgia

610. "BTE Unit Set for Atlanta." *The Living Church*, July 11, 1971, p. 4.

Discusses the plans for the Absalom Jones Theological Institute to open in the fall of 1972 as part of the Interdenominational Theological Center in Atlanta.

611. "Institute Draws Few Students." *The Living Church*, October 26, 1975, p. 7.

Notes that Absalom Jones Theological Institute in Atlanta, which opened in 1972, had few students in its first years of operation.

Arkansas Theological Chautauqua School, Arkansas, 1903-1913

612. McDonald, Margaret Simms. *White Already to Harvest: The Episcopal Church in Arkansas, 1838-1971.* Little Rock, AR: Episcopal Diocese of Arkansas, 1975.

Discusses the Arkansas Theological Chautauqua School, which operated from 1903 to 1913, and trained about 22 men for the ministry. It was established by Bishop William Montgomery Brown.

Bishop Payne Divinity School, 1878-1949, Petersburg, Virginia

613. Bragg, George F., Jr. *The Story of Old St. Stephen's, Petersburg, VA.* Baltimore, MD: Church Advocate Print, 1906.

Traces the history of the church where the Bishop Payne Seminary began in the fall of 1878 during the rectorship of Giles B. Cooke.

614.   Brydon, George Maclaren. *The Episcopal Church Among the Negroes of Virginia*. Richmond, VA: Virginia Diocesan Library, 1937.

Traces the history of the Bishop Payne Seminary from its founding at St. Stephen's Church, Petersburg, in 1878, with its first "faculty," the Rev. Thomas Spencer.

615.   Harris, Odell Greenleaf. *The Bishop Payne Divinity School, Petersburg, Virginia, 1878-1949: A History of the Seminary to Prepare Black Men for the Ministry of the Protestant Episcopal Church.* Alexandria, VA: Protestant Episcopal Theological Seminary, 1980.

Treats the history of this seminary until it closed in 1949, and its assets merged with the Virginia Theological Seminary as the Bishop Payne Library.

616.   Hawkins, John, Jr. "The Educational Development of Bishop Payne Divinity School." MSE thesis, Virginia State College, Petersburg, 1945.

Describes the Bishop Payne Divinity School for blacks which opened in 1878 and closed in 1949.

617.   Russell, James S. *Adventure in Faith: An Autobiographical Story of St. Paul Normal and Industrial School, Lawrenceville, Virginia.* New York & Milwaukee, WI: Morehouse Publishing Co., 1936.

Discusses the author's time at the Bishop Payne Seminary.

Denver Theological School and the College of St. John the Evangelist, 1879-1915, Denver, 1910-1937, Greeley.

618.   Breck, Allen DuPont. *The Episcopal Church in Colorado, 1869-1963.* Denver, CO: Big Mountain Press, 1963.

Traces the beginnings of theological education at Matthews Hall, Golden, its move to Denver in 1879 as the Denver Theological School, its closing in 1915, and the history of the College of St. John the Evangelist, "a theological school for the education of clergy for the West," at Greeley, 1910-1937.

DeLancey Divinity School, 1861-1920, Geneva, New York, 1920-1935, Buffalo, New York

619.   Burrows, G. Sherman. "Bishop William H. DeLancey." *Historical Magazine of the Protestant Episcopal Church* 5 (December 1936): 267-85.

Treats briefly the beginnings of the DeLancey Divinity School at Geneva, New York.

620.   Burrows, G. Sherman. *The Diocese of Western New York, 1897-1931.* Buffalo, NY: Diocese of Western New York, 1935.

Briefly treats the DeLancey Divinity School which began in 1861 as a "Diocesan Training School" at Geneva, and moved to Buffalo in 1920.

621.   Hayes, Charles W. *The Diocese of Western New York: History and Recollections.* Rochester, NY: Scranton, Wetmore & Co., 1904.

Traces theological education at the Fairfield Academy, 1813-1821, Geneva College, 1821-1825, and the founding of the DeLancey Divinity School (named after the Rt. Rev. William H. DeLancey, first Bishop of Western New York) at Geneva. It opened on February 1, 1861 as the Diocesan Training School and closed in 1935.

622.   *Inventory of the Church Archives of New York State Exclusive of New York City: Protestant Episcopal Church, Diocese of Rochester.* Albany, NY: Historical Records Survey, 1941.

Bishop William H. DeLancey of Western New York established a diocesan school in divinity at Geneva in April 1850, under the direction of Dr. William Dexter Wilson, which closed in 1858. On February 1, 1861, DeLancey opened the Diocesan Training School at Geneva under the direction of the Rev. James Rankine. In 1866 it was named the DeLancey Divinity School, and in 1920 moved to Buffalo. It closed in 1935.

623.   Masterman, Frederick J. "Some Aspects of the Episcopate of William Heathcote DeLancey, First Bishop of the Diocese of Western New York (1839-1865)." *Historical Magazine of the Protestant Episcopal Church* 33 (September 1964): 261-77.

Treats DeLancey's concerns about theological education and the establishment of a "Training School for Candidates" at Geneva in February 1861. Later it was named the DeLancey Divinity School.

624.   Perry, William Stevens. "The History of Hobart College, Geneva, N.Y." In *History of Ontario Co., New York*, pp. 68-76. Edited by W. H. McIntosh. Philadelphia, PA: Everts, Engigh and Everts, 1876.

While this is a history of Hobart College, Steven traces the beginning of theological education at Geneva before Hobart College was founded in 1822. On June 11, 1821, the Branch or Interior School of the New York Diocesan School opened at Geneva.

Bishop John Henry Hobart was its sponsor, and as a result some of his opponents called it "Cardinal Wolsey's College."

625.   Smith, Warren H. *Hobart and William Smith: The History of Two Colleges*. Geneva, NY: Hobart and William Smith Colleges, 1972.

While this is a history of the colleges, Smith describes the beginnings of theological education at Geneva and the work of the Branch or Interior School of the New York Diocesan School at Geneva.

626.   Turk, Milton H.   *Hobart: The Story of a Hundred Years, 1822-1922*. Geneva, NY: Hobart College, 1922.

Treats theological education at Hobart and includes early documents related to theological education.

Divinity Department of Burlington College, Burlington, New Jersey

627.   Hills, George M. *History of the Church in Burlington, New Jersey*. 2nd ed. Trenton, NJ: By the Author, 1885.

Briefly treats the Divinity Department of Burlington College which operated in the 1870's.

628.   Schermerhorn, William E. *The History of Burlington, New Jersey*. Burlington, NJ: Enterprise Publishing Co., 1927.

Notes that there were theological students at Burlington College, which was founded by Bishop George Washington Doane and operated until 1877.

Dubose Memorial Church Training School, 1921-1944, Monteagle, Tennessee

629.   Armentrout, Donald S. The DuBose Memorial Church Training School, Monteagle, Tennessee, 1921-1944. 1988. Typescript.

Treats fully the founding, history and contributions of this school which was designed to train men for rural ministry.

Episcopal Seminary of the Caribbean, 1961-1976, San Juan, Puerto Rico

630.   "Big Days for a Dean." *The Episcopalian* 127 (April 1962): 34-35.

Discusses opening of the Episcopal Seminary of the Caribbean.

631.   Elliot, Herbert. "Seminario International." *The Episcopalian* 127 (February 1962): 19-20.

Discusses beginning of Episcopal Seminary of the Caribbean which opened in September 1961.

632.   "The First Dean." *The Living Church*, February 28, 1960, pp. 7-8.

Notes that Eugene E. Crommett was first dean of ETSC.

633.   "New Dean for Caribbean Seminary." *The Episcopalian* 128 (November 1963): 47.

Reports that Richard L. Rising replaced Eugene E. Crommet as dean of the Episcopal Seminary of the Caribbean.

634.   "New Dean for Caribbean Seminary." *The Episcopalian* 134 (April 1969): 41-42.

Notes that William P. Haugaard, associate professor of church history at the Episcopal Theological Seminary of the Caribbean, became its dean in 1969.

635.   "P. R. Institution Closed." *The Living Church*, July 18, 1976, p. 6.

Notes closing of the Episcopal Seminary of the Caribbean, which opened in 1961 and trained over 70 persons for the ministry.

636.   "Seminary Elects Dean." *The Living Church*, September 22, 1963, pp. 6-7.

Notes election of Richard L. Rising as second dean of ETSC.

637.   "Seminary in the Sun." *The Episcopalian* 127 (January 1962): 35.

Notes the dedication of the Episcopal Theological Seminary of the Caribbean in San Juan, Puerto Rico, on January 11, 1962. The first dean was the Very Rev. Eugene E. Crommett.

638.   "Thanks and Expectations." *The Living Church*, January 28, 1962, pp. 6-7.

Describes the dedication of the buildings and the installation of the dean and faculty: Eugene E. Crommett, dean; James E. Griffiss, Jr., professor of systematic theology; William P. Haugaard, professor of ecclesiastical history; and Victor A Burset, professor of pastoral theology.

Episcopal Theological Seminary in Kentucky, 1834-1837, 1951-1987, Lexington, Kentucky

639.   Caswall, Henry. *America and the American Church.* London: J. G. & F. Rivington, 1839; reprint, New York: Arno Press & The New York Times, 1969.

Caswall, an Englishman who came to this country in 1828 and was professor of Sacred Literature at the Kentucky Theological Seminary, provides primary information about the early efforts at theological education. He treats fully the establishment of the Kentucky Theological Seminary.

640.   Insko, W. Robert. "Benjamin Bosworth Smith." S.T.M. thesis.
          University of the South, 1959.

          Describes the founding of the Theological Seminary of the
          Protestant Episcopal Church in Kentucky at Lexington, and traces
          its decline as a result of the financial troubles of 1837 and the
          controversy between the diocese and Bishop Smith.

641.   Insko, W. Robert, "Benjamin Bosworth Smith, 1794-1884."
          Historical Magazine of the Protestant Episcopal Church 22 (June
          1953): 146-228.

          In the section on "Bishop Smith, the Educator," describes the
          founding and difficulties of the Theological Seminary of the
          Protestant Episcopal Church in Kentucky at Lexington.

642.   Insko, W. Robert. "The Kentucky Seminary." *The Register of the
          Kentucky Historical Society* 52 (July 1954): 213-32.

          Describes establishment and development of the Theological
          Seminary of the Protestant Episcopal Church in Kentucky from the
          granting of its charter on February 24, 1834, to its quick decline as
          a result of the financial troubles of 1837 and the controversy
          between the diocese and Bishop Benjamin B. Smith. After 1840, for
          a short time, it had a nominal existence as a department of Shelby
          College in Shelbyville. It was reopened in 1951.

643.   Swinford, Frances K., and Rebecca S. Lee. *The Great Elm Tree:
          Heritage of the Episcopal Diocese of Lexington.* Lexington, KY:
          Faith House Press, 1969.

          Describes the founding and decline of the fourth seminary in
          the Episcopal Church, the Theological Seminary of the Protestant
          Episcopal Church in Kentucky at Lexington.

Fairfield Academy, 1813-1821, Fairfield, New York

644.   Hardin, George A., ed. *History of Herkimer County, New York.*
          Syracuse, NY: D. Mason & Co., 1893.

          The chapter on the town of Fairfield treats the Fairfield
          Academy, which from 1813 to 1821 was supported by Trinity
          Parish, New York. During this period it had an Episcopal
          principal, provided free instruction for four divinity students, and
          was sometime called a "Divinity School."

645.   *History of Herkimer County, N.Y.* New York: F. W. Beers & Co.,
          1879.

          The chapter on the town of Fairfield treats the Fairfield
          Academy, which from 1813 to 1821 was supported by Trinity
          Parish, New York. During this period it had an Episcopal
          principal, provided free instruction for four divinity students and

was sometimes called a "Divinity School."

646.   Smith, George W. "Fairfield Academy and Fairfield Medical
         College." *Papers Read Before the Herkimer County Historical
         Society.* II (1902): 357-69.

         The Fairfield Academy, Herkimer County, New York, began
         in 1803, with the Rev. Caleb Alexander, a Presbyterian, as
         principal. In 1813, an Episcopalian, the Rev. Bethel Judd, became
         principal, and Trinity Church of New York gave it a grant of $750
         provided it should give free tuition to four divinity students of the
         Episcopal Church. As a result it was sometimes called a "Divinity
         School."

Griswold College, Davenport, Iowa

647.   Carpenter, M. F. *A Century of the Diocese of Iowa, 1853-1953.*
         N.p. 1953.

         Briefly mentions the theological department of Griswold
         College, which was later named Lee Hall, after the first Bishop of
         Iowa, Henry W. Lee.

648.   Chitty, Arthur B. "Griswold College, 1859-1897, Davenport,
         Iowa." *Historical Magazine of the Protestant Episcopal Church* 37
         (March 1968): 73-75.

         Traces briefly the history of Griswold College and its
         theological department which opened in 1861 and closed in the
         1890s.

Hoffman Hall, Fisk University, Nashville, Tennessee

649.   "Benediction of Hoffman Hall." *The Fisk Herald* (April 1890):
         12-13.

         Treats the blessing of Hoffman Hall at Fisk University on
         March 4, 1891.

650.   "Hoffman Hall." *The Fisk Herald* (August 1891): 10-12.

         Discusses the first year of Hoffman Hall as a school to train
         black clergy.

651.   Noll, Arthur H. *History of the Church in the Diocese of
         Tennessee.* New York: James Pott, 1900.

         Notes the establishment of Hoffman Hall at Fisk University
         in Nashville in June, 1890, by the Diocese of Tennessee to train
         "colored men... for the work of the ministry." Named after its
         benefactor, the Rev. Dr. Charles F. Hoffman of New York.

Inter/Met, 1969-1977, Washington, DC

652.   Hahn, Celia Allison. *Inter/Met: Bold Experiment in Theological Education.* Washington, DC: Alban Institute, Inc., 1977.

        A study and evaluation of the Inter/Met seminary which grew out of the Washington Urban Training Program and operated from 1969 to 1977.

Jubilee College, Peoria County, Illinois

653.   Chase, Philander.   *Bishop   Chase's   Reminiscences: An Autobiography.* 2nd ed. 2 vols. Boston, MA: James B. Dow, 1848.

        Briefly refers to Jubilee College, Peoria County, Illinois, which Chase founded in 1840. It operated until 1862 and had a theological department.

654.   Pickaske, David R. "Jubilee College: Bishop Chase's School of Prophets." *The Old Northwest* 2 (1976): 281-97.

        Discusses fully the work of the theological department at Jubilee College.

655.   Smith, Laura Chase. *The Life of Philander Chase, First Bishop of Ohio and Illinois, Founder of Kenyon and Jubilee Colleges.* New York: E. P. Dutton & Company, 1903.

        Briefly mentions Jubilee College, which had a theological department.

656.   Swartzbaugh, Constance H.   *The Episcopal Church in Fulton County, Illinois, 1835-1959.* Canton, IL: Privately printed, 1959.

        Mentions briefly Jubliee College which had a theological department.

Kansas Theological School, 1876-1918, Topeka, Kansas

657.   "Kansas School Trained Clergy for 42 Years."   *The Kansas Churchman* 53 (January 1967): 3.

        Briefly describes the Kansas Theological School which operated at Topeka from 1876 to 1918.

658.   Taylor, Blanche Mercer. *Plenteous Harvest: The Episcopal Church in Kansas.* Topeka, KS: Episcopal Diocese of Kansas, 1973.

        Briefly treats the Kansas Theological School which operated from 1876 to 1918 at Topeka.

Kemper College, 1837-1845, St. Louis, Missouri

659.   Rehkopf, Charles F. "The Beginnings of the Episcopal Church in Missouri, 1819-1844." *Historical Magazine of the Protestant Episcopal Church* 24 (March 1955): 39-65.

Describes Kemper College at St. Louis, Missouri, which operated from 1837 to 1845. Henry Caswall was professor of divinity, but had no theological students.

660.   Rehkopf, Charles F. "The Episcopate of Bishop Hawks." *Bulletin of the Missouri Historical Society* 13 (July 1957): 367-80.

Reports the closing of Kemper College at St. Louis in March, 1845. Apparently its theological department never had any students.

661.   Richardson, Jack. "Kemper College of Missouri." *Historical Magazine of the Protestant Episcopal Church* 30 (June 1961): 111-26.

Kemper College was to be a Protestant Episcopal Seminary for literary and theological purposes and hired Henry Caswall as professor of theology. He had no students and the college closed in 1845.

662.   Robertson, Charles F. "The Story of Kemper College, St. Louis." *Nashotah Scholiast* 2 (October 1884): 25; (December 1884): 41; (February 1885): 58.

Traces briefly the history of Kemper College.

King Hall, Howard University, 1889-1908, Washington, DC

663.   Dyson, Walter. *Howard University: The Capstone of Negro Education. A History: 1867-1940*. Washington, DC: Graduate School, Howard University, 1941.

Mentions King Hall, a seminary for black Episcopalians, which operated from 1889 to 1908.

664.   Logan, Rayford W. *Howard University, the First Hundred Years, 1867-1967*. New York: New York University Press, 1969.

Refers to King Hall, a seminary for black Episcopalians.

665.   Winston, Michael R. *Howard University, Department of History, 1913-1973*. Washington, DC: Howard University, 1973.

Refers to King Hall, established in 1889 to train black clergy for the Episcopal Church.

Nebraska Divinity School, 1868-1885, Nebraska City, Nebraska

666.   Barnds, William J.   *The Episcopal Church in Nebraska: A Centennial History.* Omaha, NE: Episcopal Diocese of Nebraska, 1969.

         Traces the history of the Nebraska College and Divinity School which was founded in July 21, 1868, and closed on April 12, 1865. It was housed in Shoenberger Hall.

667.   Barnds, William J.   "The Episcopal Church in Nebraska Since 1875." *Historical Magazine of the Protestant Episcopal Church* 33 (September 1964): 185-223.

         Treats briefly the Nebraska Divinity School which operated from 1868 to 1885 at Nebraska City.

668.   Barnds, William J.   "The Episcopal Church in Nebraska to 1875." *Historical Magazine of the Protestant Episcopal Church* 31 (March 1962): 21-35.

         Briefly treats the Nebraska Divinity School which began in 1868 at Nebraska City.

669.   *History of the State of Nebraska.* 2 vols. Chicago, IL: Western Historical Company, 1882.

         Treats briefly Nebraska Divinity School which was a part of Nebraska College at Nebraska City.

670.   Johnson, Harrison.   *History of Nebraska.*   Omaha, NE: Henry Gibson, 1880.

         Notes briefly the Nebraska Divinity School at Nebraska City.

671.   Wilhite, Ann L.   "Cities and Colleges in the Promised Land: Territorial Nebraska, 1854-1867." *Nebraska History* 67 (Winter 1986): 327-71.

         Treats how Talbot Hall became the Nebraska College and Divinity School.

672.   Woolworth, James M.   "Episcopal Church." In *Illustrated History of Nebraska,* Vol. 2, pp. 508-515. Edited by J. Sterling Morton, Albert Watkins and George L. Miller. Lincoln, NE: Jacob North & Company, 1907.

         Treats briefly the Nebraska Divinity School founded by Bishop Robert Clarkson.

St. Andrew's Divinity School, 1876-1905, Syracuse, New York

673.   Arnold, Frederick S. *Frederic Dan Huntington, First Bishop of Central New York.* Hartford, CT: Church Missions Publishing Company, 1941.

Mentions St. Andrew's Divinity School at Syracuse.

674.   Galpin, William Freeman. *The Diocese of Central New York: The Huntington Years.* Boonville, NY: Willard Press, 1968.

Briefly traces the history of St. Andrew's Divinity School, Syracuse, from its founding in 1876 until it closed in 1905.

675.   Hubbard, Henry E. *A Short History of Saint Andrew's Divinity School at Syracuse, New York.* Syracuse, NY: Alumni Association, 1910.

Treats the history of the school and has a directory of the students.

676.   Huntington, Arria S. *Memoirs and Letters of Frederic Don Huntington, First Bishop of Central New York.* Boston, MA and New York: Houghton, Mifflin and Company, 1906.

Treats briefly the St. Andrew's Divinity School which Huntington founded at Syracuse in Septembr 1876. It closed in 1905.

St. Augustine College Theological Department, 1883-1894, Raleigh, North Carolina

677.   Halliburton, Cecil D. *A History of St. Augustine's College, 1867-1937.* Raleigh, NC: St. Augustine's College, 1937.

Notes that in 1883 a Theological Department was established and the Rev. Dr. F. M. Hubbard was added to the faculty to teach theology.

678.   London, Lawrence Foushee, and Sarah McCulloh Lemmon, eds. *The Episcopal Church in North Carolina, 1701-1959.* Raleigh, NC: Episcopal Diocese of North Carolina, 1987.

Notes the efforts at theological education at Valle Crucis, at the Ravenscroft School at Ashville revived by Bishop Athinson in 1868 and closed shortly after 1890, and the theological department at St. Augustine's Normal School and Collegiate Institute, which began before 1883 and closed in 1894.

St. Stephen's College Theological Department, 1861-1863, Annandale, New York

679.   Hopson, George B.   *Reminiscences of St. Stephen's College, Annandale, New York.* New York: Edwin S. Gorham, 1910.

St. Stephen's College (now Bard) was established on March 20, 1860, and under its second warden, the Rev. Thomas Richey, 1861-1863, a Theology Department with a three-year course was established. "Three young men began the course, but soon decided that they could accomplish their objectives more satisfactorily in some of the older seminaries."

Seminary of the Streets, 1970-1973, New York

680.   "Combined Program Offered." *The Living Church*, July 2, 1972, p. 12.

Treats the Seminary of the Streets, a ministry of Trinity Parish, New York City, which integrated traditional academic work with an involvement in the issues, struggles, and experiences of actual ministry.

681.   Dugan, George. "Church Starts 'Seminary of the Streets.'" *The New York Times*, 8 November 1970, 28 (L).

Discusses the experimental seminary headed by the Rev. John Swanson.

682.   Price, Jo-Ann. "Seminary of the Streets: 'It's Where the People Are.'" *The Tablet*, April 8, 1971, no pagination.

Describes the people and program of this experimental seminary.

683.   "Seminary of Street Protects Wild Shepherds." *Trinity Newsletter*, November-December 1971, p. 15.

Describes briefly the Seminary of the Streets which operated from 1970 to 1973.

Theological Seminary of South Carolina, 1859-1862, Camden, South Carolina, 1866-1868, Spartanburg, South Carolina

684.   Thomas, Albert S. *A Historical Account of the Protestant Episcopal Church in South Carolina, 1820-1957.* Columbia, SC: By the Author, 1957.

Treats the Theological Seminary of the Protestant Episcopal Church in the Diocese of South Carolina which opened on January 17, 1859, at Camden, and closed on June 30, 1862, because of the Civil War. It reopened in October, 1866, at Spartanburg, but closed permanently on May 16, 1868. William Porcher DuBose studied there.

William and Mary College, Williamsburg, Virginia

685.   Bruce, Philip A. *Institutional History of Virginia in the Seventeenth Century*. 2 vols. New York and London: G. P. Putnam's Sons, 1910.

       Treats the establishment of William and Mary College and its projected school of Divinity and Oriental Languages.

686.   Brydon, George Maclaren. *Virginia's Mother Church and the Political Conditions Under Which It Grew*. Vol. I: *An Interpretation of the Records of the Colony of Virginia and of the Anglican Church of That Colony, 1607-1727*; Vol. II: *The Story of the Anglican Church and the Development of Religion in Virginia, 1727-1814*. Philadelphia, PA: Church Historical Society, 1952.

       College of William and Mary and its efforts at theological education are treated throughout, but especially in volume two.

687.   Godbold, Albea. *The Church College in the Old South*. Durham, NC: Duke University Press, 1944.

       Notes effort to have a chair of divinity at William and Mary in 1821, but it lasted only until 1823.

688.   Goodwin, Edward L. *The Colonial Church in Virginia with Biographical Sketches of the First Six Bishops of the Diocese of Virginia*. Milwaukee, WI: Morehouse Publishing Co.; London: A. R. Mowbray & Co., 1927.

       Treats College of William and Mary and its professors of divinity, Bartholomew Yates, Sr., 1729, John Camm, 1749-57, and John Dixon, 1770-77.

689.   Marpurgo, Jack E. *Their Majesties Royall Colledge: William and Mary in the Seventeenth and Eighteenth Centuries*. Williamsburg, VA: Endowment Association of the College of William and Mary in Virginia, Inc., 1976.

       Briefly notes efforts to establish a Divinity School.

690.   Perry, William Stevens. *The History of the American Episcopal Church, 1587-1883*. Vol. 1. *The Planting and Growth of the American Colonial Church, 1587-1783*. Boston, MA: James R. Osgood and Company, 1885.

       Treats the founding of the College of William and Mary to train "able and faithful ministers."

691.   Tyler, Lyon G. *The College of William and Mary in Virginia: Its History and Work, 1693-1907*.   Richmond, VA: Whittet &

Shepperson, 1907.

Mentions briefly theological education at William and Mary.

692.   Tyler, Lyon G. *The History of the College of William and Mary From Its Foundation, 1660, to 1874.*   Richmond, VA: J. W. Randolph & English, 1874.

Treats   briefly   the   college's   professors   of   divinity, Bartholomew Yates, John Dixon, and Reuel Keith.

Part V. Diocesan Training Schools

Episcopal Theological School at Claremont (Bloy House), 1958-   , Claremont, California

693.   Barnes, C. Rankin.   "Late-blooming Vocations."   *The Living Church*, May 30, 1965, pp. 8-9, 12.

Explains work of Bloy House in training older men for the ministry.

694.   "Bloy House Moves to Claremont." *The Living Church*, August 23, 1970, pp. 5-6.

Notes move of Bloy House from Pasadena to Claremont, California.

George B. Mercer Jr. Memorial School of Theology, 1955-   , Garden City, New York

695.   Cain, Richard.   "Seminary for the Mature." *The Living Church*, September 12, 1965, pp. 16-18, 20.

Discusses founding of the George B. Mercer School of Theology at Garden City, New York, in February, 1955, and its mission to train men with late vocations.

CHAPTER 7
HELLENIC SEMINARIES
George C. Papademetriou

696.   "Advantages of the Monodollarion" (in Greek). *Orthodox Observer*, November 15, 1947, pp. 6, 8, 12, 16.

Gives reasons why people should contribute to the Archdiocese which also benefits Holy Cross Seminary. It includes photographs of both campuses, Pomfret, CT and Brookline, MA; a photograph of the Dean, Faculty and students and a photo of the Dean with seminarians in the higher levels of studies.

697.   "Again for our Theological School" (in Greek). *Orthodox Observer*, August 15, 1940, pp. 3-4.

Presents the reasons for financial support of the Holy Cross Seminary. It speaks of the need to support it in order to fulfill the need for American born Priests.

698.   Album (in Greek). Greek Orthodox Theological School of Holy Cross. Pomfret, CT: 1940.

Contains pictures of faculty, students and buildings of the campus of the Holy Cross Theological School in Pomfret, CT. It contains important information on the Seminary's beginnings and describes student life and programs of study.

699.   Arseniev, N. S. "Ten Years Ago." *St. Vladimir's Seminary Quarterly*, 2 - New Series (Summer 1958): 21-22.

Gives a report on the Seminary at its tenth anniversary. He gives details of the arrival of faculty, including himself, from Europe to teach as well as a description of some of the courses taught at the Seminary at that time.

700.   Athenagoras, Archbishop. "Establishment of the Orthodox Theological School" (in Greek). *Orthodox Observer*, June 20, 1937, pp. 4-7.

The Archbishop sent an announcement to all the parishes, Greek press and the entire Greek-American community to solicit their help in sending students to the Seminary in Pomfret, CT. He gives the requirements for application, lists the courses of study and the kind of life to expect in the Seminary.

701.   Athenagoras, Bishop of Elaia (Kokkinakis). "Holy Cross Greek
            Orthodox Theological School: Twenty Years of Progress,
            1937-1957." *Orthodox Observer*, October 1957, pp. 238, 240-42,
            248.

            The Dean gives some historical facts of past attempts by the
            Archdiocese to create a Seminary in this country without success
            and the overwhelming acceptance of Holy Cross by the people and
            its great progress. He asks for help to strengthen financially the
            Seminary.

702.   Athenagoras, Bishop of Elaia (Kokkinakis). "The Life of the
            Theological School" (in Greek). *Holy Cross: The Greek Orthodox
            Theological School Missionary Bulletin* 1 (April 1958): 6-8.

            The Dean gives a detailed description of life and activities in
            the Seminary. He gives valuable information about the professors,
            the programs of study, environment, donors, new buildings,
            activities of faculty and students and the trustees.

703.   Averky, Archbishop. "The Twenty-Second Commencement of Holy
            Trinity Orthodox Seminary." *Orthodox Life*, May-June 1969, pp.
            6-9.

            The Archbishop greets the visitors who came for the
            Commencement and remarks on the task of educating young men
            for the Orthodox ministry. He addresses the seminarians
            emphasizing the importance of the spiritual training and education
            offered at Holy Trinity Seminary in order to face the
            morally-decadent world.

704.   Blusin, Basil M. "Twenty Years Ago." *St. Vladimir's Seminary
            Quarterly* 2 - New Series (Summer 1958): 11-20.

            This article is an historical sketch of the origin of St.
            Vladimir's Seminary from 1938-42. It contains pictures and
            numerous details and a useful bibliography.

705.   "The Bond Between the Theological School of Athens University
            with the Greek Orthodox Theological School of America." *Holy
            Cross: The Greek Orthodox Theological School Missionary Bulletin*
            (January-February 1959): 11-12.

            Describes the close association of the Theological School of
            Athens University and Holy Cross Greek Orthodox School of
            Theology of Brookline, MA. It also gives the first address of
            Professor C. Bonis of Athens University who came to Holy Cross
            as a visiting Professor for the Spring Semester of 1959.

706.   Brooks, Arthur W. *The Greek Seminary of St. Athanasius.* Astoria,
            New York City: Office of the Trustees, 1923-1924.

This booklet contains the history of the first Greek Orthodox Seminary in New York City (Astoria) that unfortunately did not survive its financial crisis. Herein is included a list of the board of trustees, faculty, courses of study, courses of preparation, Greek studies, Seminary studies in dogmatics, Scriptures, Church History, philosophy and psychology, homiletics, canon law, apologetics, religious education, liturgics, a list of contributors, degree programs, several letters of episcopal clergy, several pictures of hierarchs, students, faculty and the buildings which were used as campus.

707. Callimachos, Demetrios. "A Sacred Defense for the Cultivation and Perpetuation of the Greek Language and Greek Ideals and Traditions for the Enrichment of American Civilization" (in Greek). "Krikos" Greek Review (July-August, 1956): 24-34.

This article is well written by a Priest-journalist arguing for the necessity for such a Seminary in this country to educate young men to teach the Orthodox faith and the Greek language. He gives important information on the purchase of the property in Brookline, MA as well as about Greeks in America compared to Roman Catholics and Jews.

708. Catalogue: Holy Cross Greek Orthodox School of Theology. Brookline, MA: Holy Cross Orthodox Press.

The Catalogue was issued: 1953-1954, 1954-1955, 1955-1956, 1956-1957, 1957-1958, 1958-1959, 1962-1963, 1963-1964, 1964-1965, 1965-1966, 1966-1967, 1967-1968, 1969-1970, 1972-1973, 1973-1974, 1974-1975, 1975-1976, 1976-1977, 1981-1982, 1983-1984, 1984-1985, 1986-1987, and 1987-1988. The catalogues published by the Holy Cross Orthodox Press contain information pertinent to the history, admission, course description, programs and degrees.

709. Chirban, John. "Istavrides Lectures at Seminary." Orthodox Observer, October 20, 1971, pp. 6-8.

Gives a brief report of the lecture of Prof. Basil Istavrides from Halki Seminary (Constantinople). The lecture topic is on the relations of Orthodoxy and Roman Catholicism.

710. "Christian-Muslim Symposium." The Greek Star, 25 April 1985.

This is a brief article on the symposium on Christians and Muslims sponsored by the faculty of Holy Cross Greek Orthodox Seminary. It also lists dignitaries and includes a picture.

711. "Chronicle of St. Vladimir's Seminary: Historical Background." St. Vladimir's Seminary Quarterly (Fall 1952): 21-31.

Includes useful information on the historical formation of the

Seminary, people involved, the president's statement, purpose and program, faculty, student choir and visiting faculties from other institutions of higher learning.

712.   *Church Almanac*. 1942.

Contains the problems of the Greek community in America, pictures of Bishops, Priests, trustees, faculty and students of Holy Cross. There are important biographical notes on faculty, trustees and students. It also contains pictures of the Priests throughout the U.S. and of the Catechetical Conference that was held on the campus in Pomfret, Connecticut.

713.   *Church Almanac*. 1949.

Contains numerous pictures of students and hierarchs. Also, there are numerous articles on the life and activities of the school, including the press, the programs, the brotherhood of supporters, the School as the center of Greek Orthodox theology and Greek learning.

714.   *Church Almanac*. 1950.

Gives important information on the Weld estate in Brookline, MA to which the Seminary moved from Pomfret, CT. It contains a long article on the "creation and activities of the Seminary in its First Twelve Years (1937-1949)" (in Greek). It gives information on all aspects of the Seminary life including programs, curriculum, faculty, buildings, degrees, and brotherhood, numerous photographs of students and faculty, publications and the Library.

715.   *Church Almanac*. 1951.

Two-thirds of this volume (pp. 60-239) is devoted to "Our Theological School." It gives pictures of the buildings, the trustees, program of studies, lists of faculty, alumni, clergy, pictures and biographies of trustees, and a description and plans of future buildings.

716.   *Church Almanac*. 1953.

Gives lists of trustees, faculty, a detailed report by the Dean, Ezekiel Tsoukalas for the year 1952, a report on the Brotherhood and the hopes for building new structures.

717.   "Crucial Shortage of Priests Threatens Greek Orthodox Church in the Americas." *Orthodox Observer*, May 4, 1983, p. 1.

In this article the Archdiocese Council discusses the seriousness of the shortage of Priests and urges the recruitment of young men for the priesthood.

718.   Dindorf,   Mainard   and   Edward   Kasinec.   "Russian

Pre-Revolutionary Religious-Theological Serials in the St. Vladimir's Seminary Library." *St. Vladimir's Theological Quarterly* (1970): 100-07.

Contains a list of theological-religious periodicals before the 1917 Russian revolution.

719.   *Diocesan Seminary of Christ the Savior in Johnstown, Pennsylvania.* Johnstown, PA: Christ the Savior Press, n.d.

An attractive booklet with pictures of buildings, students and faculty of the Seminary. It gives information on the mission, academic standing and life in the Seminary of Christ the Savior. Also included is a list of graduates.

720.   Ezekiel, Bishop of Nazianzus. "The Theological School of our Archdiocese" (in Greek). *Orthodox Observer*, December 1951, pp. 13-14; January 1, 1952, pp. 7-9, 21.

The Dean, Bishop Ezekiel, answers the constant question "why don't seminarians pay for their education." He gives reasons why theological education and training must be provided free to all future Priests. He compares Holy Cross with other American seminaries where students do not pay tuition or room and board. He also accents the need for a cafeteria, library, chapel and gymnasium.

721.   Florovsky, George. "The Responsibility of the Orthodox in America." *Russian Orthodox Journal* 23 (October 1949): 15-18.

Describes the mission of Orthodoxy in America and the role St. Vladimir's played in furthering Orthodoxy in this country. He emphasized that in America we don't need a school to train professional clergy but a band of people to set the world on spiritual fire.

722.   *40th Anniversary of St. Andrew's College in Winnipeg 1946-1986.* Winnipeg, Manitoba: St. Andrew's College, 1986.

This booklet gives important information on the College and its mission of preparing young men for the Orthodox priesthood. It gives the history, lists faculty and trustees, describes the library, the chapel and has numerous pictures. It also gives information in the Ukranian language.

723.   "From Pomfret to Brookline," *Crossroads*, 13 February 1985.

This issue of the Hellenic College (Holy Cross Greek Orthodox School of Theology) student newspaper is devoted to the history and tradition of the Seminary. It includes numerous pictures of students and buildings, several brief articles on various aspects of the life of the School, the Alumni and sports.

724.   Gianoukos, George.   "One Month's Impressions" (in Greek).
         Orthodox Observer, November 7, 1937, pp. 13-14.

         The author of this article was a professor of music and a
         seminarian preparing for the Priesthood.   He writes about his
         impressions of one month at the Seminary of the Holy Cross in
         Pomfret, CT.   He discusses the mission of the School and describes
         the courses, the environment, the discipline, and the activities of
         student life.

725.   *Golden Anniversary: St. Vladimir's Orthodox Theological Seminary
         1978-1988*.   Crestwood, NY: St. Vladimir's Seminary Press, 1988.

         A tribute to St. Vladimir's Seminary from various Church
         authorities.   It contains pictures of past and present faculty,
         administrators, trustees and lists of alumni and benefactors.

726.   Golder, Boyd E.   "Tis Better to Light One Small Candle than to
         Curse the Darkness."   *Orthodox Life*, May-June 1969, pp. 9-12.

         The author of this article speaks of the uprooted individuals
         who fled Russia in order not to submit to the evil of communism
         and how they managed to create a center in America to educate
         students who will spread the Light in the world.   He also speaks of
         problems in society and the importance of the survival of
         democracy.

727.   "Greek Orthodox Theological School of Holy Cross, Brookline,
         Mass."   *Orthodox Observer*, November 1963, pp.340-43; January
         1964, pp. 23-24; 1964, pp. 82-83; 1964, pp. 147-48.

         Includes   historical   notes,   the   Silvery   Anniversary
         (1937-1962), a list of deans who served the Seminary, the location
         of the campus, the chapel, spiritual life, the library, laboratories,
         visual aids and the bookstore. Also related is information about the
         Greek Orthodox Theological Review, the finances, charges and
         expenses, student council, the choir, Alumni Association, infirmary
         and health services, matriculation, a list of awards and information
         on the undergraduate college.

728.   *Handbook of the Orthodox Theological School of "Holy Cross"* (in
         Greek).   Pomfret Center, CT: Press of the Greek Orthodox
         Theological School, 1944.

         This booklet contains fifty-six articles on privileges and
         responsibilities of students, faculty, administrators and trustees. It
         also contains a program of studies.

729.   Harakas, Stanley Samuel. "Reflections from Brookline: Archbishop
         Iakovos and the Development of Hellenic College/Holy Cross Greek
         Orthodox School of Theology." In *History of the Greek Orthodox
         Church in America*, pp. 247-59. Edited by Miltiades B. Efthimiou

and George A. Christopoulos. New York: Greek Orthodox Archdiocese of North and South America, 1984.

Treats the development of the School under the leadership of Archbishop Iakovos. It gives facts on the creation of Hellenic College, women students, accreditation and ecumenical outreach. Also included are faculty activities and the School's participation in the Boston Theological Institute, a consortium of theological schools.

730.   "Historic SCOBA meeting on Theological Education." *Orthodox Observer*, May 25, 1977, pp. 1, 19.

Reports that all Orthodox hierarchs in America met on the campus of Holy Cross Orthodox Seminary to discuss the future of theological education. It reports on several decisions for cooperation of the theological schools in this country.

731.   Hopko, Thomas. "The St. Vladimir Story." *Russian Orthodox Journal* 60 (1987): 14-17, 24.

Gives the history of the Seminary from the beginning to the present.

732.   Kasinec, Edward. "Bibliographical Census: Russian Emigre Theologicans and Philosophers in the Seminary Library Collection." *St. Vladimir's Seminary Quarterly* 16 (1972): 40-44.

Relates important historical information on intellectuals connected to the Seminary who fled Russia after the revolution.

733.   *A Legacy of Excellence: St. Vladimir's Orthodox Seminary 1938-1988.* Crestwood, NY: St. Vladimir's Press, 1988.

This is a history of St. Vladimir's Seminary of the first fifty years. It includes the faculty, its struggles for survival, development, programs, the library, the press and bookstore, Alumni Association, the chapel, choir, and the alumni activities throughout the world. The goal of the Seminary is to be a center for Orthodox Theology and practice. It also includes numerous pictures. It is a complete history of the first fifty years of St. Vladimir's Seminary presented on its Golden Jubilee.

734.   Miloro, Frank P. "The History of Christ the Savior Seminary." *Golden Jubilee Journal*, Fall 1988.

The history, the mission and vision of the Seminary are described in this article. The beginnings, struggles and progress of Christ the Savior Seminary are related.

735.   Moskoff, Eugene A. "F.R.O.C. and St. Vladimir's Academy." *The Russian Orthodox Journal* (April 1949): 25, 32.

Presents information on the progress of St. Vladimir's Seminary and the support it receives from the Federated Russian Orthodox Clubs. It also relates the task of the Seminary to train priests and to bring together scholars to further the Orthodox theological education and scholarship.

736.   *The Orthodox Theological Day.*   St. Vladimir's Orthodox Theological Seminary. Crestwood, NY: 1970.

Issued annually since 1970. It is an annual album that includes informative articles.

737.   Papademetrious, Athanasia.   *The History of the Hellenic College/Holy Cross School of Theology Campus.* Brookline, MA: Cotsidas-Tonna Library, 1988.

This pamphlet includes the history of the campus, the original owners, the buildings and their brief history. It also includes a map of the campus.

738.   Papaioannou, George A.   "Holy Cross Theological School and Hellenic College." In *The Odyssey of Hellenism in America*, pp. 407-28.   Thessaloniki, Greece: Patriarchal Institute for Patristic Studies, 1985.

This is an excellent historical survey of the origin and development of Holy Cross. It gives information on the life of the school, its problems, programs and finances.

739.   Papson, John.   "Holy Cross School of Theology."   *Orthodox Observer*, July 20, 1977, pp. 4, 8; November 9, 1977, pp. 22, 24; December 1977, p. 3; December 21, 1977, p. 22; April 12, 1978, p. 20; May 10, 1978, pp. 4, 5, 6, 7; May 24, 1978, pp. 6, 7; June 3, 1978, p. 3.

Reflects on the mission and purpose of the Seminary. He discusses the student body, the administration and faculty, with detailed information on the life of the School and the faculty, as well as the press, bookstore, and Theological Review.

740.   Poulos, George.   *Footsteps in the Sea: A Biography of Archbishop Athenagoras Cavadas.* Brookline, MA: Holy Cross Orthodox Press, 1979.

Is about the co-founder and first Dean of Holy Cross Greek Orthodox Seminary.   The Seminary was founded and began operating in September 1937. The book covers the struggles and successes of the early years of the Seminary during war time, the life of the first students and the move from Pomfret, CT to Brookline, MA. It contains numerous pictures valuable to the history of the Seminary. The book includes important details about the life of the School, its faculty and students. The purpose of the Seminary is to project Orthodoxy and Hellenism in America. Its first Dean, Cavadas, spearheaded a public relations campaign to firmly establish its foundations and assure its perpetuation for future generations.

741.   *St. Andrew's College in Winnipeg. 1982-1983 Calendar.* Winnipeg, Manitoba, Canada.

The St. Andrew's College is sponsored by the Ukranian Greek Orthodox Church of Canada and is affiliated with the University of Manitoba. The present catalogue gives important information on the Seminary's program of studies preparing young men for the Orthodox priesthood. It includes lists of the course offerings, trustees, faculty and a brief history of the Seminary.

742.   "St. Vladimir's Seminary 1938-1958." *St. Vladimir's Seminary Quarterly* 2 - New Series (Summer 1958): 2-10.

This is an historical note on the creation of the Seminary and its early development. It contains important historical facts and names of faculty and supporters.

743.   Schmemann, Alexander. "Thoughts for the Jubilee." *St. Vladimir's Seminary Quarterly* (1969): 95-102.

Presents a theological reflection on the creation of the graduate seminary on the basis of the American educational system. He compares theological education in Russia to that in America and expresses the need for American-based theological education to keep and attract new members.

744.   "VII-Hellenic College-Holy Cross." *Orthodox Observer*, June 12, 1974, pp. 3A-4A.

Articulates the purpose and goals of the Holy Cross Seminary. It focuses on the faculty, students, academic program, facilities and vision for the future.

745.   Sister Victoria. "St. Herman's Pastoral School, Kenai, Alaska." *St. Vladimir's Seminary Quarterly* 17 (1973): 244-45.

Is a brief historical note on the creation of the pastoral seminary in Alaska. It gives brief historical facts on the Church in Alaska and names faculty.

746.   *Student Handbook.* Brookline, MA: Hellenic College/Holy Cross School of Theology, 1973-1974.

The Handbook contains rules and regulations for the religious life of the Seminarians, student government, student services, student conduct, library information and information on the campus buildings.

747.   Tsoumas, George. "The Founding Years of Holy Cross Greek
        Orthodox Theological School (1937-1942)." *The Greek Orthodox
        Theological Review* (Fall 1967): 241-82.

        Written by one who was involved as a teacher at Holy Cross
        from its beginnings. He includes theological education prior to the
        founding of Holy Cross, its establishment, the campus (at
        Pomphret, CT), the pioneer students, its Dean and faculty, the
        curriculum, choir, the printing shop, the trustees, the library and a
        description of the first closing exercises. It is rich in reference to
        articles and documents important for the early history of the
        School.

748.   Tsoumas, George. "Sentimental Journey to Pomfret, Connecticut."
        Orthodox Observer, November 1963, pp. 337-39.

        Reflects on the early years at Pomfret. It includes
        photographs of people and buildings of the first campus of Holy
        Cross Greek Orthodox Seminary in Pomfret, CT.

749.   Vaporis, N. M. *A Chronicle of Hellenic College/Holy Cross Greek
        Orthodox School of Theology.* Brookline, MA: Holy Cross
        Orthodox Press, 1988.

        Details the chronology of the School's history of the
        Seminary since its beginning. It includes stories and photographs
        of students, faculty and trustees of the School for the fifty years of
        its existence. It is well-documented and provides an excellent
        archival documentation of the Holy Cross Orthodox Seminary.

750.   Verhovsky, Serge S. "Theological Education in Our Church."
        Russian Orthodox Journal 33 (January 1960): 10-11; (February
        1960): 17-18; (March 1960): 11-12.

        This article discusses the problem of American culture,
        theological education, the necessity for theological learning, the
        need for theological literature to help lay people, the duration of
        course of study and costs.

751.   Znamensky, George. "The Philosophical Ideal of the Greatest
        Social Value for Education." *Orthodox Life*, May-June 1969, pp.
        12-15.

        Discusses the importance of the ideals and values of a
        classical education. He addresses the choice the world must make
        between Christ or chaos and confusion. True freedom and peace
        are found in the total surrender to Christ.

CHAPTER 8
INDEPENDENT SEMINARIES
William C. Ringenberg

Most American graduate theological seminaries are affiliated with a denomination. For example, of the approximately 200 institutions holding membership in the Association of Theological Schools, only about ten percent are independent. The typical non-aligned seminary is either an older, relatively liberal, divinity school branch of an academically elite university or else a conservative, self-standing institution born as a twentieth century reaction to the growth of liberal theology in either a specific Protestant denomination or in Protestantism in general. The quality of the written histories of these institutions varies widely; in general the best works are on the older seminaries. However, some first-rate studies of the newer evangelical schools are beginning to appear.

752.   Abel, Paul Frederick. "A Historical Study of the Origin and Development of Asbury Theological Seminary." M.A. thesis. Columbia University, 1951.

        Offers the best and most comprehensive history of the seminary of the Holiness wing of Methodism. It is lucid, insightful, and shows an understanding of the historical context. This is a careful work of scholarship.

753.   Arnold, Charles Harvey. *Near the Edge of Battle: A Short History of the Divinity School and the Chicago School of Theology, 1866-1966*. Chicago, IL: University of Chicago Press, 1966.

        Presents not a comprehensive history of this major institution -- no such work exists -- but rather a centennial, intellectual history of the continuing, liberal Protestant thought dominating and emanating from the divinity school both during its affiliation with the University of Chicago and also, earlier, as the independent predecessor institution, the Baptist Union Theological Seminary of Chicago suburb, Morgan Park. This sympathetic account appears as a paperback of slightly over 100 pages.

754.   Austin, Alan Kenneth. "The History of Westminster Theological Seminary, 1929-1964." M.A. thesis. East Tennessee State University, 1965.

        Places major emphasis upon the stormy conflicts at Princeton Theological Seminary and within Northern Presbyterianism in the

1920s that gave rise to the birth of Westminster in 1929 as a conservative reaction to Modernist influences. The pages beyond the founding era continue the conflict motif, especially the struggles of major Westminster founder J. Gresham Machen against the Presbyterian Church, and the Westminster debates on prohibition, premillennialism, and dispensationalism. Austin gives less attention to the more calm period since the late 1930s. This is an able and early written history; it shows a thorough knowledge of the sources.

755.   Bainton, Roland H. *Yale and the Ministry: A History of Education for the Christian Ministry at Yale from the Founding in 1701.* New York: Harper and Brothers, 1957.

Provides a model of how the history of an educational institution can be much more than institutional history. It shows how Yale so largely influenced the religious and intellectual life of southern New England, with the college, seminary, and ministerial alumni working together in the educational process and each element holding in balance, to a unique degree, theology, piety, and social concern. Although this is one of the most important works in American theological education, it would benefit from an updating; its value decreases sharply when considering the period since 1900.

756.   Collins, Marjorie A. *To Know Him and to Make Him Known: The Leadership and Philosophy of Columbia Bible College.* N.p., n.d.

Describes in a clear but uncritical style the history of the first undergraduate theological school (Bible college) to offer graduate theological instruction. What is now known as Columbia Bible College and Seminary has always placed -- even for a Bible College -- major emphasis upon foreign missions. This account gives primary attention to the institutional founders and the first three presidents, Robert McQuilkin Jr., G. Allen Fleese, and J. Robertson McQuilkin.

757.   Eberhardt, Charles R. *The Bible in the Making of Ministers.* New York: Association Press, 1949.
          Tells with the appreciation of a devoted disciple the life story of Wilbert Webster White, giving specific focus to the latter's philosophy of education. White founded the Biblical Seminary of New York (current name: New York Seminary) in 1900 with what he saw as a truly Bibliocentric curriculum. He emphasized that "the study of the Bible in the mother tongue of the student must be the organizing center of the theological curriculum." One-third of the curriculum was devoted to the direct study of the Bible, with the balance of the studies involving the integration of the Bible and the other branches of learning.

758.   Gentry, Kenneth L. "A Tenth Anniversary History of Reformed Theological Seminary." Institutional Self-study Typescript, 1982.

Stresses the origin of the seminary as a reaction to the growing liberal trends in Presbyterian seminaries in general and Columbia (South Carolina) Seminary in particular. The early history and development of Westminster Seminary was both an inspiration and model of this Mississippi institution. If updated, this clear, comprehensive account is worthy of publication.

759.   Handy, Robert T. *A History of Union Theological Seminary in New York*. New York: Columbia University Press, 1987.

Provides the field of seminary literature with one of the most important histories of an individual institution. This comprehensive, full-length history of Union is refreshingly open for an in-house publication, including significant emphasis upon conflict and controversy. Handy, a church historian leader at Union since 1950, focuses upon the faculty including such well-known scholars as Charles A. Briggs, Reinhold Niebuhr, Robert McAfee Brown, James H. Cone, Paul Tillich, Henry Sloane Coffin, Philip Schaff, Arthur C. McGiffert, and Henry Van Dusen.

760.   Harrell, David Edwin, Jr. *Oral Roberts: An American Life*. Bloomington, IN: Indiana University Press, 1985.

Contains a brief (pp. 367-70) but informative discussion of what by the mid-1980s could identify itself as the "only full accredited charismatic graduate school of Theology." This excellent biography insightfully traces the total-career of the Oral Roberts University founder and namesake.

761.   Logan, Rayford W. *Howard University: The First Hundred Years, 1867-1967*. New York: New York University Press, 1969.

Emphasizes how the theological department has been historically the weakest of the professional schools -- "the poor cousin" -- in this the most distinguished of the Black institutions of higher education in America. The scattered references to the theological department/school in this comprehensive, relatively modern history should be supplemented with John Louis Ewell, *A History of the Theological Department of Howard University* (Washington: Howard University Press, 1966).

762.   Marsden, George. *Reforming Fundamentalism: Fuller Seminary and The New Evangelicalism*. Grand Rapids, MI: Eerdmans Publishing Company, 1987.

Combines with the Handy volume on Union to provide the field of seminary bibliography in one year with two of its noteworthy recent historical studies. Marsden, whose *Fundamentalism and American Culture: The Shaping of Twentieth Century Evangelicalism, 1870-1925* (New York: Oxford, 1980) established his reputation as the leading authority on American fundmentalism, tells the story of Fuller in the full context of post-World War conservative Protestantism. After its founding in 1947, Fuller developed as the primary intellectual center of the "New Evangelical" movement which sought to rid Fundamentalism of its fighting and fortress mentality, its legalism, its fear of science and scholarship, its neglect of social concern, and its preoccupation with separatism. Thus the book title. Today Fuller has grown into the second largest and perhaps the most dynamic American seminary; unfortunately, the main body of Marsden's narrative does not continue beyond the late 1960s.

763.   Renfer, Rudolf A. "A History of Dallas Theological Seminary." Ph.D. dissertation. University of Texas, 1959.

Emphasizes the early history of one of the most important independent seminaries to be founded during the heart of the Fundamentalist-Modernist conflict. The prime virtue of the study is Renfer's ability to place the Dallas story in its larger historical context including the Bible Conference and Dispensationalist movements. Because Renfer's work focuses upon the early years, it has never been a definitive comprehensive history, however this limited focus makes it less dated now. This able study is sympathetic, informal, and clear. It should have been published.

764.   Sawyer, Kenneth. "The University of Chicago Divinity School: A Bibliographical and Archival Survey." Unpublished manuscript. University of Chicago Library, 1985.

Contains an unusually comprehensive listing of the broad variety of historical materials on the University of Chicago Divinity School. These include both works on institutional history and those by and about the faculty. This eighty-eight page manuscript includes a twenty-five page historical sketch.

765.   Shipps, Howard Fenimore. *A Short History of Asbury Theological Seminary.* Berne, IN: The Herald Press, 1963.

Represents the most recent and most readily available of the Asbury historical works. This fortieth anniversary history is less than 100 pages in length.

766.   Thompson, Bard. *Vanderbilt Divinity School: A History.* Nashville, TN: Vanderbilt Divinity School, 1958.

Provides an introduction to the early Vanderbilt history. It is ably written but very brief -- especially on the period since 1920.

767.   Williams, George H., ed. *The Harvard Divinity School: Its Place in Harvard University and in American Culture.* Boston, MA: The Beacon Press, 1953.

Remains one of the standard words on American seminary education despite its age and its unusual and sometimes disjointed organizational approach. Williams serves as the overall editor and as one of the six authors with Conrad Wright, Sideny E. Ahlstrom, Willard L. Sperry, Levering Reynolds, Jr., and Ralph Lazzaro. The book combines a chronological approach (four chapters on four periods) with a topical one (separate essays on the curriculum, faculty scholarship since 1880, and the nineteenth century students). A major contribution of the book is its effort to discuss the role of theology in the university and the uneasy relationship between faith and reason in the learning process.

768. Williamson, Glen. *Born for Such a Day: The Amazing Story of Western Evangelical Seminary*. N.p.: LeSabre Press, 1974.

Offers a light, even breezy, ninety-four page narrative of this Wesleyan-Arminian seminary from its founding in 1947 to its earning of accreditation in 1974. It is much less common for a seminary than for a liberal arts college to be founded by a dynamic individual, but in this case one man, Paul P. Petticord, was the primary early promoter and sole president through the period of this study. Pettiford had been a district superintendent in the Evangelical Church (which became part of the 1946 Evangelical United Brethren and 1968 United Methodist Church mergers), whose leadership and seminary in Naperville, Illinois had moved too far in a theologically liberal direction to please him.

769. Witmer, John A. "What Hath God Wrought -- Fifty Years at Dallas Theological Seminary." *Bibliotheca Sacra* 130 (1973): 291-304, and 131 (1974): 3-13.

Provides a supplement to the more thorough, although older Renfer study. The Witmer article, which appears in two parts in successive issues of the seminary journal, is an historical summary of the occasion of the institution's fiftieth anniversary.

CHAPTER 9
JEWISH SEMINARIES
Harold Wechsler

770.   Adler, Cyrus. *I Have Considered the Days*. Philadelphia, PA: The Jewish Publication Society of America, 1941.

Recounts Adler's relationship to the Jewish Theological Seminary of America, as an instructor, governor, and president. Discusses the Seminary's 1902 reorganization, the physical plant, finances, and its fiftieth anniversary.

771.   Adler, Cyrus. *The Jewish Theological Seminary of America*. New York: The Jewish Theological Seminary of America, 1939.

Celebrates the fiftieth Anniversary of the Jewish Theological Seminary. Relates the founding and early history of JTS. Contains chapters on individual departments. Chapter 7, by Israel Davidson, discusses the Seminary's early curriculum, which emphasized Bible and Talmud, and changes in admission and graduation requirements, in faculty composition, and in governance.

772.   Adler, Cyrus. *Selected Letters*. Edited by Ira Robinson. 2 vols. Philadelphia, PA and New York: The Jewish Publication Society of America and the Jewish Theological Seminary of America, 1985.

Includes Cyrus Adler's correspondence as president of the Jewish Theological Seminary. Subjects covered: the curriculum and the preparation of rabbis, faculty issues, institutional goals, governance, the physical plant, financial conditions, relations with other seminaries, secular institutions, the Conservative movement, and other branches of Judaism.

773.   American Jewish Archives. "Hebrew Union College-Jewish Institute of Religion: A Centennial Documentary." *American Jewish Archives* 26 (November 1974): 99-243.

Depicts the founding, early growth, development, and important events of Hebrew Union College and the Jewish Institute of Religion through original documents. The documents relate student and faculty experiences, as well as governance issues. Shows communal and national roles played by HUC-JIR's leadership, and incidents that reflect its emergence as Reform's rabbinical seminary, and as a major Jewish intellectual center.

774.   Bentwich, Norman. *Solomon Schechter: A Biography.*
         Philadelphia, PA: The Jewish Publication Society of America,
         1938. (Especially Chapter 7.)

             Shows that Schechter's long-standing interest in coming to
         the United States predisposed him to accept the presidency of the
         Jewish Theological Seminary. Schechter hoped JTS would help
         unite Jews through Jewish scholarship. It would stand for historical
         and traditional Judaism, and would appeal to the large influx of
         immigrants into urban centers. Discusses Schechter's efforts at
         curricular reform and faculty recruitment. Divides his presidency
         into two periods: five years of growth, then a decade of stasis.
         Assesses his influence on the Seminary's students.

775.   Cohon, Samuel Solis. "The History of the Hebrew Union College."
         Publications of the American Jewish Historical Society 40 (1950):
         17-55.

             Discusses the role of Rabbi Isaac Mayer Wise in HUC's
         founding. While *Wissenschaft des Judentums* (the scientific study
         of Judaism) affected the curriculum, the Higher Criticism did not.
         The College aspired to become the sole seminary for all but the most
         orthodox American Jews.   Personal and ideological discord
         thwarted this ideal. Kufman Kohler, Wise's successor, turned HUC
         into a vehicle for the education of Reform rabbis exclusively. An
         ideal of "positive, creative American Judaism" that blended
         tradition with innovation motivated Julian Morgenstern, HUC's
         third president.

776.   Davis, Moshe. *The Emergence of Conservative Judaism: The
         Historical School in 19th Century America.* Part 3. Philadelphia,
         PA: The Jewish Publication Society of America, 1963.

             Discusses the early years of the Jewish Theological Seminary
         of America: its location, goals, curriculum, faculty, and its
         founders. Sees the Seminary's 1902 reorganization as a reflection
         of the Historical School's transformation into the Conservative
         movement.   See also Marshall Sklare, *Conservative Judaism*
         (Glencoe, IL: Free Press, 1955).

777.   Davis, Moshe. "Jewish Religious Life and Institutions in America:
         A Historical Study." In *The Jews: Their History, Culture and
         Religion*, Vol. 1, pp. 354-453. Edited by Louis Finkelstein. New
         York: Harper and Brothers, 1949.

             Places the founding of each seminary in the context of late
         19th century intellectual trends. Depicts the role of seminaries in
         creating and perpetuating the major divisions in American Judaism.
         Each group was built upon three pillars: seminaries, a union of
         congregations, and a conference of rabbis. Traces evolution of the
         major seminaries -- especially the need to define consistent
         intellectual positions after an initial period of organization and

expansion. Discusses tendencies of theological schools to expand into universities, with rabbinical schools remaining at the core. Sees higher Jewish education as one of several unifying forces among American Jewry.

778.   Fierstien, Robert E. "The Founding and Early Years of the Jewish Theological Seminary of America." *History of Higher Education Annual* 7 (1987): 69-78.

Depicts JTS's founding as a response to the changing demography of American Jewry and to the "extreme" beliefs of HUC's Isaac M. Wise. While academically successful, leadership and financial problems led to its 1902 reorganization. Draws parallels between the Seminary's early history and the evolving concept of "Conservative Judaism." Based on "From Foundation to Reorganization: The Jewish Theological Seminary of America, 1886-1902" (dissertation, Jewish Theological Seminary, 1986). See also Herbert Rosenblum, "The Shaping of an Institution: The 1902 Reorganization of the Seminary," *Conservative Judaism* 27 (Winter 1973): 35-48.

779.   Fliegel, Hyman. "The Creation of the Jewish Institute of Religion." *American Jewish Historical Quarterly* 58 (December 1968): 260-70.

Sees the Jewish Institute of Religion as providing a liberal institution in America's greatest Jewish center. Other factors that led to its founding: to make up for the small enrollments at Hebrew Union College; to provide a forum where Zionists could freely speak; and to promote academic freedom in a seminary environment. Early overtures to HUC and to the Union of American Hebrew Congregations came to naught; union between JIR and HUC occurred a generation later.

780.   Ginzberg, Eli. *Keeper of the Law: Louis Ginzberg.* Philadelphia, PA: The Jewish Publication Society of America, 1966.

Offers a faculty perspective on the Jewish Theological Seminary, its 1902 reorganization, and the administrations of Solomon Schechter and Cyrus Adler. Portrays Schechter, who appointed Ginzberg professor of Talmud in 1902, sympathetically. Ginzberg's appointment pointed JTS toward a concern for Jewish scholarship. Depicts Cyrus Adler's leadership as bureaucratic, not intellectual. Adler was unable to lift JTS out of its financial straits. Sees Louis Finkelstein's presidency as salutary for Jewish scholarship.

781.   Greenberg, Simon. "Jewish Educational Institutions." In *The Jews: Their History, Culture and Religion.* Vol. 3, pp. 916-49. Edited by Louis Finkelstein. New York: Harper and Brothers, 1949.

Contains brief descriptions and histories of major Jewish institutions of learning in America. Shows that for Jews, as for others, institutions of higher learning preceded primary and secondary institutions. Shows the transition from yeshivot to theological seminaries in nineteenth and twentieth century America.

782. Gurock, Jeffrey S. "From Exception to Role Model: Bernard Drachman and the Evolution of Jewish Religious Life in America, 1880-1920." *American Jewish History* 76 (June 1987): 456-84.

Examines the traditionalists among those who founded the Jewish Theological Seminary, especially Bernard Drachman. While an instructor at JTS, Drachman recruited students who worked with Jewish immigrants to ensure that immigrants did not depart from Jewish tradition while acquiring American ways. Although early efforts did not halt assimilation, they prepared the groundwork for later, more broad-based anti-assimilation work. They gave training to those who wold lead this work. Sees in the Young Israel movement the coming of age of American Traditionalist ideals. Drachman also influenced the transformation of the Rabbi Isaac Elchanan Seminary from a transplanted European yeshiva to an American orthodox seminary. See also Bernard Drachman, *The Unfailing Light: Memoirs of an American Rabbi.* (New York: Rabbinical Council of America, 1948).

783. Gurock, Jeffrey S. *The Men and Women of Yeshiva University: Higher Education, Orthodoxy and American Judaism.* New York: Columbia University Press, 1988.

Uses the institution's history to understand the changes in American Orthodoxy and American Jewish life. Looks at the backgrounds and experiences of the school's students, and compares them with Conservative and Reform students in several historical periods. Examines the Revel and Belkin presidencies, and the role of education for the rabbinate as part of the institution's greater mission.

784. Hartstein, Jacob I. "Yeshiva University." *American Jewish Yearbook* 50 (1948-1949): 73-84.

Stresses the continuity of the Yeshiva ideal and its compatibility with collegiate and university ideals as the institution evolved from an Orthodox Jewish seminary into a full university, the only one of the major rabbinical seminaries to do so. Provides a short chronicle of this evolution.

785. Heller, James G. *Isaac Mayer Wise: His Life, Work and Thought.* New York: Union of American Hebrew Congregations, 1965.

Places the life of Isaac M. Wise in the context of late 19th century America. Findings: Wise, though inconsistent on lesser matters, held his objectives constant; he disavowed the use of Reform Judaism as a way "out of Judaism"; he was knowledgeable about Jewish sources; he had a strong sense of Jewish unity; he was a product of "the spirit of the age"; his concept of America was central to his thinking; he was a complex, sometimes mercurial, human being. The founding of a seminary was a consistent purpose. Contains an account of HUC's early years and an extensive bibliography. See also Joseph H. Gumbiner. *Isaac Mayer Wise: Pioneer of American Judaism* (Cincinnati, OH: U.A.H.C., 1959), Joseph Gutman. "Watchman on the Rhine: New Light on Isaac Mayer Wise." *American Jewish Archives* (October 1958): 135-44, Max B. May [Wise's grandson]. *Isaac Mayer Wise: The Founder of American Judaism* (New York, G. P. Putnam's Sons, 1916), Israel Knox. *Rabbi in America: the Story of Isaac M. Wise* (New York: Little, Brown and Co. 1957), and Dean Wilansky. *Sinai to Cincinnati: Lay Views on the Writings of Isaac M. Wise* (New York: Renaissance Book Co., 1937).

786.   Helmreich, William. "Old Wine on New Bottles: Advanced Yeshivot in the United States." *American Jewish History* 69 (December 1979): 234-56.

Traces history of the Rabbi Isaac Elchanan Theological Seminary, and Yeshiva College, which dominated the Orthodox community. Also examines less well-known yeshivot. Discusses opposition to Bernard Revel's dream of conducting secular and religious studies at one institution. Outlines the founding of the next group of American yeshivot, the graduates of which became an influential "intellectual elite of sorts." These institutions facilitated the migration of orthodox Holocaust survivors in the late 1940s. Sees a split between "Strictly Orthodox" and "Modern Orthodox." The "Modern Orthodox" supported RIETS and Chicago's Hebrew Theological College. Discusses post-War developments: the prominence of Rabbi Joseph B. Soloveitchik of Yeshiva, the move of the Telshe Yeshiva to the United States, and Rabbi Aharon Kotler's establishment of the Beth Medrash Govohi in Lakewood, New Jersey. Says that yeshiva heads are displacing pulpit rabbis in influence, and that the yeshiva world is a vital, growing force.

787.   Helmreich, William. *The World of the Yeshiva.* New York: The Free Press, 1982.

Gives a comprehensive portrait of the advanced (equivalent to college-level) "Lithuanian-style" yeshivot in the United States that together service about 5,000 students. Examines their history in America, the sociology of yeshiva life, the demographic composition of the student body, the conditions for success or failure, and the relationship of the yeshiva to other social institutions. Evaluates the yeshiva in terms of its self-stated goals.

788.   Karff, Samuel E., ed. *Hebrew Union College-Jewish Institute of Religion at 100 Years.* Cincinnati, OH: Hebrew Union College Press, 1976.

Contains Michael A. Meyer's extensive "Centennial History," and a "Survey of Scholarly Contributions" that includes essays on "Bible," "Rabbinics," "Theology and Philosophy," "History," and "Hebrew and Hebrew Literature." Notes tension between scholarship and the defence of the faith. Concludes that HUC-JIR views the rabbinate as a learned profession. Other themes: HUC-JIR's relationship to Reform Judaism, its quest for self-definition, academic freedom and the Jewish faith, student-faculty relations, and expectations for the rabbi. See also Stanely Chyet, *Hebrew Union College-Jewish Institute of Religion 1947-1967* (Cincinnati, OH: Hebrew Union College Press, 1961).

789. Karp, Abraham J. "A Century of Conservative Judaism in the United States." *American Jewish Yearbook* 86 (1986): 3-63.

Argues that the Jewish Theological Seminary was established by traditionalists and members of the Historical School who believed that the Union of American Hebrew Congregations was a Reform organization and that Hebrew Union College graduates would articulate Reform Judaism. JTS soon defined a "conservative" role for itself while attracting an acculturated East European clientele. Under Solomon Schechter, it gained leadership, intellectual strength, and heterogeneity. It matured under Cyrus Adler. Discusses the Seminary faculty: Louis Ginzberg, Mordecai Kaplan, Louis Finkelstein, and Robert Gordis. During Finkelstein's presidency, Conservative Judaism became America's largest Jewish grouping. JTS added a graduate school, a music college, and a Cantors Institute to the Rabbinical School, Teachers Institute, and College of Jewish Studies. Under Gerson D. Cohen, JTS hired new faculty, recruited students from Conservative, not traditional backgrounds, and gave greater attention to advocates of change. Recounts the history of the admission of women to the Rabbinical College.

790. Karp, Abraham J. *Haven and Home: A History of the Jews in America.* New York: Schocken Books, 1985.

Sees Hebrew Union College as the educator of an emerging American rabbinate caught between the demands of tradition and innovation, and performing more roles than European rabbis. Discusses Rabbi Simon Tuska, who studied in an American college and in European seminaries -- the author of guidelines for an American Reform seminary. Sees Jewish Theological Seminary as forming a rabbinate that "would be true to the traditions of Judaism and fully at home in the culture of America." Calls JTS president Solomon Schechter the Conservative movement's first charismatic leader. (See also Karp, Abraham J. "Solomon Schechter Comes to America." *American Jewish Historical Quarterly* 57 (June 1969): 42-62.)

791. Kiev, I. Edward, and John J. Tepfer. "Jewish Institute of Religion." *American Jewish Yearbook* 49 (1947-48): 91-100.

Views the Institute as a liberal alternative to Hebrew Union College. It attracted more mature students, and offered a less dogmatic curriculum. Under the guidance of Rabbi Stephan S. Wise, the College recruited an intellectually heterogeneous faculty that reflected the contemporary Hebrew renaissance. Among the innovations: JIR offered graduate instruction in modern Hebrew; the curriculum addressed practical communal problems.

792.   Klaperman, Gilbert. *The Story of Yeshiva University.* New York: Macmillan, 1969.

Offers a history of Yeshiva University from its origins as the Rabbi Isaac Elchanan Seminary through the 1960s. Contains descriptions of the founding of Yeshiva College and of the rise of a full scale university after World War II. Emphasizes two presidents: Bernard Revel and Samuel Belkin.

793.   Klaperman, Gilbert. "Yeshiva University: Seventy-five Years in Retrospect." *American Jewish Historical Quarterly* 54 (September and December 1964): 5-50, 198-201.

Discusses the founding of the Rabbi Isaac Elchanan Seminary, Yeshiva's predecessor, and the decision to embark upon creation of a secular college (Yeshiva College) under Jewish auspices during the 1920s.

794.   Kohler, Kaufman. *Hebrew Union College and Other Addresses.* Cincinnati, OH: Ark Publishing, 1916.

Ascribes two goals to his collection of sermons and addresses: "To give permanency to those memorable events in the history of Hebrew Union College, of which it has been vouchsafed to me to be witness, or participant, [and] to acquaint the general public with the views and aims of Reform Judaism and with the great personalities." See also Kaufman Kohler, "The HUC of Yesterday and a Great Desideratum in its Curriculum Today," in David Philipson, et al., eds., pp. 71-78. *Hebrew Union College Jubilee Volume (1875-1925)* (Cincinnati, OH: Hebrew Union College, 1925), in which Kohler calls for increased attention to contemporary problems, especially to relations with Christians and Christianity, and for increased spirituality among students.

795.   Korn, Bertram W. "The First American Jewish Theological Seminary: Maimonides College 1867-1873." In *Eventful Years and Experiences*, pp. 151-213. Cincinnati, OH: American Jewish Archives, 1954.

Traces parallel plans by Leeser and Isaac Mayer Wise for institutions that would train rabbis. Wise's Zion College gained no support outside of Cincinnati and closed. Attempts by New York's Temple Emanu-El and by the Independent Order of B'nai B'rith also came to naught. A Philadelphia group, led by Leeser, established Maimonides College, despite concerns about student recruitment and preparation. Several Philadelphia rabbis and laymen volunteered to assist Leeser as faculty members. The College never had more than a handful of ill-prepared students. Its financial condition quickly deteriorated. Lack of leadership (Leeser died in 1867) and of students, and Jewish insularity and isolationism all contributed to Maimonides' demise. See also Bertram W. Korn, "The Temple Emanu-El Theological Seminary of New York City." In Melvin Urofsky, ed., *Essays in American Zionism: Herzl Yearbook Number 8* (New York: Herzl Press, 1958).

796.   Liebman, Charles S. "Orthodoxy in American Jewish Life." *American Jewish Year Book* 66 (1965): 21-97.

Discusses Yeshiva University, the Hebrew Theological College of Chicago, and advanced *yeshivot*. Traces Yeshiva's growth under Samuel Belkin. Yeshiva's core units espouse no particular philosophy within the Orthodox spectrum. Examines its faculty, students, alumni, and its relationship to the community. Traces the evolution of post-high school yeshivot, founded by sectarian Orthodox Jews who arrived in America at the time of World War II.

797.   Liebman, Charles S. "The Training of American Rabbis." *American Jewish Yearbook* 69 (1968): 1-112.

Praises curricula at Yeshiva, The Jewish Theological Seminary, and Hebrew Union College-Jewish Institute of Religion. Notes however that change often comes slowly, and preparation for daily life as a rabbi could be improved. Analyzes a questionnaire administered to rabbinical students. Finds that rabbis become socialized to communal, rather than to institutional, values. Students are dissatisfied with the state of Jewish belief and practice, with the possibilities for preservation of Judaism, and with Jewish education. They see their influence on the personal, not the communal level, mainly because the seminaries say little about the Jewish community.

798.   Marcus, Jacob R. "The Americanization of Isaac Mayer Wise." In *Studies in American Jewish History*, edited by Jacob R. Marcus. Cincinnati, OH: Hebrew Union College Press, 1969.

Presents an autobiographical account of Hebrew Union College's founder, based on material from *Asmonean* (March 17-24, 1854) on his life in Bohemia, from his *Reminiscences*, and from *The American Israelite*.

799.   Marcus, Jacob R., and Abraham J. Peck, eds. *The American Rabbinate*. New York: KTAV, 1985.

Offers essays on the American rabbinate and the American

seminaries that educate its members. Jeffrey Gurock depicts the Jewish Theological Seminary as an accommodation to America, "a desire to be traditional and modern at the same time." He suggests that the Orthodox rabbinate must confront the tension between resistance and accommodation. Conservative Judaism, writes Abraham Karp, is similarly caught between "traditionalists" and "progressives." However, Conservative rabbis consider change legitimate, whereas Orthodox rabbis do not. Similarly, Conservative rabbis see JTS as a unifying symbol, whereas Orthodox Jews have no similar institution. Reform rabbis are also caught between tradition and change, but tradition includes the nineteenth century Reform Judaism. Reform rabbis have HUC-JIR as a common training ground, but do not consider themselves bound by its dictates.

800.   Meyer, Harry A. "What Price Conservatism? Louis Ginzberg and the Hebrew Union College." *American Jewish Activities* 10 (1958): 145-50.

         Suggests that Hebrew Union College's 1898 decision to rescind an appointment offer made to Louis Ginzberg when Isaac M. Wise incorrectly surmised that Ginzberg subscribed to the Higher Criticism. Deciding that the occupant should be someone "to whom Judaism stands higher than the learning of the Universities," HUC offered the chair to Rabbi Henry Malter.

801.   Moore, Deborah Dash. "Yeshiva College: Orthodox Hedge." In *At Home in America: Second Generation New York Jews.* New York: Columbia University Press, 1981.

         Discusses Yeshiva College's mission: assurance of a continual supply of rabbis. The College broadened the pool of students to include potential rabbis and students aspiring to other professions. It sought the proper curricular balance between elements from the traditional yeshiva and from the American liberal arts college. Rabbis educated in both Jewish and secular subjects could address modern concerns while deciding ritual questions.

802.   Neuman, Abraham A. *Cyrus Adler: A Biographical Sketch.* New York: The American Jewish Committee, 1942.

         Examines Cyrus Adler's role as president of the Jewish Theological Seminary's Board of Trustees after its 1902 reorganization. Adler believed the Seminary would redeem American Judaism. Discusses the relationship between JTS and the United Synagogue of America, and the reasons for Adler's assumption of the JTS presidency upon Solomon Schechter's death.

803.   Ohles, John F. and Shirley N. Ohles, eds. *Private Colleges and Universities.* 2 vols. Westport, CT: Greenwood Press, 1982.

         Includes brief historical articles on Jewish seminaries,

including Hebrew Theological College, Hebrew Union College, and Jewish Theological Seminary of America. Also includes articles on Baltimore Hebrew College, Cleveland College of Jewish Studies, Dropsie University, Hebrew College, and Spertus College of Judaica.

804.   Parzen, Herbert. *Architects of Conservative Judaism.* New York: Jonathan David, 1964.

Depicts Conservative Judaism as a heterogeneous movement. Traces its evolution through the history of the Jewish Theological Seminary and the biographies of its administrative and intellectual leaders: Sabato Marais, Solomon Schechter, Cyrus Adler, Louis Ginzberg, Israel Friedlander, and Mordecai M. Kaplan. Discusses President Louis Finkelstein's resolution "to steer the Seminary decisively rightward, irrespective of the attitude of the United Synagogue or the Rabbinical Assembly."

805.   Parzen, Herbert. "The Purge of the Zionists: Hebrew Union College and Zionism." *Jewish Social Studies* 37 (Spring-Fall 1975): 291-322.

Shows the attenuation of academic freedom and intellectual pluralism at Hebrew Union College after Kaufman Kohler's assumption of the presidency in 1903. Kohler believed that Judaism had to be "Westernized" and "Americanized," and that HUC trained religious leaders, not scholars. Kohler hired Max Margolis for his Biblical scholarship and for his theological standpoint. But Margolis and two colleagues differed with Kohler on Zionism and other fundamental issues. When Kohler insisted that a seminary was not a university, and that academic freedom was limited, the three dissidents resigned. This allowed Kohler to place his stamp upon HUC and American Reform Judaism for a generation.

806.   Philipson, David. "History of the Hebrew Union College, 1875-1925." In *Hebrew Union College Jubilee Volume (1985-1925),* pp. 1-70. Edited by David Philipson, et al. Cincinnati, OH: 1925.

Places the founding of seminaries in Europe and the United States in the context of Jewish emancipation. Reform Judaism, a product of that emancipation, required new institutions and new rabbis. Sees the primary reason for establishing the Union of American Hebrew Congregations as the creation of Hebrew Union College. Discusses the preparatory and collegiate curricula, faculty, governance, physical plant, and students. Kohler stressed the universalistic interpretation of Judaism as defined by the Reform movement. See also Stanley Chyet, "I. M. Wise: Portraits by D. M. Philipson." In *A Bicentenniel Festschrift for Jacob Rader Marcus* (New York: KTAV, 1976).

807.   Rothkoff, Aaron. *Bernard Revel: Builder of American Jewish*

Orthodoxy.   Philadelphia, PA: Jewish Publication Society of
America, 1972.

Places Bernard Revel's life and his presidency of Yeshiva
College in the context of Orthodox Jewry's status in the early
twentieth century. Discusses his role in Yeshiva's transition from
a seminary to a multi-divisional college, in opposing a projected
merger with the Jewish Theological Seminary, in confronting
Orthodox criticisms of his actions, in maintaining contact with the
rabbis graduated by the institution, and in seeing the College
through the economic problems resulting from the Depression.

808.   Rubinstein, Aryeh. "Isaac Mayer Wise: A New Appraisal." *Jewish
         Social Studies* 39 (Winter/Spring 1977): 53-74.

Offers a revisionist assessment of Isaac Mayer Wise, founder
of Hebrew Union College. "Wise was a radical, not a moderate.
He talked a lot about unity, but the reform he introduced made for
disunity. He indeed made many enemies, but that was more his
fault than theirs." Sees Wise as an opportunist whose "conservative
pronouncements were only lip-service, while his rationalist,
Deist-like statements represented his true opinions."

809.   Schechter, Solomon. *Seminary Addresses and Other Papers*. New
         York: Burning Bush Press, 1959.

Pleas for traditional Judaism, "which it is the mission of the
[Jewish Theological] Seminary to teach and preach in this country."
Schechter, JTS president from 1902 to 1915, also calls for adopting
in scholarship "all the methods which distinguish modern research
from the mere erudition of olden times." Stresses the need for
strong secular education before turning to the advanced study of
Jewish learning.

810.   Tannenbaum, Marc H. "Seminaries." *American Jewish Yearbook*
         60 (1959): 53-56.

Depicts the liberalization of Yeshiva's rabbinical curriculum
and the parallel move at the Jewish Theological Seminary towards
a "more traditional mode of preparing rabbis" during the late 1950s.

811.   Urofsky, Melvin. *A Voice That Spoke for Justice: The Life and
         Times of Stephen S. Wise*. Albany, NY: State University of New
         York Press, 1982. (Especially chapter 13.)

Sees the founding of the Jewish Institute of Religion as part
of Stephen Wise's attempt to bring American Judaism into line with
twentieth century conditions. Distinguishing features:
graduate-level instruction, intellectual diversity, and social activism.
Emphasizes Wise's personal stamp: his academic and social
liberalism, enthusiasm, and sense of mission. Discusses the
Institute's precarious finances, and relations with Hebrew Union

College.   While discrimination by Reform leaders against JIR graduates compromised its influence, other seminaries eventually adopted its distinguishing features.

812.   Wise, Isaac Mayer. *Reminiscences.* Translated by David Philipson. Cincinnati, OH: Leo Wise, 1901.

Traces Wise's arrival and experiences in the United States. Emphasizes the need for individual religious freedom and for order that prevents freedom from degenerating into anarchy. These needs underlie Wise's call for an educated ministry, and for an end to chaotic congregationalism.   Recounts Wise's campaign for an American rabbinical seminary that would impart both an American education and a knowledge of Judaism. Discusses failed efforts to organize Zion College, which offered rabbinical and secular education, and the successful effort to organize Hebrew Union College.

813.   Wise, Stephen S. *Challenging Years: The Autobiography of Stephen Wise.* New York: G. P. Putnam's Sons, 1949. (Especially Chapter 8.)

Recounts Stephen Wise's decision to found the Jewish Institute of Religion. Considerations included: the need to provide an alternative to Orthodoxy and Reform; the lack of social service education in the curricula of existing seminaries; the importance of New York City to American Jewish life; and the need for a seminary free from all dogmas.   Discusses funding, faculty recruitment, the physical plant, governance and administration, and relations with Hebrew Union College through the merger of the two seminaries.

CHAPTER 10
LUTHERAN SEMINARIES
Richard W. Solberg and Jon Diefenthaler

814.   Adams, James E. *Preus of Missouri and the Great Lutheran Civil War*. New York: Harper and Row, Publishers, 1977.

Sets forth the assessment of a St. Louis newspaper editor and outsider on the theological controversy of the 1970s in the Lutheran Church-Missouri Synod and the dismantling of its "moderate" stronghold at Concordia Seminary, St. Louis. Focuses on "conservative" Synod President J. A. O. Preus, describing his Norwegian Lutheran background and training, his tenure as faculty member and president of the Springfield seminary, synodical presidency, and role in the upheavals at the St. Louis seminary.

815.   Allbeck, Willard D. *Theology at Wittenberg 1845-1945*. Springfield, OH: Wittenberg Press, 1946.

816.   Anderson, H. George, and Robert M. Calhoon, eds. *A Truly Efficient School of Theology: The Lutheran Theological Seminary in Historical Context, 1830-1980*. Columbia, SC: Lutheran Theological Southern Seminary, 1981.

Contains a series of four interpretative historical essays prepared for the seminary's sesquicentennial in 1980. Views Lutheranism in relation to cultural patterns in the antebellum South, including evangelicalism and the struggle for confessional identity. Deals with curricular trends at the turn of the century and the seminary's growing interaction with its parent denomination in the twentieth century.

817.   Arden, G. Everett. *The School of the Prophets*. Rock Island, IL: Augustana Theological Seminary, 1960.

Gives the story of theological education among Swedish Lutherans in America. Focuses on the seminary of the Augustana Synod established at Rock Island, Illinois, and subsequently moved to Chicago when Augustana merged with the United Lutheran Church in America to form the Lutheran Church in America (LCA).

818.   Board of Control, Concordia Seminary. *Exodus from Concordia*. St. Louis, MO: Concordia Seminary Publicity Office, 1977.

Assesses the controversy in the Missouri Synod of the 1970s and the trauma at Concordia in St. Louis that led to the walkout of most of the student body and the firing of almost the entire faculty from the standpoint of conservatives who took and maintained control of the school's administration.

819.   Bredemeier, Herbert G. *Concordia College, Fort Wayne, 1839-1957.* Fort Wayne, IN: Fort Wayne Public Library, 1978.

Provides details of the early years of Concordia Theological Seminary, the "practical" school of the Missouri Synod, first established in Ft. Wayne, Indiana, but separated from the college during the Civil War and combined with the St. Louis seminary until it was relocated in 1874 in Springfield, Illinois.

820.   Chrislock, Carl. *From Fjord to Freeway.* Minneapolis, MN: Augsburg College, 1969.

Describes the founding of Augsburg Seminary in 1869 and the subsequent shaping of its tradition by the distinguished Norwegian-American theologian, Georg Sverdrup. In the face of the American pattern of liberal college preparation for theological study, Sverdrup contended for a nine-year unified program, including a prep school, a Greek department, and a theological course. Shows how, in the course of Lutheran synodical and institutional mergers beginning in 1963, Augsburg Seminary became a part of Luther Northwestern Seminary in St. Paul, Minnesota.

821.   Christensen, William E. *Saga of the Tower.* Blaire, NE: Dana College, 1959.

Recounts the establishment and early history of Trinity Seminary by the pietistic branch of Danish Lutherans in 1884 in Blair, Nebraska, where its preparatory department became Dana College in 1899 and shared the same campus until the seminary moved in 1956 to Dubuque, Iowa, where, with the formation of The American Lutheran Church in 1960, Trinity Seminary merged with Wartburg Seminary, also in Dubuque.

822.   Clark, William S. and Arthur H. Wilson. *The Story of Susquehanna University.* Selinsgrove, PA: Susquehanna University Press, 1959.

Describes the establishment of Missionary Institute by Benjamin Kurtz in 1858 as an independent seminary to provide missionary pastors for the frontier. Points out that because its preparatory department grew more rapidly, the institution in 1894 was renamed Susquehanna University, with the theological department continuing to train pastors until it was merged into the Hamma School of Theology at Wittenberg College, Springfield, Ohio.

823.   Danker, Frederick W.   *No Room in the Brotherhood: The Preus-Otten Purge of Missouri.* St. Louis, MO: Clayton Publishing House, 1977.

        Gives the perspective of a "moderate" insider and member of the faculty on the traumatic events at Concordia Seminary, St. Louis, that were at the heart of the theological storm that swept the Missouri Synod during the 1970s. Provides details on the events leading up to the days of crisis in 1974 and emphasizes the crucial role of the seminary body in protesting the removal of John Tietjen as president of the school and the walkout that led to the formation of a seminary-in-exile.

824.   *Evangelical Lutheran Theological Seminary, 1830-1930.* Columbus, OH: Lutheran Book Concern, 1930.

        Contains materials relating to the seminary of the Joint Ohio Synod which in 1930 merged with the Iowa Synod and the tiny Buffalo Synod to form the "first" American Lutheran Church.

825.   Evenson, George O.   *Adventuring for Christ: The Story of the Evangelical Lutheran Church of Canada.*   Calgary, AB: The Foothills Lutheran Press, 1974.

826.   Graebner, Theodore.   *Concordia Seminary: Its History, Architecture, and Symbolism.* St. Louis, MO: Concordia Publishing House, 1927.

827.   Hansen, Thorvald. *We Laid Foundations Here: The Early History of Grand View College.*   Des Moines, IA: Grand View College, 1972.

        Contains material relating to the founding of Grand View Seminary of the Danish Church.

828.   Harstad, Peter T. *Sigurd Christian Ylvisaker 1884-1959.* Mankato, MN: Bethany College, 1984.

        Contains material relating to the founding of Bethany Seminary of the conservative Norwegian Evangelical Lutheran Synod.

829.   Hausmann, Carl Frederick. *Kunze's Seminarium.*   Philadelphia, PA: American Germanica Press, 1917.

        Focuses on one of the earliest efforts on the part of John Christopher Kunze of Philadelphia in 1773 to establish some "sort of seminary" on American soil and describes the short life of this particular school because of the Revolutionary War and the British occupation of Philadelphia in 1777.

830.   Heins, Henry Hardy. *Throughout All the Years: The Bicentennial Story of Hartwick in America, 1746-1946.* Oneonta, NY: Hartwick

College, 1946.

Tells the story of the oldest Lutheran theological seminary in America, established in 1797, according to the terms of the will of a Lutheran pastor, John Christopher Hartwick. Traces the course of theological instruction, emphasizing that while there was a first professor in New York City, the seminary building itself, together with an academy, was built on Hartwick's land in upper New York State in 1815. Describes how in 1930 the seminary was moved to Brooklyn and in 1941 concluded its 144-year history in New York City.

831.   Heintzen, Erich H. *Prairie School of the Prophets: The Anatomy of a Seminary.* Springfield, IL: Concordia Theological Seminary, 1975.

Provides a comprehensive overview of the development of the "practical" seminary of the Missouri Synod, relocated on the old campus of Illinois State University in Springfield in 1874, where it remained for the next century, until it was moved again to Ft. Wayne, Indiana, and located on the grounds of the former Concordia Senior College.

832.   Kaufmann, John A., ed. *Biographical Record of the Lutheran Theological Seminary of Philadelphia, 1864-1962.* Philadelphia, PA: n.p. 1964.

833.   Kinnison, William A. *An American Seminary: A History of Hamma School of Theology.* Columbus, OH: Ohio Synod, LCA, 1980.

Describes the American pattern of theological education established by the founders of Wittenberg College in 1845, modeled after the New England colonial colleges, integrating theological courses with both classical and liberal studies. Recounts change in 1905, when in recognition of a generous endowed gift, the theological department was named Hamma School of Theology. It remained under the administrative structure of Wittenberg College until the merger of Hamma during the 1970s with the Evangelical Lutheran Seminary in Columbus, Ohio, to form Trinity Lutheran Seminary in Columbus.

834.   Koehler, John Phillipp. *The History of the Wisconsin Synod.* 2nd ed. Edited by Leigh D. Jordahl. Sauk Rapids, MN: The Protestant Conference, 1981.

Contains valuable references (pages 118-24, 146-49, 188-89, 207-08, 218-19, 234-36, 252-53) to the seminary, presently located in Mequon, Wisconsin, of the conservative Wisconsin Evangelical Lutheran Synod, in the context of the theological development of that synod from 1864 to 1925.

835.   Kowalke, Erwin E. *Centennial Story: Northwestern College, 1965.*

Contains important background material on the German model that shaped theological education at the preparatory and seminary levels in the Wisconsin Synod.

836.   Marquart, Kurt E. *Anatomy of an Explosion: Missouri in Lutheran Perspective*. Ft. Wayne, IN: Concordia Theological Seminary Press, 1977.

Discusses the controversy of the 1970s in the Missouri Synod and its impact upon theological education from the standpoint of a "conservative" insider.

837.   McCullough, Paul, et al., eds. *A History of the Lutheran Church in South Carolina*. Columbia, SC: R. L. Bryand Co., 1971.

Contains references to the origin, history, and program of the Lutheran Theological Southern Seminary and its relation to southern Lutheranism.

838.   Meyer, Carl S. *Log Cabin to Luther Tower*. St. Louis, MO: Concordia Publishing House, 1965.

Provides a detailed institutional history of the Missouri Synod's Concordia Seminary, St. Louis, from its humble beginnings in 1839 to its emergence in the post-World War II era as the largest Lutheran seminary in America. Focuses on changes in the curriculum, key faculty members, and student life, all of which were affected by the acculturation of the German church body with which the school was closely aligned.

839.   Quanbeck, Warren, et al. *Striving for Ministry: Centennial Essays Interpreting the Heritage of Luther Theological Seminary*. Minneapolis, MN: Augsburg Publishing House, 1977.

840.   Rholl, Arthur, ed. *Red Wing Seminary: Fifty Years of Service*. Red Wing, MN: Red Wing Seminary, 1929.

841.   Rinde, Thomas. *After 74 Years: A History of Western and Central Seminaries, 1893-1967*. Fremont, NE: Lutheran Book Concern, 1967.

842.   Sheatsley, C. V. *History of the First Lutheran Seminary of the West*. Columbus, OH: Lutheran School of Theology at Chicago, 1930.

843.   Skillrud, Harold C. *LSTC: Decade of Decision*. Chicago, IL: Lutheran School of Theology at Chicago, 1969.

Contains the documentary history of the formation of the Lutheran School of Theology at Chicago in 1962. Recounts the merger of four Lutheran seminaries representing Swedish, German, Danish, and Finnish Lutheran traditions: Augustana at Rock

Island, Illinois; Chicago Lutheran Seminary at Maywood, Illinois; Grand View Seminary at Des Moines, Iowa; and Suomi Seminary at Hancock, Michigan. In addition to the historical account of the merger process, it contains bibliography, reports of advisory committees, official constituting documents of the seminary, lists of participating personnel, and dedicatory orders of service.

844.   Stadius, Arnold. "Suomi College and Seminary." In *The Finns in North America: A Social Symposium*, pp. 91-123. Edited by Ralph J. Jalkanen. East Lansing, MI: Michigan State University Press, 1969.

845.   Tappert, Theodore, G.   *History of the Lutheran Theological Seminary at Philadelphia, 1864-1964*.   Philadelphia, PA: Lutheran Theological Seminary, 1964.

         Describes the founding and development of the Lutheran Theological Seminary at Philadelphia from 1864 to 1964.   Also includes an introductory chapter on earlier efforts in Lutheran theological education in America.   Recounts the theological tensions which were responsible for the founding of the Philadelphia seminary.   Traces the development of its faculty and curriculum, student life, and its role in the life of the Lutheran Church in this country.

846.   Threinen, Norman.   *Fifty Years of Lutheran Convergence: The Canadian Case Study*.   Lutheran Historical Conference Publication No. 3, Dubuque, IA: Lutheran Historical Conference, 1983.

847.   Vig, P. S.   *Trinitatis Seminarium*.   Blair, NE: n.p. 1911.

848.   Voigt, Gilbert P.   *A Historical Sketch: Lutheran Theological Southern Seminary*.   Columbia, SC: Lutheran Theological Southern Seminary, 1955.

849.   Wentz, Abdul Ross.   *History of Gettysburg Lutheran Theological Seminary, 1826-1965*.   2 vols.   Harrisburg, PA: The Evangelical Press, 1965.

         Recounts the origin and development of the oldest currently operating Lutheran theological seminary in America, founded by Samuel S. Schmucker, whose thinking became the focal point of the "American Lutheran theology" in the confessional controversies of the mid-nineteenth century.

850.   Hubbard, Walter M. "History of the First Seven Years of Nazarene
         Theological Seminary."   B.D. thesis. Nazarene Theological
         Seminary, 1953.

         Describes the founding of Nazarene Theological Seminary
         and its organization and operation during the first seven years of its
         existence.   Draws upon minutes of denominational boards and
         faculty committees, letters, personal interviews, and published
         materials. Includes brief biographies of the first faculty.

851.   Miller, William Charles.   "The Governance of Theological
         Education: A Case Study of Nazarene Theological Seminary,
         1945-1976." Ph.D. dissertation. Kent State University, 1983.

         Examines the governance of Nazarene Theological Seminary
         from its opening in 1945 until July, 1976 in terms of four
         governance models. Analyzes administrative decisions and actions,
         trustee,   faculty,   staff,   and   student   involvement,   and
         church-seminary interaction. Concludes that seminary presidents
         have been the most consistently dominant influences in decision
         making, that the denomination has regularly exercised its influence
         through its Board of General Superintendents, that selected
         governance models do account for governance behavior, and that a
         definable pattern of governance behavior has existed under each
         presidential administration.

852.   Robinson, Kenneth. "Educational Development in the Church of
         the Nazarene." B.D. thesis. Nazarene Theological Seminary, 1948.

         Surveys higher education efforts in the Church of the
         Nazarene up to 1948.   Traces in these a central concern with
         preparing persons for church ministries which culminates in the
         founding of Nazarene Theological Seminary in 1945.   Final
         chapter sets forth the basic facts of the seminary's founding and
         first three years of operation.

853.   Spindle, Oran Randall. "An Analysis of Higher Education in the
         Church of the Nazarene, 1945-1978."   Ed.D. dissertation.
         Oklahoma State University, 1981.

Analyzes the factors leading to changes in educational policy and practice in the denomination since the end of World War II. Mainly examines liberal arts colleges, but includes a brief section on the founding and subsequent development of Nazarene Theological Seminary. Includes the seminary in some appendices comparing earned degrees of faculty members, salary structures, and the like among Nazarene schools.

854.   "A Study of the Educational Structure of the Church of the Nazarene." A Report from the Education Commission of the Church of the Nazarene, 1964.

Reports on the state of higher education in the Church of the Nazarene. A major concern is to evaluate the education of ministers and Christian workers. Includes numerous tables representing questionnaire data collected from college and seminary faculty members and administrators, ministers, and lay people. Several sections focus directly on Nazarene Theological Seminary. Two new liberal arts colleges and Nazarene Bible College, Colorado Springs were organized partly as a result of this study.

CHAPTER 12
PRESBYTERIAN SEMINARIES
William J. Weston

Presbyterian Theological Education in General

855.   Baird, Samuel. "A history of the early policy of the Presbyterian Church in the training of her ministry, and of the first years of the Board of Education, with sketches of its deceased members." Philadelphia, PA: Published by the Board, 1865.

   A thirty-seven page pamphlet, "prepared at the request of the Board."

856.   Kelly, Robert L. *Theological Education in America: A Study of 161 Theological Schools in the U.S. and Canada.* New York: George H. Doran Company, 1924.

   This landmark study, written by the executive secretary of the Council of Church Boards of Education, contains occasional notes and comments on specific Presbyterian seminaries and on Presbyterian seminaries as a group.

857.   Presbyterian Church in the USA. "Annual Reports" of the Committee on Theological Seminaries, printed in the *Minutes of the General Assembly.*

   Brief factual accounts of the status and major events at each of the denomination's seminaries.

858.   Presbyterian Church in the USA. Curriculum Survey of the Committee on Theological Education. 1955, 1956, 1957. Typescript.

   Starting with a concern in the denomination over the teaching of Biblical languages, the committee decided to survey the facts and mission of PCUSA theological education as a whole.

859.   Wilson, J. Christy, ed. *Ministers in Training: A Review of Field Work Procedures in Theological Education.* Presbyterian Church in the U.S.A., 1957.

   Chapters written by the "Directors in Field Work in the Seminaries of the Presbyterian Church, U.S.A., representatives of the Boards of the Church and other specialists." Designed to promote supervision and integration overall, there is little on specific institutions except a fifteen page chapter on "Field work in our seminaries."

Histories

Austin

860.   Currie, Thomas, Jr. *Austin Presbyterian Theological Seminary: A Seventy-fifth Anniversary History.* San Antonio, TX: Trinity University Press, 1978.

A detailed history, based on the author's Th.D Thesis.

861.   Currie, Thomas, Jr. "A History of Austin Presbyterian Theological Seminary, 1884-1943." Th.D. thesis, Union Theological Seminary, 1958.

A detailed narrative history by the son and namesake of a central figure in the history of Austin Presbyterian Seminary.

Columbia

862.   Columbia Theological Seminary. *Semi-Centennial of Columbia Seminary, 1831-1881.* Columbia, SC: Presbyterian Publishing House, 1884.

A memorial volume of the celebration, including fifty pages on the history of the seminary and its missionary influences. The bulk of the book consists of memorials to graduates.

863.   Farmer, James O., Jr. *The Metaphysical Confederacy: James Henry Thornwell and the Synthesis of Southern Values.* Macon, GA: Mercer University Press, 1986.

A new study of the leading figure of Southern Presbyterianism and of Columbia Seminary before the Civil War, treated as a representative figure of the Southern intellectuals. Winner of the Brewer Prize of the American Society of Church History.

864.   Lamotte, Louis. *Colored Light: The Story of the Influence of Columbia Theological Seminary, 1828-1936.* Richmond, VA: Presbyterian Committee for Publication, 1937.

A fond, detailed narrative by a graduate of the Seminary.

865.   Palmer, Benjamin Morgan. *The Life and Letters of James Henley Thornwell.* Richmond, VA: Whittet and Shepperson, 1875; reprint New York: Arno, 1969.

The standard, large (600 pp.), and friendly biography of the leading figure of the southern Old School before the Civil War, written soon after Thornwell's death in 1862. Though most of his career was spent at South Carolina College, where he eventually served as president, Thornwell spent the last seven years of his life as professor of Columbia Seminary (then still in Columbia, SC), where he became the leading advocate of separation from the northern Old School church.

866.   Richards, J. McDowell. *As I Remember It: Columbia Theological Seminary, 1932-1971*. Decatur, GA: CTS Press, 1985.

A short popular history of the Seminary and memoir by its long-time President, who served from 1932 to 1970.

867.   Robinson, William C. *Columbia Theological Seminary and the Southern Presbyterian Church*. Decatur, GA: CTS Press, 1931.

A scholarly history of the seminary by a professor in the institution after its move to Decatur, GA, based on his Harvard Th.D. dissertation. Presented as the centennial history of the seminary in 1928.

Dubuque

868.   Fox, Harry Clifford. *German Presbyterianism in the Upper Mississippi Valley*. Ypsilanti, MI: University Lithoprinters, 1942.

A scholarly depiction of the religious context of Dubuque University and Seminary. Based on a University of Iowa doctoral dissertation.

869.   Mihelic, Joseph. "A Survey of the University of Dubuque, 1846-1979." 1979. Typescript.

A brief chronicle of the seminary that developed to serve German-speaking Presbyterians, as well as its outgrowth, the University, done for the use of the University by a longtime seminary professor and University archivist. Most interesting, though sketchy, is its treatment of the unionization of the seminary faculty in the early 1970s, the first such in the nation.

870.   Schnucher, Calvin. *The Development of the Rural Concept at the Theological Seminary of the University of Dubuque, 1941-1954*. Dubuque, IA: University of Dubuque, 1954.

An article, reprinted as a pamphlet, describing the development of the seminary's concept of its distinctive mission.

Erskine

871.   Allison, Leon McDill. A Sketch of Erskine Theological Seminary, 1836-1968. N.d. Manuscript.

A brief account of the major events of the seminary's history.

Louisville/Danville

872.   Groves, Walter. "A School of the Prophets of Danville." *Filson
        Club History Quarterly*, 1953.

        The founding of Danville Seminary, now part of Louisville
        Presbyterian Theological Seminary. (Twenty-five pages.)

873.   McElroy, I. S. *Louisville Presbyterian Theological Seminary*.
        Charlotte, NC: Presbyterian Standard Publishing Co., 1929.

        A short, readable history of the attempts of Kentucky
        Presbyterians to provide for their own theological education. A
        brief account is given of failed attempts at a seminary at Centre
        College in 1828, the more successful Danville Seminary (1853),
        through the northern Presbyterians' control of Danville Seminary,
        and then the southern church's theological department at Central
        University. The rest of the story, from the consolidation of the
        northern and southern synod's theological schools in Louisville in
        1901, until 1928, is told by McElroy, on the last surviving founders
        of the consolidated institution.

874.   Saunders, Robert S. *History of Louisville Theological Seminary,
        1853-1953*. Louisville, KY: Louisville Theological Seminary, 1953.

        A friendly account of the history of the Seminary from the
        founding of its predecessor Danville Theological Seminary until
        1953. It is intended as a somewhat more scholarly supplement to
        McElroy's volume.

McCormick -- including Cumberland, Lane, and Northwest

875.   Bone, Winstead P. *A History of Cumberland University*. Lebanon,
        TN: Published by the author, 1935.

        A standard institutional history by a president and graduate;
        of particular interest here are the chapters on "The Theological
        School, 1854-1909" and "Teachers in the Theological School,
        1854-1909."

876.   *General Catalogue 1829-1899*. Cincinnati, OH: Lane Theological
        Seminary.

        Brief biographical sketches of alumni and faculty. The
        edition of 1881 covers 1829-1881; a subsequent edition updates to
        1899.

877.   *General Catalogue*. Several editions, McCormick Theological
        Seminary.

        Short biographical entries for all faculty and alumni by class.
        The edition of 1900 covers the classes of 1834-1900 of the
        "McCormick Theological Seminary of the Presbyterian Church,"

with an update in 1912. The 1928 edition reflected the (temporary) name change to "Presbyterian Theological Seminary, Chicago."

878.   Halsey, LeRoy. *A History of the McCormick Theological Seminary of the Presbyterian Church.* Chicago, IL: McCormick Theological Seminary, 1893.

A large (550 pages) institutional history of the first six decades of McCormick and its predecessor institutions by a longtime professor. Detailed accounts of the battles over the early moves of the institution, slavery, and theology are given.

879.   Lesick, Lawrence T. *The Lane Rebels: Evangelicalism and Antislavery in Antebellum America.* Methuchen, NJ: Scarecrow, 1980.

A history of the Lane Seminary "rebellion" of 1834, with an emphasis on the role of Finney's revival theology in the antislavery commitments of the dissenters. A substantial, though narrowly focused historical study, originally a Vanderbilt dissertation.

880.   McClure, James G. K. *The Story of the Life and Work of the Presbyterian Theological Seminary, Chicago (Founded by Cyrus McCormick)* (as told briefly and swiftly by James G. K. McClure for the Centennial Celebration). N.p. 1929.

An informal account of the first century (1829-1929) of the seminary, as told by the president. Readable, short (140 pages), and downplaying the controversy of the era of the fundamentalist/modernist battles.

881.   *McCormick Theological Seminary Historical Celebration.* Chicago, IL: McCormick Theological Seminary, 1910.

The addresses from the eightieth anniversary celebration, including those by Augustus H. Strong of Rochester Seminary, J. Ross Stevens (later of Princeton Seminary), and Woodrow Wilson, the president of Princeton University. Includes a sixteen page history of the seminary and a thirty page appreciation of Cyrus McCormick.

882.   Morris, Edward. *Thirty Years in Lane and Other Lane Papers.* Cincinnati, OH: The Lane Club, 1896.

An affectionate memoir by a Lane history and theology professor, 1867-1897, published as a retirement memento by an alumni group.

883.   Presbyterian Theological Seminary of the Northwest. *Correspondence concerning the Presbyterian Theological seminary of the North-West between Rev. Willis Lord [et al.] and Cyrus McCormick [et al.].* New York: AC Rogers, 1869.

A pamphlet bringing together the historical papers of the founding of one of the predecessors of McCormick Theological Seminary.

884.   Sellars, Ovid. *The Fifth Quarter Century of McCormick: The Story of the Years 1929-1954 at McCormick Theological Seminary.* Chicago, IL: McCormick Theological Seminary, 1955.

Sellars, professor and dean at the seminary, was commissioned to write this history for the 125th anniversary, updating the series begun by Halsey and McClure. An ironic memoir, emphasizing faculty and administration, and downplaying controversy.

885.   Stephens, John Vant. *The Cumberland University Theological School.* Cincinnati, OH: (probably printed by the author), 1939.

Three pamphlets, bound together, telling the history of the seminary of the Cumberland Presbyterian Church in its forms as the Lebanon Theological Seminary of Cumberland University (Lebanon, TN), as the Seminary of the South, and then as it was merged into Lane Seminary, and thus eventually into McCormick Seminary.

Omaha

886.   Hawley, Charles A. *50 Years on The Nebraska Frontier: A History of Presbyterian Theological Seminary at Omaha.* Omaha, NE: Ralph Printing Co., 1941.

An institutional history written for the semi-centennial, plus appendices, describing some of the faculty, directors and graduates, as well as historical correspondence important to the seminary. Note: Omaha Seminary graduated its last class in 1943. It has since been transformed into the Omaha Presbyterian Seminary Foundation, which supports Presbyterian ministerial training in the West and Midwest.

Pittsburgh -- including Western and Xenia

887.   McNaugher, John. *The History of Theological Education in the United Presbyterian Church and its Ancestries.* Pittsburgh, PA: United Presbyterian Board of Publication & Bible School Work, 1931.

Basic facts of the Service (PA), Philadelphia, Canonsburg, Xenia, New York, Newburgh, Pittsburgh, Allegheny, Oxford (Ohio), Monmouth and Knoxville Seminaries of the United Presbyterian Church of North America, by the president of the successor of all of these institutions, Pittsburgh-Xenia Theological Seminary.

888.   Pittsburgh Theological Seminary. *Alumni Directory.* Pittsburgh,

PA: published by the seminary, 1965.

Brief biographical sketches of alumni and faculty.

889.   Sweetnam, George. "'Star in the West' -- History of Pittsburgh Theological Seminary 1794-1963." *PTS Perspective* 4 (December 1963).

A forty page article in the Pittsburgh Seminary magazine, inspired by the consolidation of Pittsburgh-Xenia and Western Seminaries into the New Pittsburgh Theological Seminary in 1958, which brought together institutions having roots in the Associate, Associate Reformed, United Presbyterian of North America, and Presbyterian in the USA denominations.

890.   *Western Theological Seminary General Biographical Catalogue.* Allegheny City, PA: Western Theological Seminary, 1885, 1927.

The edition of 1885 (200 pages) covers the period 1827-1885. Another edition covers 1827-1927 (400 pages). Includes brief biographical sketches of faculty and graduates of the seminary, along with lists of the directors.

891.   Xenia Theological Seminary. *Testimonial and Memorial to William Gallogly Moorehead.* Xenia, OH: Xenia Theological Seminary, 1913.

Brief reminscences and short historical accounts of the United Presbyterian Xenia Seminary, first created in Service, 1794, and of Professor Moorehead, in honor of his forty-one years of service to the institution.

Presbyterian School of Christian Education

892.   McComb, Louise. *A History of the Presbyterian School of Christian Education.* Richmond, VA: Presbyterian School of Christian Education, 1985.

A brief institutional history of the Presbyterian lay training school, established with close relations to its neighbor, Union Theological Seminary in Virginia.

893.   Presbyterian School of Christian Education. Self Study Report for the Southern Association of Colleges and Schools. 1967. Mimeo.

A detailed account of (then) current conditions at the Richmond school, with brief sections of historical background.

Princeton

894.   Alexander, Archibald. *Biographical Sketches of the Founder and Principal Alumni of the Log College, together with an account of the revivals of religion under their ministry.* Princeton, NJ: J. T.

Robinson, 1845.

Accounts of the life and labors of the Tennent family and other graduates of the predecessor of Princeton Seminary, written by Princeton's founder.

895. Clutter, Ronald. "The Reorientation of Princeton Theological Seminary, 1900-1925." Th.D. thesis, Dallas Theological Seminary, 1982.

A careful, scholarly consideration of the events leading up to the reorganization of Princeton Seminary and the withdrawal of the Machen party. Although the author is generally conservative, he does not support Machen's contention that the position of his opponents represented a liberal or "indifferentist" betrayal of Presbyterian theology.

896. *General Biographical Catalogue.*   Princeton, NJ: Princeton Theological Seminary.

Short biographical entries for graduates and faculty in several editions, including [1818]-1881, 1894, and 1909.

897. Haines, George L. "The Princeton Theological Seminary, 1925-1960." Ph.D. dissertation, New York University, 1966.

An account emphasizing developments in the seminary after the reorganization, which is largely sympathetic to the "broadening" trend that occurred after the removal of the Machen party.

898. Hart, John. "The Controversy within the Presbyterian Church, U.S.A., in the 1920's with Special Emphasis on the Reorganization of Princeton Theological Seminary." Senior thesis, Princeton University, 1978.

A solid, straightforward chronicle of the events in the seminary and the denomination surrounding the battle between moderates and fundamentalists for control of Princeton Seminary.

899. Kerr, Hugh T., ed. *Sons of the Prophets: Leaders in Protestantism from Princeton Seminary.*   Princeton, NJ: Princeton University Press, 1963.

Assembled for the seminary's sesquicentennial by a longtime professor at the seminary and editor of *Theology Today*, who provides a short foreword. Most useful for seminary history are essays by President Emeritus John Mackay on Archibald Alexander, and by Leonard Trinterud on Charles Hodge; the others mostly concern the later careers of famous students of the seminary.

900. Loetscher, Lefferts. *Facing the Enlightenment and Pietism: Archibald Alexander and the Founding of Princeton Theological Seminary.*   Westport, CT: Greenwood Press and Presbyterian

Historical Society, 1983.

A scholarly account of the founder, and something of the founding, of Princeton Seminary, by a noted historian of the Presbyterian Church and longtime professor of the seminary.

901.   Machen, J. Gresham. "The Attack Upon Princeton Seminary: A Plea for Fair Play." Pamphlet published by the author, December, 1927.

A short, but detailed, polemical brief for the losing side in the struggle within Princeton Seminary, written by the leader of the militant conservative "majority" party.

902.   Noll, Mark A., ed. *The Princeton Theology, 1812-1921: Scripture, Science, and Theological Method from Archibald Alexander to Benjamin Breckenridge Warfield.* Grand Rapids, MI: Baker Books, 1983.

Selections from Archibald Alexander, Charles and A. A. Hodge, and B. B. Warfield, with short introductions. Noll also gives a good forty page introduction to the context and work of the nineteenth century Princeton theologians.

903.   [Princeton Theological Seminary.] *Brief Account of the Theological Seminary, 1822.* (No author given -- possibly by Philadelphia bookseller A. N. Finley).

A ninety page compilation of the "Plan" and other regulations of the early days of the Seminary.

904.   [Princeton Theological Seminary.] *The Centennial Celebration of the Theological Seminary of the Presbyterian Church in the United States of America at Princeton, New Jersey.* Princeton, NJ: Printed "at the Theological Seminary," 1912.

While most of this large volume is given over to congratulatory letters from other institutions, the texts of eleven speeches given at the centennial celebration are also included. The most useful of these for understanding the history of the Seminary are by Francis Patton (reviewing the faculty), William McEwen (eminent pastors among the graduates), Robert Speer (eminent missionaries among the graduates), William Hallock Johnson (Princeton theology), and Charles Beatty Alexander (memoirs of the seminary's earlier days).

905.   Princeton Theological Seminary." *Necrological Reports.* Published by the seminary, 1875-94, 1895-1912, 1913-22, 1923-32.

Annual collections of one-page obituaries of the Seminary's graduates, made to the alumni association.

Reformed

906.   Gentry, Kenneth L. "A Ten Year History of Reformed Theological
          Seminary." 1976. Manuscript.

          A student paper recounting the early history of the
          independent Reformed Theological Seminary of Jackson, MS.

Reformed Presbyterian

907.   Copeland, Robert. *Spare no Exertions: 175 Years of the Reformed
          Presbyterian Theological Seminary.* Pittsburgh, PA: Reformed
          Presbyterian Theological Seminary, 1986.

          An institutional history, more scholarly than most, of the
          Reformed Presbyterian Church of North America ("Covenanter")
          institution, written by the Secretary of the Board of Trustees.

San Francisco

908.   Baird, J. H. *The San Anselmo Story.* Stockton, CA: California
          Lantern, 1963.

          A "personalized history" of San Francisco Theological
          Seminary from its founding in 1871, through the move to San
          Anselmo in 1892, to Baird's retirement in 1957. Written by the
          President emeritus, who was moderator of the PCUSA General
          Assembly in 1948-49.

909.   Curry, James. *History of San Francisco Theological Seminary of the
          Presbyterian Church in the U.S.A. and its Alumni Association.*
          Vacaville, CA: Reporter Publishing, 1907.

          A short (forty page) basic institutional history, written by a
          graduate, plus biographical sketches of eminent graduates and
          biographical entries for all alumni.

910.   San Francisco Theological Seminary. "Twenty-fifth Anniversary,
          1972-1987." San Rafael, CA: Marin Journal, 1897.

          This pamphlet contains addresses on the history and future
          of the seminary by Profs. William Alexander and Robert
          Mackenzie.

Union (New York) -- including Auburn

911.   Adams, John Quincy. *History of the Auburn Theological Seminary,
          1818-1918.* Auburn, NY: Auburn Seminary Press, 1918.

          A straightforward institutional history, commissioned for the
          centennial of the seminary, done as a "labor of love" by a member
          of the faculty.

912.   Auburn Theological Seminary. "Auburn Theological Seminary."

The Auburn Seminary Record, January 19, 1911.

An official description, with illustrations of the seminary.

913.   Coffin, Henry Sloane. *A Half Century of Union Theological Seminary, 1896-1945: An Informal History.* New York: Scribners, 1954. A chapter on Coffin was written by Morgan Phelps Noyes.

A readable and affectionate history by a graduate, professor, and retired president. Coffin's emphasis is on breadth and openness as distinctive features of Union from the beginning. Includes assessments of faculty from graduates of all eras.

914.   *General Biographical Catalogue.* Auburn, NY: Auburn Theological Seminary. (Two editions), *1818-1919, 1919-1940.*

Brief sketches of graduates and faculty from the founding in 1818. The second edition includes the move and association with Union Seminary in New York City.

915.   Handy, Robert T. *A History of Union Theological Seminary in New York.* New York: Columbia University Press, 1987.

A scholarly review of the whole history of the seminary by a longtime Union professor and noted historian of American religion.

916.   Prentiss, George Lewis. *The Union Theological Seminary in the City of New York: Its Design and Another Decade of its History.* Asbury Park, NJ: Pennypacker, 1899.

Prentiss had just published a large, ordinary institutional history of the first five decades of Union Seminary when the seminary was caught up in the Charles Briggs case. This called forth an even larger volume, mostly given to defending the seminary and, to a lesser extent, Briggs.

Union (Richmond)

917.   *Centennial Catalogue of Union Theological Seminary, Virginia, 1807-1907.* Richmond, VA: Union Theological Seminary, 1907, 1924.

Brief biographical sketches of faculty and graduates, with a twenty page history of the Seminary. The edition of 1924 has the same format, with an updated history.

918.   Gamble, Connolly C., Jr. "The Education of Southern Presbyterian Ministers: A Study of the Program and Possibilities of Union Theological Seminary, Richmond, Virginia." Th.M. thesis. Union Theological Seminary, 1950.

A critique of the seminary program, based on a survey of 359 PCUS ministers.

919.   *A General Catalogue of Trustees, Officers, Professors, and Students
        of Union Theological Seminary in Virginia.* Richmond, VA: Union
        Theological Seminary in Virginia, 1977.

        Short biographical entries on students from 1807-1976, as
        well as other information on the staff and officers of the seminary,
        compiled by Eleanor R. Millard. Also includes a serviceable twenty
        page "History of Union Theological Seminary in Virginia" by
        well-known historian and Union professor Ernest Trice Thompson.

920.   Kay, Martha W. "The Literary Contributions of the Faculty of
        Union Theological Seminary [in Virginia], 1807-1941." M.R.E.
        thesis. Training School for Lay Workers (Richmond, VA), 1942.

        A conventional history of the seminary, emphasizing the
        writings of the faculty.

921.   Mahler, Henry, Jr. "A History of Union Theological Seminary in
        Virginia, 1807-1865." Th.D. dissertation. Union Theological
        Seminary in Virginia, 1951.

        A straightforward, scholarly account of the southern
        Presbyterian school, from the theological professorship of Moses
        Hoge at Hampden-Sydney College in 1807, through its move to
        Richmond, to the end of the Civil War.

922.   Union Theological Seminary in Virginia. *"The Days of Our Years."*
        Richmond, VA: published by the Seminary, 1962.

        Four lectures on the history of the seminary by Ernest Trice
        Thompson, Dean Frank Lewis, and James Appleby, for the
        sesquicentennial.

923.   Union Theological Seminary in Virginia. "Self Study Report for the
        American Association of Theological Schools," 1967. Mimeo.

        The emphasis is on current conditions, with little history.
        Another report was made in 1974.

Westminster

924.   Rian, Edwin H. *The Presbyterian Conflict.* Grand Rapids, MI:
        Wm. Eerdmans, 1940.

        A partisan, but fact-filled account of the struggle over
        Princeton Seminary in the 1920s, and the founding of Westminster
        Seminary in Philadelphia by J. Gresham Machen and the
        unsuccessful party in that struggle. Rian was a member of the
        Westminster board, and of the Orthodox Presbyterian Church with
        which Westminster was associated.

925.   Vander Stelt, John C. *Philosophy and Scripture: A Study in Old
        Princeton and Westminster Theology.* Marlton, NJ: Mack, 1978.

A criticism of the theology of pre-1929 Princeton and later Westminster seminaries, from a conservative Dutch Calvinist who is generally sympathetic to conservative American Presbyterianism. Reviews the work of Princeton University and Princeton Seminary theologians from John Witherspoon through C. W. Hodge, and Westminster theologians J. Gresham Machen and Cornelius Van Til. Treats Scottish Common Sense philosophy as the key to Princeton and Westminster theology, and as the source of its errors.

CHAPTER 13
REFORMED SEMINARIES
Peter De Klerk

926.   Brownson, William C. "At Work in the modern World: the Practical Field." *The Reform Review* 19 (May 1966): 51-60.

Explains that the subjects in the Practical Field involve "practice" as well as theory. It focuses on the task of communication. The students are taught the technical skills of the preparation and delivery of sermons (Homiletics), and of the educational ministry of the church (Christian Education). The author maintains that a well-rounded practical department also includes adequate instruction in the history and principles of missions, of evangelism, of worship, of church administration and government, and of pastoral care. An important integral part at Western Theological Seminary is also the practical experience known as Field Education.

927.   Bruggink, Donald J. "One Hundred Years in the Task of Theological Education: the Historical Background of Theological Education." *The Reformed Review* 19 (May 1966): 2-17.

Traces the task of Theological Education from the time of the church fathers through the Middle Ages and the Reformation, periods knwn for the first-rate theological education for the ministry, to the Netherlands of the 1600s. The Dutch in North America had their sons trained for the ministry in the Netherlands till the Dutch Church in America, amidst bitter strife, adopted a Plan of Union in 1771 to educate its students in the professor's own dwelling place. New Brunswick Theological Seminary was founded in 1784, but for financial reasons it was not until 1810 that John H. Livingston, the first theological professor, settled in New Brunswick. By 1830 the curriculum had expanded and the seminary had supplied the church with a good number of trained men, of whom a few had gone into foreign missions.

928.   Bruins, Elton J. "The Church at the West: a Brief Survey of the Origin and Development of the Dutch Reformed Church in the Middle West." *The Reformed Review* 20 (December 1966): 2-20.

Describes the arrival of the Dutch at Manhattan Island, the language struggle in the Dutch Reformed Church, the failure of the

church to move with the mobile frontier, the later growth of the
church in the West due to migration of Dutch landseekers
(farmers), the schisms in 1857 (sociological protest) and in 1881
(freemasonry), and the educational ventures such as the Academy
(Hope College) and Western Theological Seminary. The Church
of the West did not produce a great systematic theologian; nor did
it develop a publishing house as an outlet for Reformed Church
authors. The professors and graduates of Western Theological
Seminary filled that vacuum through theological education, through
church extension, through mission work and through their seminary
publication, *The Reformed Review*.

929.   Bruins, Elton J. "The Contribution of the Theological Seminary in
         New Brunswick to the Church in the West, 1850-1884." *The
         Reformed Review* 13 (December 1959): 42-47.

         After describing the union of Classis of Holland (Michigan)
         with the Reformed Protestant Dutch Church in North America
         (now Reformed Church in America), Bruins outlines the benefits
         of this union for the West. New Brunswick graduates taught at the
         Academy which evolved into Hope College, sons of the western
         colonists went to New Brunswick for their theological training, a
         graduate taught in the theological department established at Hope
         in 1866, and finally in 1884 three graduates of New Brunswick
         came to the West to teach theology and thus initiated Western
         Theological Seminary.

930.   Bruins, Elton J. "The New Brunswick Theological Seminary,
         1844-1959." Ph.D. dissertation. New York University, 1962.

         Investigates the changed role of New Brunswick founded in
         1784 as the seminary of the Reformed Church in America, after the
         founding of Western Theological Seminary in 1884 through the year
         1959. In those 75 years three major revisions of the curriculum took
         place and a sixth chair, that of Christian Education, was established
         in 1925. Bruins then traces the contributions of the teaching
         faculty, giving emphasis to their loyalty to and their participation
         in the life of the church, and to their awareness of the field of
         biblical criticism. The seminary became also the missionary center
         of the church, in that it produced from among the graduates many
         who devoted themselves to missionary work, especially in foreign
         missions. Meanwhile, it continued to train ministers and leaders for
         the church at large.

931.   *Centennial of the Theological Seminary of the Reformed Church in
         America 1784-1884* (formerly Ref[ormed] Prot[estant] Dutch
         Church). Edited by David D. Demarest, Paul D. Van Cleef and
         Edward T. Corwin. New York: Board of Publication of the
         Reformed Church in America, 1885.

         Gives a full account of the proceedings of the centennial
         celebration of New Brunswick Theological Seminary. Besides a

detailed and scholarly history of the seminary, it contains chapters on historical theology, on the influence of the seminary on the denominational life, on theological instruction in the West, and letters of congratulation from the Netherlands and America. Historical documents are added, describing the beginnings of literary and theological education in New York and New Jersey before the school moved to New Brunswick. It also contains biographical sketches of the professors who served the seminary.

932.   Decker, Robert D. "New Testament Studies." *The Standard Bearer* 57 (1980/81): 36-37.

Notes that the Protestant Reformed Seminary lays a great deal of emphasis on biblical-exegetical studies which include the study of the original languages, both Hebrew and Greek. The New Testament areas of study are listed.

933.   Decker, Robert D. "Practical-Theological Studies." *The Standard Bearer* 57 (1980/81): 37-39.

Identifies the courses in this branch of the curriculum, such as, homiletics, catechetics, liturgics, poimenics, missions and church polity being taught at the Protestant Reformed Seminary.

934.   De Klerk, Peter, comp. and ed. *A Bibliography of the Writings of the Professors of Calvin Theological Seminary*. Grand Rapids, MI: Calvin Theological Seminary, 1980.

A listing of the writings penned by those who have served on the faculty of the seminary. It also includes those writings penned when they were not on the faculty. The bibliography is very inclusive, noting all printed publications, such as books, articles in scholarly and popular journals and book reviews, up to 1980. A brief biographical sketch of each faculty member is provided.

935.   De Vries, Robert C. "A Thousand Sermons in a Hundred Places." *The Banner*, February 6, 1984, pp. 16-17.

Stresses the importance of the field education program at Calvin Theological Seminary. The goals of this program for the students are for spiritual growth, for personal development, for understanding the theological aspect of the ministry and for an effective ministry.

936.   Eenigenburg, Elton M. "The History of the Seminary." *The Reformed Review* 19 (May 1966): 18-32.

Seven seniors of Hope College desiring theological education in the west instead of in the east (New Brunswick) petitioned the general synod of the Reformed Church in America in 1866 for such training in a theological department of the college in Holland, Michigan. This training commenced in the fall of 1866. In 1877 financial difficulties led to the suspension of this education till 1884. The history is an external one with emphasis on the listing of those who taught at the seminary, on the raising of funds for the physical plant, on the growth of the student body, and on the development of the theological library.

937.   Eenigenburg, Elton M. "The New Curriculum at Western Seminary." *The Reformed Review* 20 (December 1966): 59-63.

Argues that new times demand new ways of doing things. The present curriculum has its faults: duplication of course materials; no one faculty team effort; a static character; too many courses per quarter; and lacking in unity and meaningful relationships. He proposes: emphasis on the original biblical languages (Hebrew and Greek); concentration on biblical studies in the light of the original languages; large units of systematic theology; and one theological development of the church. The new curriculum will have an organic character. A description of the curriculum plan is briefly summarized.

938.   Engelhard, David H. "Calvin Seminary: what lies ahead?" *The Banner*, February 6, 1984, pp. 11-13.

Describes the changes that have taken place at the seminary, involving a revised curriculum, a greater emphasis on research and writing by the faculty, a concerted effort to provide theological education for minority students, and a consideration of a graduate program towards a research degree.

939.   Hageman, Howard C. "The Story of New Brunswick Seminary." In *Two Centuries Plus*. The Historical Series of the Reformed Church in America, 13. Grand Rapids, MI: Wm. B. Eerdmans Publishing Co., 1984.

Relying heavily on the centennial volume of 1885, Hageman tells the history of the seminary like a story. It is a straightforward chronological narrative, without the pedantic material entrusted in the footnotes. The seminary's weaknesses are clearly portrayed, such as the uncertainty of its mission and the fact that it enjoyed only fitful support but also its strengths such as the services of its ingenious and innovative administrators and the personal sacrifices of its teaching staff. The volume concludes with a chapter on a "New Vision for a New Day" by Benjamin Alicea which tells of the seminary's accommodation of its ethnic heritage and of its mission ot the nearby burgeoning pluralistic communities.

940.   Hanko, Herman. "Church Historical Studies." *The Standard Bearer* 57 (1980/81): 34-36.

Argues the importance of Church History in Theological Education and describes briefly the areas being covered at the Protestant Reformed Seminary.

941.   Hoeksema, Homer C. "Dogmatics and Old Testament Studies."
         The Standard Bearer 57 (1980/81): 33-34.

         Outlines briefly the Old Testament courses being taught at
         the Protestant Reformed Seminary.

942.   Huisken, Jon. "The Seminary: the View from the T[heological]
         S[chool] C[ommittee]." *The Standard Bearer* 57 (1980/81): 41-43.

         Details the work of this committee in cooperation with the
         faculty of the Protestant Reformed Seminary in overseeing and in
         upgrading its theological education. The seminary opened its doors
         in 1925 and has now three full-time professors.

943.   Kromminga, John H. "Calvin Seminary in the Life of the Church."
         In *One Hundred Years in the New World. The Story of the Christian
         Reformed Church from 1857 to 1957: its Origin, Growth, and
         Institutional Activities; together with an Account of the Celebration
         of its Anniversary in its Centennial Year.* Grand Rapids, MI:
         Centennial Committee of the Christian Reformed Church, 1957.
         pp. 69-78.

         Records that already in 1861, four years after the founding
         of the Christian Reformed Church in North America, the first
         formal mention of the need for theological education was expressed.
         After a few years in which such education was provided through
         private tutoring, the school installed its first professor in 1876.
         Kromminga traces the growth of the teaching faculty, the student
         body, the curriculum, and the buildings. The development was
         made possible through the loyalty of the members of the church.

944.   Kromminga, John H. "Calvin Seminary: then and now." *The
         Banner*, February 6, 1984, pp. 8-10.

         The author muses about the years he served as president of
         the seminary. He touches on the faculty and its commitment to the
         seminary and to the Christian Reformed Church as a whole; on the
         students and their contributions to the theological instruction and
         social life of the seminary; and on the outreach of the seminary
         towards the community. He notes, however, that the ultimate
         mandate is to prepare ministers for the church.

945.   Kromminga, John H., Harold Dekker and Martin Geleynse.
         "Master of Divinity Program at Calvin Seminary." *The Banner*,
         November 2, 1973, pp. 10-11.

         Describes the reasons for the introduction of the M.Div.
         program and its basic features: (1) a greater emphasis on practical
         training; (2) a bringing together of regular course curriculum and
         practical training in church work; and (3) a provision for
         supervision and evaluation of student ministry and for theological
         reflection on field experience. A prescribed number of field

education credits must be earned before a student can receive his M.Div. degree.

946.   Osterhaven, M. Eugene. "At Work in the Modern World: the Theological Field." *The Reformed Review* 19 (May 1966): 43-51.

Emphasizes the marked interest in theology and theological education is the motivating force in the life of Western Theological Seminary. He states that the theological field consists of "church history and historical theology, systematic theology, and Christian ethics and philosophy of religion." He stresses that theology is an organized body of knowledge which is derived from God's revelation in the Scriptures. The study of theology is to safeguard the church from error; for this reason it is essential for the training of students for the ministry.

947.   Piet, John H. "At Work in the Modern World: the Biblical Field." *The Reformed Review* 19 (May 1966): 34-43.

Stresses that the study of the Bible is basic to the curriculum of Western Theological Seminary. He argues that the study of the English Bible is essential for the student but also the study of the original languages of the Old Testament (Hebrew) and the New Testament (Greek) in order to grasp the nuances of biblical thought and to be well-equipped for a well-balanced ministry. A study of biblical criticism (lower and higher) may not be overlooked so that the student will see the place of the books of the Bible in the history of literature, in oral tradition and in the sociological setting of the day when the Bible books were written.

948.   Raven, John Howard. *Biographical Record* Theological Seminary New Brunswick 1784-1911.

Provides biographical sketches of those who taught and graduated from the seminary. The names of the graduates are arranged in alphabetical order under the year of their graduation.

949.   Richards, George Warren. *History of the Theological Seminary of the Reformed Church in the United States, 1825-1934, [and] Evangelical and Reformed Church, 1934-1952.* Lancaster, PA: Rudisill and Company, 1952.

Relates that the German Reformed Church obtained its ministers from Germany and Switzerland for a hundred years. Private theological education led eventually to the establishment of a theological seminary in Carlisle, Pennsylvania, in the midst of much controversy. Of the different locations of the seminary in Pennsylvania [York (1829-1837), Mercersburg (1837-1871) and Lancaster (1871-)] Mercersburg is distinctively remembered for its faculty and its theology. In this creative period the recognized educators were Frederick A. Rauch, John W. Nevin and Philip Schaff, who were thoroughly familiar with the new German theological currents. Richards draws much of the illustrative material from private letters, church and school documents, and published sources. Added are biographies of eighteen professors, written by individuals other than Richards.

950.   Ridder, Herman J. "Hopes and Expectations: the Seminary and the church into Century II together." *The Reformed Review* 19 (May 1966): 60-71.

Maintains that the Reformed Church in America and Western Theological Seminary have been closely intertwined over the years. The church has a duty towards the seminary in providing sufficient funds for maintaining an adequate faculty, in sending its most promising sons and daughters, in praying for the day to day decision making which might have wide implications for the church, and in insisting on a trained ministry for service in the real world. The seminary's duty towards the church is in training students for its parish ministry, in offering a critique of its actions and programs, and in providing theological leadership for the denomination.

951.   Ridder, Herman J. "Western Seminary and the Churches' Need for Ministers." *The Reformed Review* 19 (March 1966): 5-9.

Argues for a long-range program for the recruitment of seminary students. A seminary's need for ministers is difficult to predict from year to year, but a seminary should look beyond the needs of its own denomination to those of the larger church. The seminary wants to find the best possible candidate, to train him for the best possible profession, and to place him in the best possible environment.

952.   Rottenberg, Isaac C. "Tendencies and Trends in a Century of Theological Education at Western Theological Seminary." *The Reformed Review* 20 (December 1966): 22-24, 41-49.

Traces the spiritual and theological climate in the Netherlands and in the Michigan and Iowa settlements before asking the question in what way the professors of Western Theological Seminary contributed to theological leadership in the church. The author stresses the fact that because of the great need in the churches for a practical and catechetical education the faculty's main theological endeavors were focused on instructions in the denominational press. After some initial failures, the periodicals to which the professors contributed were *The Leader* and its successor *The Church Herald*, and *The Reformed Review*. It is clear that their writings had an apologetic strain, an openness to new ideas and methods, including biblical criticism, and a missionary emphasis.

953.   Rynbrandt, Abraham. "History of Western Theological Seminary." *The Reformed Review* 9 (June 1956): 1-6.

Outlines theological education, with a listing of those teachers who taught their areas of discipline at Western. The instruction started first as a theological department at Hope College from 1866 to 1877, when the training was suspended till 1884. In 1885 the seminary was separated from Hope College, thereafter having its own governing board, faculty and curriculum. The history is a rather external one.

954.   *Semi-Centennial Volume.* Theological School and Calvin College, 1876-1926. Grand Rapids, MI: The Semi-Centennial Committee, Theological School and Calvin College, 1926.

Contains a collection of twelve essays portraying the development of pastor's training and higher education in the Christian Reformed Church in North America. From the humble beginning of a school in a parsonage there emerged in fifty years a theological school and a liberal arts college. The essays give an account of the principles that led to the establishment of Calvin, portray something of its life and influence, and indicate the ideals which guided its development. Included are chapters on the school and Christian education, the school and its social task, the school and missions, and the school and American life.

955.   Stob, George. "The Christian Reformed Church and her Schools." Th.D. dissertation. Princeton Theological Seminary, 1955.

Discusses in elaborate detail the Theological School (Calvin Theological Seminary) and its development since its inception in 1876, and also the interrelationship between members of the faculty, the faculty and the Curatorium (the Board of Trustees), and the faculty and the Synod of the Christian Reformed Church in North America. The seminary reflects the religious and theological temper of the church in a significant way.

956.   Timmerman, John J. *Promises to Keep. A Centennial History of Calvin College.* Grand Rapids, MI: Calvin College and Seminary with Wm. B. Eerdmans Publishing Co., 1975.

Traces the college's origin in the Theological School (Calvin Theological Seminary) established in 1876. In the first chapter the author describes the appointment of the first seminary instructor, who bore the awesome responsibility of teaching at least seventeen different subjects over a period of seven years. After two more theological instructors were appointed, the Literary Department was opened up to nontheological students in 1894. Only in 1919 did Calvin College become a separate institution.

957.   Vanden Berge, Peter N. *Historical Directory of the Reformed Church in America 1628-1978.* The Historical Series of the Reformed Church in America, vol. 6. Grand Rapids, MI: Wm. B. Eerdmans Publishing Co., 1978.

This volume has the basic biographical information of some 8,000 ministers who are serving or have served the Reformed Church in America. A very large number of the ministers received their theological training either at New Brunswick Theological Seminary or at Western Theological Seminary.

958.   Van Oene, W. W. J.   *Inheritance Preserved. The Canadian Reformed Churches in Historical Perspective.* Winnipeg, Manitoba: Premier Printing, 1975.

Dutch immigrants to Canada after World War II brought with them their religious beliefs, which led to the organization of the Canadian Reformed Churches in 1950. In a few pages Van Oene relates how the church in 1962 decided that the training of ministers should be entrusted to a number of ministers rather than left in the hands of only one professor. In 1969 the Theological College opened its doors with three full-time professors and two lecturers. It has now four full-time professors.

959.   Weber, William A.   "Theological Education in the Reformed Church in America." Ph.D. dissertation. Yale University, 1934.

Traces briefly the roots of the Reformed Church in America, the reason for the establishment of a seminary for theological education at New Brunswick, and the control which the church exercises over the doctrinal soundness of the student before he enters the active ministry. The author then discusses the changes that have taken place in the curriculum from the founding of the seminary in 1784 till 1925. On the basis of a questionnaire forwarded to the ministers of the church, the strengths and weaknesses of the curriculum are examined. The scope of this study is limited, however, to the eastern area of the Reformed Church which has drawn its ministers mainly from graduates of New Brunswick Theological Seminary; the western area of the church, with ministers drawn mainly from graduates of Western Theological Seminary, is excluded because the response to the questionnaire was too meager to provide a fair representation of the whole. The author concludes that many changes in content and method of the curriculum are necessary to make theological education in the church more effective.

960.   Wichers, Wynand. *A Century of Hope 1866-1966.* Grand Rapids, MI: Wm. B. Eerdmans Publishing Co., 1968.

Western Theological Seminary began its life as a theological department of Hope College in 1866. In a few pages the author outlines the financial plight which was the main reason for the suspension of theological education as part of the college in 1877.

CHAPTER 14
SEVENTH-DAY ADVENTIST SEMINARIES
George R. Knight

961.   Dower, Edward L. "A Needs Assessment of the Seventh-day Adventist Theological Seminary's Master of Divinity Program as Perceived by the Graduates, Faculty, Students, and Employers of Graduates." Ed.D. dissertation. Andrews University, 1980.

        A helpful study that briefly traces the historic training and role of SDA ministers prior to discussing the needs assessment of the M.Div. program. The conclusions of the needs assessment deal both with issues in SDA seminary education and the SDA ministry.

962.   Evans, I. H. *Our New Theological Seminary.* Washington, DC: n.p. [1937].

        An early history of the Advanced Bible School, which was in the process of becoming the Seventh-day Adventist Theological Seminary at the time the document was published.

963.   Land, Gary. "The SDA Theological Seminary: Heading Toward Isolation?" *Spectrum* 18 (October 1987): 38-42.

        Argues the thesis, with statistical support, that the SDA Theological Seminary has become too ingrown since the early 1980s.

964.   "The Seminary at 50 Years: An Observation." *FOCUS*, Summer 1984, pp. 7-25, 34.

        Written for the fiftieth anniversary of the founding of the SDA Theological Seminary, these "observations" contain an interview with the Dean of the Seminary, a report on the current status of the Seminary, and a historical sketch of the institution.

965.   Vande Vere, Emmett K. *The Wisdom Seekers.* Nashville, TN: Southern Publishing Association, 1972.

        Discusses the history of Andrews University and its predecessors -- Battle Creek College, Emmanuel Missionary College, and Potomac University. The last two chapters offer some insight into the history of the Seventh-day Adventist Theological Seminary.

966.   Vanterpool, Donald Leander. "A History of the Seventh-day
         Adventist Theological Seminary, 1951 to 1952: A Preliminary
         Search." Term paper, Andrews University, 1977. (Copy available
         from the Adventist Heritage Center, Andrews University).

         A cross-sectional sketch of the SDA Theological Seminary
         from 1951 to 1952. Discusses the administration, enrollment,
         physical aspects, degree programs, and the school's extension work
         for the selected time period.

967.   Welch, Shirley Annette. "History of the Advanced Bible School,
         1934-1937." Term paper, Andrews University, 1977. (Copy
         available from the Adventist Heritage Center, Andrews University).

         The Advanced Bible School was the forerunner of the SDA
         Theological Seminary. Welch traces the origin and early
         development of the school, its purposes, faculty, and academic
         policies and practices.

CHAPTER 15
UNITED CHURCH OF CHRIST SEMINARIES
Lowell H. Zuck

Fifteen theological seminaries are currently related to the United Church of Christ which began in 1957 when the former Congregational-Christian Churches united with the Evangelical and Reformed Church. The former descended from the earliest New England Pilgrims and Puritans; the latter was a union of German Reformed and German Evangelical (= Lutheran/Reformed) people in the United States.

The closely related United Church of Christ seminaries are the seven denominationally oriented schools, while the eight others have become interdenominational or university related divinity schools.

The closely related seminaries include Andover-Newton, Bangor, Chicago Theological Seminary, Eden, Lancaster, Pacific School of Religion, and United Theological Seminary (Twin Cities).

The other U. C. C. seminaries include the Seminario Evangelico de Puerto Rico, Harvard Divinity School, Howard Divinity School, the Interdenominational Theological Center, Union (New York), Vanderbilt Divinity School, and Yale Divinity School.

Part I: Closely Related Seminaries

Andover-Newton, Bangor, Chicago, Eden, Lancaster, Pacific, and United

A twice-yearly journal, *Prism: A Theological Forum for the U. C. C.*, Box 12092, St. Paul, MN 55112, is currently published by the closely related U. C. C. seminaries. See also *New Conversations*, Fall 1986, "Heritage and Horizon: Higher Education and the Church," published by the Board for Homeland Ministries, 132 W. 31 St., New York, NY 10001.

968.   Alden, Joseph Price. *Central Theological Seminary, Continuing Heidelberg Theological Seminary and the Ursinus School of Theology, 1850-1934.* Dayton, OH: Typescript, 1957. (Copy in Eden Seminary Library.)

Recounts anti-Mercersburg and midwestern German Reformed theological school developments before the Evangelical and Reformed merger; supplements Stabitz.

969.   Althausen, Johannes, et al. "Report on the 1985 Visit with the U. C. C. by Theologians from the (German) Evangelische Kirche der Union." *U. C. C. - E. K. U. Newsletter* 6 (May 1986): 2-15.

An effort by visiting East/West German theologians from the (German) Evangelical Church of the Union to encourage increased denominational/theological support for U. C. C. seminaries.

970. Arpke, Jerome C. *Das Lippe-Detmolder Settlement in Wisconsin.* Milwaukee, WI: Germania Publishing Co., 1895.

Tells the story of German Reformed settlers in Wisconsin from Lippe who began Mission House Seminary in 1862 (now part of United Theological Seminary in the Twin Cities).

971. Bacon, Leonard. *A Commemorative Discourse, on the Completion of Fifty Years from the Founding of the Theological Seminary at Andover.* Andover, MA: W. F. Draper, 1858.

A fifty-year Andover commemorative speech, by a beloved New Haven pastoral mediator between Congregational factions.

972. Bass, Dorothy C. "The Congregational Training School for Women." In *Hidden Histories in the United Church of Christ.* Vol 2, pp. 149-67. Edited by Barbara Brown Zikmund. New York: United Church Press, 1987.

The story of a Chicago Congregational seminary for women, which did not ordain, between 1909 and 1926.

973. Brauer, Jerald C. "American Religion Studies at the University of Chicago." In *The Lively Experiment Continued*, pp. 3-23. Edited by Jerald C. Brauer. Macon, GA: Mercer University Press, 1987.

A discussion of teaching by a Chicago Divinity School Dean which sheds light on the Federated Theological Faculty there.

974. Brueggemann, Walter E. *Ethos and Ecumenism, An Evangelical Blend: A History of Eden Theological Seminary, 1925-1975.* St. Louis, MO: Eden Publishing House, 1975.

Continuing Schneider's short history of Eden Seminary from 1925 onward, Brueggenmann's work is based on a 1974 St. Louis University Ph.D. dissertation.

975. Chrystal, William G. *A Father's Mantle: The Legacy of Gustav Niebuhr.* New York: Pilgrim Press, 1982.

Educational and churchly ideals of an Evangelical immigrant pastor and home missionary (1863-1913) whose sons and daughters became the famous Niebuhrs.

976. Chrystal, William G. "Samuel D. Press: Teacher of the Niebuhrs." *Church History* 53 (1984): 504-21.

The story of the beloved president of Eden Seminary who helped Americanize the Evangelicals and tutored the Niebuhrs.

977.   Chrystal, William G., ed. *Young Reinhold Niebuhr: His Early Writings, 1911-1931*. St. Louis, MO: Eden Publishing House, 1977.

        These early writings of Reinhold Niebuhr help to explain his Evangelical near-immigrant background in the Midwest, and pre-Yale seminary training at Eden.

978.   Clark, Calvin Montague. *History of Bangor Theological Seminary*. New York: Pilgrim Press, 1916.

        The centennial history of Bangor Seminary.

979.   Cook, Walter L. *Bangor Theological Seminary: A Sesquicentennial History*. Orono, ME: University of Maine Press, 1971.

        Bangor's history is carefully brought up to date after 150 years.

980.   Diefenthaler, Jon. "H. R. Niebuhr: A Fresh Look at His Early Years." *Church History* 52 (June 1983): 172-85.

        Gives evidence of the importance of his youthful Evangelical education for Richard Niebuhr's theology.

981.   Diefenthaler, Jon. *H. Richard Niebuhr: A Lifetime of Reflections on the Church and the World*. Macon, GA: Mercer University Press, 1986.

        Briefly tells the story of Richard Niebuhr's theological training and teaching.

982.   Faulkner, John Alfred. "The Tragic Fate of a Famous Seminary." *Bibliotheca Sacra* 80 (October 1923): 449-64.

        Recounts how the liberal doctrine of future probation produced a student decline at Andover until the entire senior class married the daughter of President McGiffert from Union. The 1908 Andover move to Harvard was voided by law in 1925, by which time Andover left its faculty and most of its students at Harvard.

983.   Gambrell, Mary Latimer. *Ministerial Training in Eighteenth Century New England*. New York: Columbia University Press, 1937.

        Describes ministerial training primarily among colonial Congregationalists prior to the founding of seminaries.

984.   Godsoe, Mrs. Helen A. *Historical Catalog of Bangor Theological Seminary: Biographical Data for 1814-1964. Supplementing the General Catalog of 1928*. Bangor, ME: n.p. 1964.

        A useful biographical dictionary of Bangor graduates.

985.   Hinke, William J. *Ministers of the German Reformed Congregations in Pennsylvania and Other Colonies in the Eighteenth Century.* Lancaster, PA: n.p. 1951.

An alphabetical series of ministerial biographies from the colonial German Reformed Church.

986.   Jaberg, Eugene C., et al., eds. *A History of Mission House - Lakeland.* Philadelphia, PA: Christian Education Press, 1962.

A careful centennial history of the Wisconsin German Reformed founders of Mission House Seminary, later part of United Theological Seminary, Twin Cities.

987.   Kedzie, A. S. *Chicago Theological Seminary: A Quarter Centennial Sketch.* Chicago, IL: Chicago Theological Seminary Press, 1879.

An official history written by an enthusiastic Congregational home missionary founder of the seminary.

988.   Kuklick, Bruce. *Churchmen and Philosophers: From Jonathan Edwards to John Dewey.* New Haven, CT: Yale University Press, 1985.

Kuklick interweaves theology and philosophy, primarily Congregational, in order to show how Edward's theology culminated in Dewey's instrumentalism.

989.   Leis, Walter Benjamin. *An Historical Sketch of the Central Theological Seminary of the Reformed Church in the United States from Its Origins Through Its Merger with Eden Theological Seminary, Webster Groves, Missouri, 1934, 1850-1934.* 1976. Typescript.

A recent 154 page typed manuscript recounting the history of Central Seminary of the German Reformed Church, including lists of graduates and faculty.

990.   McGiffert, Arthur Cushman, Jr. *No Ivory Tower: The Story of Chicago Theological Seminary.* Chicago, IL: Chicago Theological Seminary Press, 1965.

A lively history by a retired President, stressing the openness of the seminary to practical social concerns.

991.   Mooar, George. "The Seminary of 1869-94." In *Quarter-Centennial Addresses.* N.p. 1894.

A founding Congregational pastor recalls the beginnings of Pacific School of Religion 25 years earlier.

992.   Nevin, John Williamson. *The Anxious Bench*, 2nd ed. Chambersburg, PA: n.p. 1844, and *The Mystical Presence*,

Philadelphia, PA: n.p. 1846. Reprint. Bard Thompson and George H. Bricker, eds. Philadelphia, PA: United Church Press, 1966.

Two important writings by the American theological leader at the Mercersburg German Reformed seminary.

993. Nichols, James Hastings. *The Mercersburg Theology*. New York: Oxford University Press, 1966.

An excellent theology, with bibliography, about Mercersburg.

994. Nichols, James Hastings. *Romanticism in American Theology: Nevin and Schaff at Mercersburg*. Chicago, IL: University of Chicago Press, 1961.

An important historical sketch of the character of the Mercersburg theology, stressings its German Romantic roots.

995. Pierce, Richard D. "The Legal Aspects of the Andover Creed." In *Church History* 15 (1946): 28-47.

Recounts the story of how Andover and Harvard were separated, includes bibliography.

996. Praikschatis, Louis and H. A. Meier. *Das Missionhaus*. Cleveland, OH: Deutsches Verlagshaus, 1897.

A German Reformed church editor helped write this early history of Mission House Seminary, WI.

997. Rasche, Ruth W. "The Deaconess Sisters: Pioneer Professional Women." In *Hidden Histories in the United Church of Christ*. Vol. 1, pp. 95-109. Edited by Barbara Brown Zikmund. New York: United Church Press, 1984.

Describes the extensive development of a nursing order of Deaconesses, semi-ordained, within the former Evangelical Synod.

998. Richards, George Warren. *History of the Theological Seminary of the Reformed Church in the United States, 1825-1934, Evangelical and Reformed Church, 1934-1952*. Lancaster, PA: n.p. 1952.

A massive history of Lancaster Seminary, written by its former President.

999. Richards, George Warren. "The Mercersburg Theology - Its Purpose and Principles." *Church History* 20 (September 1951): 42-55.

The Mercersburg theology interpreted by a Lancaster Seminary President, himself influenced by later Neo-Orthodox theology.

1000.   Rowe, Henry K. *History of Andover Theological Seminary.*
          Newton, MA: n.p. 1933.

          A standard history of Andover Seminary.

1001.   Ruger, Anthony, ed. "The Financial Status and Trends of the
          Seven Closely Related Seminaries of the United Church of Christ
          Committee on the funding of the Closely Related Seminaries."
          1988. Typescript.

          One recent evidence of cooperation between the seven closely
          related U. C. C. seminaries.

1002.   Schaff, Phillip. *The Principle of Protestantism.* Chambersburg,
          PA: n.p. 1854. Reprint. Bard Thompson and George H. Bricker,
          eds. Philadelphia, PA: United Church Press, 1964.

          A seminal work by an immigrant church historian leading
          the Mercersburg, Pennsylvania high-church Reformed theology.
          Mercersburg Seminary was later moved to Lancaster.

1003.   Schneider, Carl E. *The German Church on the American Frontier:
          A Study in the Rise of Religion Among the Germans of the West:
          Based on the History of the Evangelischer Kirchenverein des
          Westerns, 1840-1866.* St. Louis, MO: Eden Publishing House, 1939.

          An extensive scholarly study of German Evangelical
          beginnings in the Midwest, including beginnings of Eden Seminary.

1004.   Schneider, Carl E. *History of the Theological Seminary of the
          Evangelical Church* (also in German).   St. Louis, MO: Eden
          Publishing House, 1925.

          A brief but authoritative sketch of the beginnings of Eden
          Seminary in Missouri, founded in 1850.

1005.   Schroeder, W. Widick. "The United Church of Christ: The Quest
          for Denominational Identity and the Limits of Pluralism." *Chicago
          Theological Seminary Register* 75 (Spring 1985): 14-28.

          A contemporary reflection upon the relation between
          denominational identity and pluralism within the U. C. C.

1006.   Shewmaker, William O. "The Training of the Protestant Ministry
          in the United States of America, Before the Establishment of
          Theological Seminaries." In *Papers of the American Society of
          Church History*, 2nd series. Vol. 6, pp. 71-202. Edited by Frederick
          William Loetscher. New York: G. P. Putnam's Sons, 1921.

          An adequate sketch of the education of ministers in colonial
          America before seminaries had begun.

1007.   Stibitz, George. "An Historical Sketch of the Central Theological

Seminary of the Reformed Church in the U.S., Published on the Occasion of the 75th Anniversary of the Seminary." *Central Theological Seminary Quarterly* 2 (1925).

A brief history of anti-Mercersburg German Reformed theological education until 1925.

1008.   Ulrich, Reinhard. "The School of Prophets: A Study of the Cultural and Theological Patterns in the Establishment and Early Development of the German Reformed Mission House in Wisconsin." Ph.D. dissertation. Lutheran School of Theology at Chicago, 1963.

A careful study of Wisconsin German Reformed theological education, partially reproduced in Jaberg (see number 986).

1009.   Vriesen, D. W., ed. *Geschichte des Missionhaus.* Cleveland, OH: Deutsches Verlagshaus, 1885.

Articles giving various reasons for German Reformed immigration to Wisconsin, religious and economic/political, are here collected in German.

1010.   Williams, Daniel Day. *The Andover Liberals: A Study in American Theology.* New York: Octagon Books, 1970.

Williams recounts the colorful history of Andover, begun to oppose Boston Unitarianism, but eventually itself becoming liberal.

1011.   Woods, Leonard. *History of the Andover Theological Seminary.* Boston, MA: James R. Osgood & Co., 1885.

A classical account of Andover's founding, by the defender of Congregational orthodoxy against Unitarianism, the "Wood 'n Ware" debate.

1012.   Zikmund, Barbara Brown. "Theology in the United Church of Christ: A Documentary Trail." *Prism* 1 (Fall 1985): 7-25.

A thorough bibliographical survey of the scattered theological writings produced by persons within the U. C. C.

1013.   Zuck, Lowell H. "Evangelical Pietism and Biblical Criticism: The Story of Karl Emil Otto:". In *Hidden Histories in the United Church of Christ.* Vol. 2, pp. 66-79. Edited by Barbara Brown Zikmund. New York: United Church Press, 1987.

An unknown heresy trial of the Eden Seminary President in 1880 by his conservative Evangelical Synod for teaching biblical criticism in the liberal German way.

1014.   Zuck, Lowell H. *Socially Responsible Believers: Puritans, Pietists, and Unionists in the History of the United Church of Christ.* New

York: United Church Press, 1986.

Gives the European and American settings in biography for the ministry of United Church people from their four different backgrounds.

Part II: Other U. C. C. Seminaries. (Basic histories, articles, and broader survey materials relating to Congregational-originated seminaries which have become interdenominational or university-related divinity schools.)

Seminario Evangelico de Puerto Rico, Hartford, Harvard Divinity School, Howard Divinity School, the Interdenominational Theological Center, Union (New York), Vanderbilt Divinity School, and Yale Divinity School

1015.   Ahlstrom Sydney E. and Jonathan S. Carey. *An American Reformation: A Documentary History of Unitarian Christianity.* Middletown, CT: Wesleyan University Press, 1985.

An excellent source-book telling of Unitarian developments leading to liberalization at Harvard and the founding of its divinity school.

1016.   Allen, Yorke. *A Seminary Survey: A Listing and Review of the Activities of the Theological Schools and Major Seminaries Located in Africa, Asia and Latin America.* New York: Harper & Row, 1960.

Includes a summary, pp. 184-87, of the ecumenical founding in 1919 of the Seminario Evangelico de Puerto Rico.

1017.   Bainton, Roland H. "Yale and German Theology in the Middle of the Nineteenth Century." *Zeitschrift fur Kirchengeschichte* 66 (1954): 294-302.

Tells how German critical scholarship played a significant role in modernizing theology in the older Congregational schools.

1018.   Bainton, Roland H. *Yale and the Ministry: A History of Education for the Christian Ministry at Yale from the Founding in 1701.* New York: Harper & Row, 1957.

A lively and biographically oriented study of religion at Yale, centering especially in the Divinity School.

1019.   Bass, Dorothy C. and Kenneth B. Smith, eds. *The United Church of Christ: Studies in Identity and Polity.* Chicago, IL: Exploration Press, Chicago Theological Seminary, 1987.

Susan B. Thistlewaite, W. Widick Schroeder, and others argue in a series of essays for pluralism as characterizing the United Church of Christ.

1020.   Beull, Lawrence. "The Unitarian Movement and the Art of Preaching in 19th Century America." *American Quarterly* 14 (1972): 166-90.

         An excellent article which connects learning and religious literature, especially through preaching.

1021.   Cannon, Katie G., et al. *God's Fierce Whimsy: Christian Feminism and Theological Education.* New York: Pilgrim Press, 1985.

         Appeals for increasing feminist concerns within theological education.

1022.   Carr, Aute L. "The Interdenominational Theological Center." *Theological Education* 4 (Summer 1968, Suppl. 1): 33-46.

         A description is given of the Black Interdenominational Theological Center, begun at Atlanta in 1958.

1023.   Coffin, Henry Sloane. *A Half Century of Union Theological Seminary, 1896-1945.* New York: Charles Scribner's Sons, 1954.

         President Coffin informally relates the early 20th century tensions and triumphs at Union.

1024.   Cremin, Lawrence A. *American Education: The National ·Experience, 1783-1876.* New York: Harper & Row, 1980.

         A continuation of 19th American education history, including "Institutions."

1025.   Cremin, Lawrence A., David A. Shannon, and Mary Evelyn Townsend. *American Education: The Colonial Experience, 1607-1783.* New York: Harper & Row, 1970.

         A comprehensive scholarly account of colonial education including "Institutions."

1026.   Day, Heather F. *Protestant Theological Education in America: A Bibliography.* Metuchen, NJ: The Scarecrow Press, 1985.

         An unannotated bibliography of 5,249 items on American Protestant theological education, originating from a Lilly Endowment study led by Robert Lynn.

1027.   Dyson, Walter. *Howard University, the Capstone of Negro Education: A History, 1867-1940.* Washington, DC: Graduate School, Howard University, 1941.

         The history of a pioneer Black seminary begun in Washington, D.C. by Congregationalists in 1868.

1028.   Eliot, Charles W. "Theological Education at Harvard between 1816 and 1916." In *Addresses Delivered at the Observance of the 100th Anniversary of the Establishment of Harvard Divinity School.* pp. 32-68. Cambridge, MA: Harvard University, 1917.

An appreciative commemorative address by a Harvard President at the centennial of the Divinity School.

1029.   Farley, Edward. *The Fragility of Knowledge: Theological Education in the Church and the University.* Philadelphia, PA: Fortress Press, 1988.

Farley describes and prescribes how theological education does and should occur in the university, the seminary, and the church.

1030.   Farley, Edward. *"Theologica": The Fragmentation and Unity of Theological Education.* Philadelphia, PA: Fortress Press, 1983.

The sharpest current critical reflection upon the nature of theological education, arguing that diverse disciplines detract from the theological virtue of wisdom.

1031.   Fenton, Jerry. *Understanding the Religious Background of the Puerto Rican.* Cuernava, Mexico: Centro Intercultural de Documentacion, 1969.

Discusses religious practices in Puerto Rico and in New York, where Puerto Ricans seek to give meaning to the progress they have achieved.

1032.   Figueroa, Juan and Eliezer Alvarez. "Puerto Rico: A Disciple's Report on the Present State of the Ecumenical Climate in Puerto Rico." *Midstream* 25 (January 1986): 114-18.

A recent Disciples report about ecumenical cooperation at the Seminario Evangelico de Puerto Rico and in the churches.

1033.   Fiorenza, Francis Schuessler. "Thinking Theologically About Theological Education." *Theological Education* 24 (1988 Suppl. 2): 89-119.

Evaluates and criticizes three diverse approaches to theological education: theological, ecclesiological, and professional.

1034.   Fletcher, Robert Samuel. *A History of Oberlin College from Its Foundation through the Civil War.* 2 Vols. Oberlin, OH: Oberlin College, 1943.

A classic study of Oberlin College, in two volumes, including its Graduate School of Theology, which joined the Vanderbilt Divinity School in 1966.

1035.   Fox, Richard Wightman. *Reinhold Niebuhr: A Biography.* New

York: Pantheon Books, 1985.

A thorough biography which tells much about Eden, Yale, and Union seminaries and other institutions in the 20th century.

1036.   Gabriel, Ralph H. *Religion and Learning at Yale: The Church of Christ in the College and University.* New Haven, CT: Yale University Press, 1958.

A careful, inside study of religious activity at Yale both within the College and the Divinity School, with more focus on the former, while Bainton is more concerned with the latter.

1037.   Geer, Curtis Manning. *The Hartford Theological Seminary, 1834-1934.* Hartford, CT: Case, Lockwood & Brainard Co., 1934.

An outstanding history of Hartford Seminary, written for the 100th anniversary.

1038.   Gunnemann, Louis W. *The Shaping of the United Church of Christ: An Essay in the History of American Christianity.* New York: United Church Press, 1977.

A history, both of the preceding denominations briefly reviewed, and of the actual union leading up to the United Church of Christ.

1039.   Gunnemann, Louis W. *United and Uniting: The Meaning of an Ecclesial Journey.* New York: United Church Press, 1987.

An interpretative effort to recover the original "united/uniting" ecclesiological vision of the United Church of Christ.

1040.   Gustafson, James M. assisted by Todd D. Swanson. "Reflections on the Literature on Theological Education Published Between 1955 and 1985." *Theological Education* 24 (1988 Suppl. 2): 9-86.

A lengthy reflection on what has happened in theological education since the Niebuhr-Williams-Gustafson report in 1956, along with an appendix on "The Opportunities of a University Divinity School."

1041.   Hall, David. *Faithful Shepherd: A History of the New England Ministry in the Seventeenth Century.* Chapel Hill, NC: University of North Carolina Press, 1972.

A careful study of Congregational ministerial patterns before seminaries had begun.

1042.   Handy, Robert T. *A History of Union Theological Seminary in New York.* New York: Columbia University Press, 1987.

A candid and interestingly written history of Union, bringing its development up to date through the troubled sixties and beyond.

1043.   Harrison, Paul M. *Theological Education and the United Church of Christ: A Draft Report Prepared for the Commission on Theological Education and the United Church of Christ.* University Park, PA: Pennsylvania State University, Dept. of Religious Studies, 1967.

A study revealing the problem of how to combine the independent institutional traditions of Congregational seminaries with the denomination-supported practice of the Evangelicals and Reformeds.

1044.   Hartford Theological Seminary. *A Memorial of the Semi-Centenary Celebration of the Founding of the Theological Institute of Connecticut.* Hartford, CT: Press of the Case, Lockwood & Brainard Co., 1884.

A fiftieth anniversary history of Hartford Seminary.

1045.   Herrick, Everett Carleton. *Turns Again Home: Andover Newton Theological School and Reminiscences from an Unkept Journal.* Boston, MA: Pilgrim Press, 1949.

An informal account by the former President of the Newton Baptist seminary which Andover joined after the courts voided Andover's reunion with Harvard in 1925.

1046.   Hodgson, Peter C. *Revisioning the Church: Ecclesial Freedom in the New Paradigm.* Philadelphia, PA: Fortress Press, 1988.

An effort to outline a new theology of the church, making use of democratic-participative-secular models of ministry instead of hierarchial-authoritarian-sacerdotal models.

1047.   Holmes, Dwight O.W. "Fifty Years of Howard University." *Journal of Negro History* 3 (April 1918): 128-38; (October 1918): 368-80.

A celebration of Howard's ministerial training after fifty years.

1048.   Hough, Joseph C., Jr., and John B. Cobb, Jr. *Christian Identity and Theological Education.* Chico, CA: Scholars Press, 1985.

An influential effort to make theological education more critical, inclusive, and universal.

1049.   Howe, Daniel Walker. *The Unitarian Conscience: Harvard Moral Philosophy, 1805-1861.* Cambridge, MA: Harvard University Press, 1970.

A penetrating study of how the Unitarian conscience affected theology, the church, and society at Harvard.

1050.   Hutchison, William R. *The Modernist Impulse in American Protestantism.* Cambridge, MA: Harvard University Press, 1976.

A well-documented study, favorable to liberals, which studies modernism among Protestants from the 1870s to the 1930s.

1051.   Koyama, Kosuke. "Ecumenical and World Christianity Center, Union Theological Seminary, New York City." *Theological Education* 22 (Spring 1986): 132-37.

A case description of globalized theological education at Union Seminary.

1052.   Kuklick, Bruce. *The Rise of American Philosophy: Cambridge, Massachusetts, 1860-1930.* New Haven, CT: Yale University Press, 1978.

This thorough study of Harvard's philosophy department from the post-Civil War years through the post-World War I era preceded his equally perceptive later work on churchmen and philosophers.

1053.   Lindbeck, George A. *The Nature of Doctrine: Religion and Theology in a Postliberal Age.* Philadelphia, PA: Fortress Press, 1984.

A difficult, but influential proposal about how theology might be done in a post-liberal era, making use of a linguistic model for theological education.

1054.   Lindbeck, George A. *University Divinity Schools: A Report on Ecclesiastically Independent Theological Education.* New York: Rockefeller Foundation, 1976.

A critical, but approving evaluation of university-related divinity schools.

1055.   Logan, Rayford W. *Howard University: The First Hundred Years, 1867-1967.* New York: New York University Press, 1969.

A history of the first hundred years of Howard University.

1056.   Lynn, Robert Wood. "Notes toward a History: Theological Encyclopedia and the Evolution of Protestant Seminary Curriculum, 1808-1968." *Theological Education* 17 (Spring 1981): 118-44.

Preliminary conclusions from a careful study of the early use by Protestant seminaries of theological "encyclopedia."

1057.   Miles, Margaret B. "Hermeneutics of Generosity and Suspicion: Pluralism and Theological Education." *Theological Education* 23 (1987 Suppl.): 34-52.

Current pluralism at Harvard Divinity School, with special emphasis upon feminism. Bibliography and Readings are included.

1058.   Miller, Glenn and Robert Wood Lynn. "Christian Theological Education III." In *Encyclopedia of the American Religious Experience: Studies of Traditions and Movements*, pp. 1627-52. Edited by Charles H. Lippy and Peter W. Williams. New York: Charles Scribner's Sons, 1988.

The best up-to-date comprehensive article about American Protestant theological seminaries.

1059.   Mims, Edwin. *History of Vanderbilt University.* Nashville, TN: Vanderbilt University Press, 1946.

The Vanderbilt Divinity School is related to the United Church of Christ through the Oberlin Graduate School of Theology, which joined it in 1966. (See Fletcher, number 1034.)

1060.   Moore, Donald T. *Puerto Rico Para Cristo: A History of the Progress of the Evangelical Missions on the Island of Puerto Rico.* Cuernavaca, Mexico: Centro Intercultural de Documentacion, 1969.

A study of Protestant missions and indigenization, including self-support, Puerto Rican leadership, and local autonomy.

1061.   Niebuhr, H. Richard. "Seminary in the Ecumenical Age." *Princeton Seminary Bulletin* 54 (July 1960): 38-45.

Richard Niebuhr's mature reflections on the nature of seminary education.

1062.   Niebuhr, H. Richard, Daniel Day Williams, and James M. Gustafson. *The Purpose of the Church and Its Ministry: Reflections on the Aims of Theological Education.* New York: Harper & Row, 1956.

The most influential recent survey of theological education which popularized the somewhat unclear conception of "pastoral director."

1063.   Paton, Lewis Bayles, ed. *Recent Christian Progress: Studies in Christian Thought and Work During the last 75 Years, by Professors and Alumni of Hartford Seminary.* New York: Macmillan, 1909.

A remarkable collection of contributed articles summarizing seminaries and disciplines in the early twentieth century.

1064.   Paul, Robert S. *Freedom With Order: The Doctrine of the Church in the United Church of Christ*. New York: United Church Press, 1987.

         More congregational than Gunnemann, Paul calls for an open-ended, dynamic, and inclusive ecclesiology.

1065.   Paul, Robert S. "Theology in Connecticut, 1860-1960:" In *Contributions to the Ecclesiastical History of Connecticut, 1860-1960*, Vol. 2, pp. 34-57. Edited by James F. English. Hartford, CT: Conference, United Church of Christ, 1960.

         Helpful in comparing the histories of Yale and Hartford Seminaries.

1066.   Prentiss, George Lewis. *The Union Theological Seminary in the City of New York: Historical and Biographical Sketches of Its First 50 Years*. New York: A.D.F. Randolph & Co., 1889.

         An accurate official history of the first fifty years of Union Seminary.

1067.   Prentiss, George Lewis. *The Union Theological Seminary in the City of New York: Its Design and Another Decade of Its History. With a Sketch of the Life and Public Services of Charles Butler, LL.D.* Asbury Park, NJ: M., W. & C. Pennypacker, 1899.

         Still another decade of Union's history, told by Prentiss.

1068.   Richardson, Harry V. *Walk Together, Children: The Story of the Birth and Growth of the Interdenominational Theological Center*. Atlanta, GA: I T C Press, 1987.

         The most recent history of the Atlanta Black seminary complex, begun in 1958.

1069.   Robinson, David. *The Unitarians and the Universalists*. Westport, CT: Greenwood Press, 1985.

         A recent synthesis of American Unitarian-Universalist histories, together with a 130-page biographical dictionary.

1070.   Rooks, Charles S. "A New Day Dawns [Address Given at Dedication of Howard University Divinity School]." *Journal of Religious Thought* 38 (Spring - Summer 1981): 5-11.

         An address celebrating the dedication of a new building at the Howard Divinity School in Washington.

1071.   Scott, Donald M. *From Office to Profession: The New England Ministry, 1750-1850*. Philadephia, PA: University of Pennsylvania Press, 1978.

Shows how increasing professionalism changed ministerial work and training in the nineteenth century.

1072. Shriver, Donald W. "The Use of an Ecumenical Seminary." *Christian Century*, February 1-8, 1984, pp. 106-08.

The present Union Seminary President describes his ecumenical ideals.

1073. Shockley, Grant S. "Living Out the Gospel in Seminary Life [Interdenominational Theological Center]." *The Christian Century*, February 2-9, 1977, pp. 90-91.

A description of seminary life at the Interdenominational Theological Center, Atlanta.

1074. Shockley, Grant S. "National Church Bodies and Interdenominational Theological Education." *Theological Education* 15 (Spring 1979): 155-61.

Discusses denominational support for interdenominational, inter-racial theological education.

1075. Smith, Jane I. "Globalization in the Curriculum of Harvard Divinity School." *Theological Education* 22 (Spring 1986): 85-91.

A case description of globalized theological education at Harvard Divinity School.

1076. Stoltz, Karl Ruf, ed. *Sketches of Life in the Hartford School of Religious Education, 1885-1935.* Hartford, CT: Case, Lockwood & Brainard Co., 1935.

Reflects a special religious education concern at Hartford.

1077. *The Union Theological Seminary in the City of New York: Alumni Directory, 1836-1970.* New York: Union Theological Seminary, 1970.

A massive biographical dictionary of all of the graduates of Union Seminary.

1078. Wayland, John T. "The Theological Department in Yale College, 1822-1858." Ph.D. dissertation. Yale University, 1933.

An unpublished dissertation relates the interesting beginnings of Yale Divinity School.

1079. Williams, George H., ed. *The Harvard Divinity School: Its Place in Harvard University and in American Culture.* Boston, MA: Beacon Press, 1954.

An interesting and authoritative collective history of

Harvard Divinity School.

1080.   Williams, George H.   "The Seminary in the Wilderness: A
Representative Episode in the Cultural History of Northern New
England [Gilmanton Seminary, 1835-46]." *Harvard Library Bulletin*
13 (Autumn 1959): 369-400; 14 (Winter 1960): 25-58.

Tells about a forgotten 1836 New Hampshire Congregational
seminary.

1081.   Williams, George H.   "Translatio Studii: The Puritans' Conception
of Their First University in New England, 1636." *Archiv für
Reformationsgeschichte* 47 (1966): 7-288.

How the early Puritans transferred the Cambridge, England
tradition of theological scholarship to America.

1082.   Williams, George H.   *Wilderness and Paradise in Christian
Thought.* New York: Harper & Row, 1962.

Recalls the learned and Scripturally imaginative academic
tradition of early Harvard theology.

1083.   Wright, Conrad, ed. *A Stream of Light: A Sesquicentennial History
of American Unitarianism.*   Boston,   MA: The
Unitarian-Universalist Association, 1975.

The standard recent history of Unitarianism, well-written,
by an authority on Unitarian history.

1084.   Yale University Divinity School. *Education for Christian Service,
by Members of the Faculty of the Divinity School of Yale University:
a Volume in Commemoration of Its One Hundredth Anniversary.*
New Haven, CT: Yale University Press, 1922.

A   centennial   commemorative   volume,   comprised   of
interesting articles contributed by faculty members.

1085.   Youngs, J. William T., Jr. *God's Messengers: Religious Leadership
in Colonial New England, 1700-1750.*   Baltimore, MD: Johns
Hopkins University Press, 1976.

Develops the later colonial New England view of ministry,
before the emergence of seminaries.

1086.   Zikmund, Barbara Brown, ed.   *Hidden Histories in the United
Church of Christ.* Vols. 1 and 2, New York: United Church of
Christ, 1984, 1987.

Twenty-one essays by different authors attempt to go beyond
the inherited historic traditions of the United Church of Christ in
order to recover the histories of women and selected racial and
ethnic minorities.

1087.   Zuck, Lowell H. *Four Centuries of Evangelism in the United Church of Christ.* New York: The United Church Board for Homeland Ministries, 1987.

    A brief survey of the growth of the various parts of the United Church of Christ, with short bibliography.

CHAPTER 16
UNITED METHODIST SEMINARIES
L. Glenn Tyndall

Acknowledgements

Gary Hauk, Reference Librarian and Assistant to the Director, Pitts Theology Library, Candler School of Theology, Emory University, Atlanta, GA; Allen W. Mueller, Director, Library, Wesley Theological Seminary; Laura H. Randall, Reference Librarian, and Roger Loyd, Associate Librarian, Bridwell Library, Perkins School of Theology, Southern Methodist University, Dallas, TX; Joseph Troutman, Librarian, Robert W. Woodruff Library, Interdenominational Theological Center, Atlanta, GA; Phyllis Cole, Communications Coordinator, Methodist Theological School in Ohio, Delaware, OH; and David K. Himrod, Assistant Librarian, The United Library, Garrett-Evangelical Theological Seminary, Evanston, IL.

Introduction

The denomination that today bears the name "United Methodist" is one whose history is one of bringing together groups into a unified whole. Consequently the names of the denomination and its antecedent churches caused no small amount of confusion. Perhaps a brief explanation would lead to clarity.

From its inception in 1784, the Methodist movement in the United States was referred to as "The Methodist Episcopal Church." A group left in 1828 over the issue of bishops and lay rights to form The Methodist Protestant Church. Another split came in 1844 over slavery, resulting in the formation of The Methodist Episcopal Church, South. These groups stayed apart for nearly 100 years, but united as The Methodist Church in 1939, with all the Black churches in a segregated (or Central) Jurisdiction. In 1968 the Central Jurisdiction was abolished, and The Methodist Church joined with The Evangelical United Brethren Church to form The United Methodist Church. Antecedent churches of the Evangelical United Brethren (formed in 1946) were The Church of The United Brethren in Christ and The Evangelical Church.

These are the thirteen theological schools currently related to the United Methodist Church:

- Boston University School of Theology - Boston, MA
- Candler School of Theology, Emory University - Atlanta, GA
- Drew University Theological School - Madison, NJ
- Duke University Divinity School - Durham, NC
- Gammon Theological Seminary (part of the Interdenominational

Theological Center) - Atlanta, GA
- Garrett-Evangelical Theological Seminary - Evanston, IL
- Iliff School of Theology, University of Denver - Denver, CO
- Methodist Theological School in Ohio - Delaware, OH
- Perkins School of Theology, Southern Methodist University - Dallas, TX
- School of Theology at Claremont - Claremont, CA
- St. Paul School of Theology - Kansas City, MO
- United Theological Seminary - Dayton, OH
- Wesley Theological Seminary - Washington, DC

1088.   Bailey, Kenneth K. *Southern White Protestantism in the Twentieth Century.* New York, Evanston, IN: Harper and Row, Publishers, 1964.

Gives in Chapter Two an account of educational developments in southern white churches. Notes the development of Vanderbilt University by the Methodist Episcopal Church, South. Describes also Vanderbilt's subsequent disassociation with the Church in 1914, leading to the beginning of two new theological schools by The Methodist Episcopal Church, South: Candler School of Theology (at Emory University), and Southern Methodist University School of Theology (later Perkins School of Theology).

—1089.   Behney, J. Bruce, and Paul Himmell Eller, *The History of the Evangelical United Brethren Church.* Nashville, TN: Abingdon Press, 1979.

Notes that in 1946 there were three theological schools in the Evangelical United Brethren denomination as the new church took shape: Evangelical School of Theology (with Albright College in Reading, Pennsylvania); Bonebrake Theological Seminary (later called United) in Dayton, Ohio; and Evangelical Theological Seminary (Garrett-Evangelical after merger with the Methodist Church) in Naperville, Illinois. Describes study which took place resulting in the union of the schools in Reading and Dayton into United Theological Seminary at Dayton in 1954. Cites how formation of Union Biblical Institute (a forerunner of Evangelical Theological Seminary) in 1876 helped overcome fears of "educated" ministers by choosing at first to be primarily a training school for missionaries.

1090.   Bowen, Boone M. *The Candler School of Theology: Sixty Years of Service.* Atlanta, GA: Candler School of Theology, Emory University, 1974.

Begins its historical narrative with an account of the crisis in Methodist higher education brought on by the decision of the Supreme Court of Tennessee that separated Vanderbilt University from Methodist control. Gives a narrative of the following sixty years at Candler, relating theological controversies, personal anecdotes, faculty profiles, and student life. Provides the definitive work on the history of Candler School of Theology. Contains a list of all graduates through 1973, as well as illustrations.

1091.   Brawley, James P. *Two Centuries of Methodist Concern: Bondage, Freedom, and the Education of Black People.* New York: Vantage Press, 1974.

Surveys educational development for blacks within the Methodist Episcopal Church. Contains specific information in Part IV on Gammon Theological Seminary, including the original development of Gammon as a department within Clark University in Atlanta. Notes that in spite of the close affiliation of these two institutions (Gammon and Clark), the two remained administratively distinct. Gives a brief historical sketch of Gammon in Chapter 16, down to and including its association in 1958 with The Interdenominational Theological Center, joining together several black educational institutions in the Atlanta area.

1092.   Bucke, Emory Stevens, et al., ed. *The History of American Methodism in Three Volumes.* New York: Abingdon Press, 1964.

Discusses in Volume II, Chapter 24, Section 1 the doctrinal controversy affecting Boston University School of Theology, when Professor Hinckley G. Mitchell was accused of doctrinal heresy in 1900 and 1905. Relates how Mitchell was censured by the Central New York Annual Conference, then later vindicated by the General Conference. Notes how Professor Borden Parker Browne, another Boston professor, was censured and later vindicated. Places Methodism right in the middle of the "fundamentalist-modernist" controversy, with conservative forces struggling to keep the Conference Course of Study (non-seminary training of ministers) "pure."

Describes in Chapter 24, Section 7, the development of the Conference Course of Study as an alternative to formal theological education. Notes earliest efforts at establishing Methodist seminaries which were really biblical institutes. Cites Nineteenth Century opposition to seminary-trained pastors. Records origin of first Methodist Protestant seminary in 1884 -- Westminster Theological Seminary (later Wesley Theological Seminary). Lists three United Methodist seminaries no longer in existence: Kimball School of Theology in Salem, Oregon; Norwegian-Danish Theological Seminary in Evanston, Illinois; and Swedish Theological Seminary, also in Evanston.

Gives in Volume III, Chapter 29, Section 3, an account of the Vanderbilt controversy resulting in the separation in 1914 of Vanderbilt University and Divinity School from The Methodist Episcopal Church, South. States how this event led to the development of two new theological schools in the South, Candler (Emory) and Perkins (Southern Methodist).

Provides in Chapter 29, Section 5, a survey of the development of theological education up to the unification of The Methodist Church in 1939 (including The Methodist Episcopal Church, The Methodist Episcopal Church, South, and The Methodist Protestant Church). Includes information on the doctrinal controversies at Boston University School of Theology and the development of the Conference Course of Study.

1093.   Cameron, Richard Morgan. *Boston University School of Theology 1839-1968*. Boston, MA: Boston University School of Theology, 1968.

Provides a comprehensive historical account of the development of the Boston University School of Theology, dating back to 1839, earliest of any of the institutions currently related to The United Methodist Church. Gives consideration to the anti-education views that tended to hold back the development of theological education. Notes Boston University School of Theology's origin at Newbury, Vermont, and follows it through Concord, New Hampshire to two different locations in Boston. Credits John Dempster, who later went on to help at Garrett, with helping to keep the early institution financially solvent. Records in Chapter III, Section 2, the heresy controversy in the early Twentieth Century. Surveys attempts in later years to keep the school current in its structure and curriculum content.

1094.   Carr, Aute L. "The Interdenominational Theological Center." *Theological Education* 4 (Summer 1968, Supplement I): 33-46.

Provides a comprehensive overview of the structure of the Interdenominational Theological Center and its relationship to its member institutions, including Gammon Theological Seminary. Contains statistical information on enrollment of member institutions from 1959 to 1966. Stresses the positive side of the ecumenical relationship, especially in terms of making ministerial education available to far more black individuals than before. Continues to raise questions about Gammon's role as a black seminary apparently in the shadow of Candler (Emory), i.e., two Methodist theological schools in the same city.

1095.   Chandler, Douglas R. *Pilgrimage of Faith: A Centennial History of Wesley Theological Seminary, 1882-1982*. Cabin John, MD: Seven Locks Press, 1984.

Provides a definitive historical account of this theological school founded in 1882 by a dissenting element in Methodism which stressed lay rights and equality in the Church, The Methodist Protestant Church. Ties this important ecclesiastical development with the egalitarian movement in American history. Describes Wesley's development in terms of the men and women who made it happen, especially the eight Presidents who served during the first one hundred years. Traces the first seventy-five years of the

institution as Westminster Theological Seminary in Western
Maryland, prior to its move to Washington and change of name to
Wesley Theological Seminary. Calls attention to Wesley's historical
and strategic location in our nation's capital, adjacent to one of our
great universities.

1096.   Clark, Kenneth Willis. "Four Decades of the Divinity School."
         Duke Divinity School Review 32 (Spring 1967): 160-83.

         Provides a personal and rather detailed historical survey of
         developments at the Duke Divinity School from 1926 to 1966.
         Suffers somewhat from Professor Clark's subjective viewpoint, but
         on the whole relates helpful information on the seminary and its
         history from one of its principal characters during that era. Notes
         attempts at Duke to provide extension theological opportunities for
         black ministers in the Durham area, often in cooperation with
         North Carolina Central College (later University).

1097.   Culver, Dwight W. *Negro Segregation in The Methodist Church.*
         New Haven, CT: Yale University Press, 1953.

         Provides helpful insight into the extent of racial inclusiveness
         in Methodist theological schools as of 1953. Points out actual
         enrollment figures in 1946 at Iliff, School of Theology at Southern
         California (later Claremont), Garrett, Boston, and Drew. Notes
         collegiality and moves toward integration at Candler and Perkins in
         the early 1950s.

1098.   Cummings, Anson Watson. *The Early Schools of Methodism.* New
         York: Phillips and Hunt, 1886.

         Gives from late nineteenth Century perspective an account
         of developments in theological education in The Methodist
         Episcopal Church. Provides specific historical information on
         Boston University School of Theology, Garrett Biblical Institute,
         and Drew Theological School. Focuses on seminary education in
         the overall context of The Methodist Episcopal Church's role in
         higher education in the nineteenth Century.

1099.   Cushman, Robert E. "Fifty Years of Theology and Theological
         Education at Duke." *Duke Divinity School Review* 42 (Winter
         1977): 3-22.

         Provides a theological perspective on the development of the
         Duke Divinity School from the viewpoint of one former Dean.
         Focuses on the rather unique quality of Duke's context -- on the one
         hand, closely related to The United Methodist Church and its
         heritage as a denomination, but, on the other hand, offering
         theological instruction as "broadly catholic and not narrowly
         denominational." Cites the blend of educational offering that is at
         the same time denominational and ecumenical, helping the growth
         of the school as well as its mission to the wider Church.

1100.   Day, Heather F. *Protestant Theological Education in America: A Bibliography*. Metuchen, NJ: The American Theological Library Association and The Scarecrow Press, 1985.

        Lists more than five thousand bibliographical entries covering the whole range of topics and concerns related to Protestant theological education. Provides basic bibliographical information without annotations.

1101.   Dickhaut, John W. "The Latest and Lasting Word." *Journal: Methodist Theological School in Ohio* 2 (September 1963): 1-5.

        Gives an informative account of the early days at Methodist Theological School in Ohio in the context of the Commencement Address for the first graduating class. Lifts up the unique challenge which METHESCO has always tried to offer its students.

1102.   Eller, Paul Himmell. *Evangelical Theological Seminary, 1873-1973: Shaping Ministry*. Naperville, IL: Evangelical Theological Seminary, 1973.

        Portrays the early years, 1865-1900; the years of development, 1900-1930; and "Today's Seminary Takes Shape," 1930-1972. Surveys history of Evangelical Theological Seminary through its first one hundred years on the threshold of its eventual union with Garrett Theological Seminary to form Garrett-Evangelical in 1974.

1103.   *Emory at 150: A Report on the State of the University*. Atlanta, GA: Emory University, Office of the President, 1987.

        Reports on the recent decade 1978-87, with an eighty-page overview providing significant views of the most recent developments of the Candler School of Theology, its faculty, curriculum, institutes, and related programs.

1104.   Ferguson, Charles W. *Organizing To Beat the Devil: Methodists and the Making of America*. Garden City, NY: Doubleday and Co., Inc., 1971.

        Provides in Chapter twenty-three an account of the development of Methodist theological schools in the context of the overall emphasis on an educated ministry characteristic of the Methodist movement in the United States.

1105.   Foster, Charles, ed. "A Discussion On Theological Education." *Journal: Methodist Theological School in Ohio* 2 (Fall 1972): 16-23.

        Records a taped conversation between the Editor, the Dean, a Professor of Christian Education, the Dean of Admissions, and a pastor, in the context of changes in contemporary theological education, especially in terms of METHESCO's response.

Highlights such changes and challenges as the following: democratization of the classroom, theological and cultural pluralism, the civil rights movement, the Vietnam War, the counter-culture and "Jesus movement," and the rise of Black Theology. Notes that the school now takes the Church and the ministry more seriously. States that with so many changes taking place around it, the school must also take the world and its needs more seriously, and allow students the freedom to help design a curriculum that responds to those needs in responsible ways.

1106.   Harmon, Noland B., Albea Godbold, and Louise L. Queen, eds. *Encyclopedia of World Methodism.* Nashville, TN: United Methodist Publishing House, 1974.

Contains brief articles on each of the thirteen United Methodist theological schools, their origins, history, benefactors, etc. Provides the standard reference on all aspects of United Methodism.

1107.   Hauk, Gary. "The Pitts Theology Library." In *A Sesquicentennial Chronicle of the Emory University Library.* Prepared by Thomas H. English. Atlanta, GA: Friends of the Emory University Libraries, 1987.

Chronicles in a nine-page chapter the dramatic rise of the University's theological library into a position of world renown and prominence, primarily during the most recent decade.

1108.   Herberg, Will. "Crisis at Drew." *Christianity and Crisis*, February 20, 1967, pp. 25-27.

Describes the crisis at Drew University surrounding President Robert F. Oxnam, Drew's President beginning in 1960. Shows how the President was apparently obstructing efforts of the Theological School to strengthen its academic position. Tells how a controversy arose over the filling of a major vacancy in Systematic Theology in 1966 because of the death of Carl Michalson, and how it became an almost insurmountable problem. Relates how the controversy resulted in President Oxnam's having the Dean of the Theological School dismissed. Suggests the serious threat this case generated to the future of the Drew Theological School, as an example of the question of academic freedom, particularly in a church-related school.

1109.   Howe, Leroy T., ed. "Special Issue in Honor of Retiring Dean Joseph D. Quillian, Perkins School of Theology." *Perkins Journal* 34 (Spring 1981): 1-33.

Contains articles on the relationship of the seminary to the University; Dean Quillian's special contributions; the policy process at Perkins under Quillian; and an appreciation of the Quillian years with a look ahead to the future.

1110.   Johnson, Dick. "Homosexuals and the Seminaries." *ESA: Engage/Social Action* 6 (August 1978): 44-45.

         Raises the issue, possibly for the first time, whether it is appropriate for a United Methodist theological seminary to dismiss students who are "admitted homosexuals." Focuses on the question of whether the determination of "fitness for ordination" is the proper function of the institution. Offers a prophetic statement on an issue which was likely to become far more significant in subsequent years with restrictive rulings adoped by the General Conferences in the 1980s.

1111.   Joy, James Richard, ed. *The Teacher of Drew, 1867-1942.* Madison, NJ: Drew University, 1942.

         Provides a primary focus, not on historical details, but on the faculty and leaders who served the Seminary well in its first seventy-five years. Gives an historical sketch in the first forty pages, and then switches to the individual sketches for the remainder of the book.

1112.   Kidder, Daniel P. "Ministerial Education and Training in The Methodist Episcopal Church." *Bibliotheca Sacra* 33 (July 1876): 558-84.

         Describes early efforts in theological education by the Methodists, who required of seminary students in the nineteenth Century that they have Certification by a Quarterly Conference, i.e., local church, and also required them to preach while attending school. Notes the commitment of the Church as well to try to ease the financial burden for theological education for young ministers.

1113.   Lansman, Quentin Charles. *Higher Education in The Evangelical United Brethren Church.* Nashville, TN: Division of Higher Education, The United Methodist Church, 1972.

         Examines the theological seminaries affiliated with the forerunner denominations of The Evangelical Brethren Church in the overall context of higher education. Focuses on the difficulties in maintaining close ties between Church and educational institution without control of the latter by the former.

1114.   Leiffer, Murry and Dorothy Leiffer. *Enter the Old Portals: Reminiscences -- Fifty Years.* Evanston, IL: Garrett-Evangelical Theological Seminary, 1987.

         Provides a chronological narrative of Garrett through fifty years from the perspective of a retired Professor of Church and Society. Offers reflections and reminiscences of life at Garrett in anecdotal style, with personal glimpses of other faculty members by Dr. Leiffer, who taught at Garrett for more than forty years. Tells the stories behind the dates and historical facts.

1115.   Marsh, Daniel L. "Methodism and Early Methodist Theological
         Education." *Methodist History* 1 (1962): 3-13.

         Lists four distinctive marks of Methodism, including a strong
         emphasis on education. Points out that the early circuit riders were
         self-educated men, but in spite of this, six theological schools were
         developed by The Methodist Episcopal Church from 1784 to 1884.
         Focuses on the importance of theological education and the
         development of the Conference Course of Study as a means of
         educating ministers who could not attend theological school. Cites
         Boston University School of Theology as an example of the early
         development of theological education in The Methodist Episcopal
         Church, following it from its origin in Newbury, Vermont, to its
         current location adjacent to Boston University.

1116.   McCulloh, Gerald O. *Ministerial Education in the American
         Methodist Movement.* Nashville, TN: United Methodist Board of
         Higher Education and Ministry, Division of Ordained Ministry,
         1980.

         Provides a comprehensive study of the actors and actions
         that have produced one of the largest and most successful families
         of theological schools in the United States. Relates the history of
         each of the thirteen United Methodist seminaries to basic themes
         and trends in theological education over the past century. Includes
         attention to diversity of curriculum, development of practical
         studies, emphasis on concerns of women and ethnic minorities, and
         the development of financial support for theological education
         through the Ministerial Education Fund. Calls attention to the
         strategic location of these seminaries in large urban centers, often
         adjacent to major universities with Methodist backgrounds.
         Contains an exhaustive bibliography, making it the definitive work
         on theological schools in the Methodist tradition.

1117.   Minus, Paul M. "Ferment Along the Olentangy." *Journal:
         Methodist Theological School in Ohio* 6 (Fall 1967): 13-17.

         Presents a preliminary sketch of what one person has gleaned
         from METHESCO's attempt to move creatively toward the future,
         on the eve of the tenth anniversary of the school's founding in 1958.
         Notes emphasis on field education, raising questions about
         problems connected with it. Cites a need for more theological
         "wholeness" in the seminary curriculum. Notes discussion
         underway concerning an advanced degree beyond the Master of
         Divinity. Describes inter-institutional relationships with other
         educational institutions, especially with United Theological
         Seminary in Dayton following the upcoming denominational merger
         in 1968.

1118.   Niebuhr, H. Richard, Daniel Day Williams, and James M.
         Gustafson. *The Advancement of Theological Education.* New York:
         Harper and Brothers, Publishers, 1957.

Offers in the Appendix of this more general work a specific look at the role of The Methodist Church in the education of black ministers. Cites 1948 statistics showing far more blacks in The Methodist Church than in any other predominantly white denomination. Cites also a 1948 study showing improved educational status of the ministerial members of the Central (Negro) Jurisdiction. Makes clear, however, that there was still a huge gap between black and white ministerial members in The Methodist Church.

1119.   Norwood, Frederick Abbott.   *Dawn to Mid-Day at Garrett.* Evanston, IL: Garrett-Evangelical Theological Seminary, 1978.

Organizes, interprets, and preserves in compact form Garrett's one hundred and twenty-five years of tradition and history up to 1978. Treats the history of Garrett only, and not Evangelical Theological Seminary, until the two were brought together in 1974. Contains a very informative section dealing with special challenges for theological education in the 1960s: the Vietnam War, racial issues, women's issues, etc.

1120.   Norwood, Frederick Abbott. "The Shaping of the Methodist Ministry." *Religion in Life* 43 (Autumn 1974): 337-51.

Looks at the nature of educated ministry during the first forty years of the Methodist movement in the United States. Cites the practice of traveling with a circuit rider in order to learn from him "in the field." Shows that this practice generally continued until the seminary movement surfaced around 1840 in New England.

1121.   Norwood, Frederick Abbott. *The Story of American Methodism: A History of the United Methodists and Their Relations.* Nashville, TN: Abingdon Press, 1964.

Provides in Chapter 27, "Education and the Printed Word," a comparison of The Methodist Episcopal and The Evangelical United Brethren in their approaches to higher education and the starting of theological schools. Notes a bias in both denominations against formal education for ministers. Notes how the Course of Study came into being as a way of dealing with this bias. Credits developers like John Dempster and benefactors like Daniel Drew with providing both the impetus and the inspiration for the advancement of theological education in the Methodist tradition.

1122.   *The Perkins 40th Story.*   Dallas, TX: The Perkins School of Theology, 1986.

Focuses on the generous endowment gift made by Joe and Lois Perkins in 1946 which enabled the transition from Southern Methodist University's School of Theology to The Perkins School of Theology in the same year. Provides a brief sketch of major changes and developments in the forty years since the change in name.

1123.   Porter, Earl W. *Trinity and Duke, 1892-1924: Foundations of Duke University*. Durham, NC: Duke University Press, 1964.

Places the origin of the Duke Divinity School within the context of the transition from Trinity College to Duke University in 1924 due to a major endowment gift from Mr. James B. Duke. Notes that a major thrust of the college had always been the education of ministers, and so it was a natural turn of events when, two years later, a formal school of Religion was begun, which soon became known as The Divinity School. Focuses on some of the tension between the church interests calling for education in religion to be more "spiritual," and those academics who yearned for it to continue to be "scholarly." Offers the best available historical account of the background of Duke University.

1124.   Richardson, Harry V. *Dark Salvation: The Story of Methodism As It Developed Among Blacks in America*. Garden City, NY: Anchor Press/Doubleday, 1976.

Gives an overview of developments within the Methodist movement in America. Focuses on the work of the Freedmen's Aid Society in The Methodist Episcopal Church as a major force in educating blacks following the Civil War. Cites formation of Gammon Theological Seminary as part of Clark University as a natural development from the earlier work of the Society.

1125.   Richardson, Harry V. *Walk Together, Children: The Story of the Birth and Growth of the Interdenominational Theological Center*. Atlanta, GA: The Interdenominational Theological Center Press, 1981.

Gives thorough coverage to the background, issues, etc., which led to the move by Gammon Theological Seminary to become a part of the Interdenominational Theological Center, especially from the perspective of Dr. Richardson, President of Gammon at the time. Describes negotiations with the Sealantic Fund, a Rockefeller educational foundation, which led to the eventual formation of the Center in 1957, followed by major funding from Sealantic in 1958. Contains historical sketches of all participating institutions at the end of the book.

1126.   Ryan, Michael Daniel. "Theology at Drew: Between Its Past and Future." *Drew Gateway* 41 (Winter 1971): 70-82.

Cites the relationship between Drew's Theological School and The Methodist Church as allowing a response to the task of "the free criticism of Church and society." Compares earlier criticism of slavery and slaveholders with current criticism of racism in Church and society, economic injustice, and war. Calls for a seminary philosophy that continues to be a responsible critic in these areas.

1127.   *Self-Study Report of The Methodist Theological School in Ohio to The Association of Theological Schools and The North Central Association of Colleges and Schools.* Delaware, OH: The Methodist Theological School in Ohio, 1987.

Contains a section on "The Mission of the School in Historical Perspective." Relates the Purpose Statement as it has been re-affirmed in 1987, and looks at it in the light of the school's stated objectives. Notes how the School was begun because of a serious need for Methodist ministers in Ohio, but has more recently broadened to include lay education and service to society. Gives a brief historical sketch of the development of The Methodist Theological School in Ohio (METHESCO), incorporated in 1958. Notes problems relating to being one of two United Methodist theological schools in Ohio after the 1968 EUB merger. Cites unique features of the school, including the Council for the Study of Ethics and Economics, and a degree program in Alcoholism and Drug Abuse Ministry, perhaps the only one of its kind in the country. Notes recent attempts by the seminary to combat racism and sexism, both within the institution and without.

1128.   *Semi-Centennial Celebration: Garrett Biblical Institute.* Evanston, IL: Garrett Biblical Institute, 1906.

Provides a collection of essays, addresses, programs, etc. from the Semi-Centennial Celebration of Garrett Biblical Institute in 1906. Gives a brief historical sketch of Garrett's beginnings. Offers a helpful account of President Little's Commemorative Address, pp. 139-161. Puts Garrett's development into an historical and philosophical context.

1129.   Shipps, Howard Fenimore. *A Short History of Asbury Theological Seminary.* Berne, IN: The Herald Press, 1963.

Describes the historical background of Asbury Theological Seminary and its relationship with Methodism, noting that, while it has not been considered a Methodist school, it does trace its roots historically to New Testament times through the same route as Methodism (Wesley, Asbury, etc.). Relates how The Rev. John Wesley Hughes, a Kentucky Methodist, felt God's call to found a college, which he did in 1890, calling it Kentucky Holiness College. States the goal of this college as that of "purifying reform within Methodism and Christianity." Notes how this concern broadened to include ministerial education, with Asbury College adding a full-fledged seminary in 1923. Cites continuing struggles with accreditation by the American Association of Theological Schools, with accreditation finally restored in 1960.

1130.   Sitterly, Charles Fremont. *The Building of Drew University.* New

York: The Methodist Book Concern, 1938.

Notes the historical beginnings of the Drew Theological School. Covers the expansion of the Theological School as it joined forces with the Undergraduate College of Liberal Arts (formerly known as Brothers College), resulting in the formation of Drew University in 1928. Contains a great deal of biographical information on distinguished Drew faculty and presidents.

1131.   Smith, Horace Greeley. *The Story of Garrett, 1853-1953.* Evanston, IL: Garrett Biblical Institute, 1954.

Divides the story of Garrett Biblical Institute into three parts: 1) implementing the dream up to 1853; 2) four periods of growth -- pioneer, stabilization, expansion, forward; and 3) a "bird's-eye view" of faculty, students, curriculum, endowment, etc. Shows from the perspective of a twentieth century Garrett President how the need for trained ministers followed the pioneering westward movement of The Methodist Church.

1132.   *A Study of Theological Education in The Methodist Church, 1952-1956.* Nashville, TN: Study Commission on Theological Education, 1956.

Provides results of a Study commissioned in 1952 by the General Conference to consider: 1) the size of existing Methodist seminaries; 2) possible need for more seminaries; and 3) possible Methodist sanction and support for non-Methodist schools. Cites enrollment figures from 1941 to 1954. Notes in 1956 that 72.8 percent of Methodist ministers who are members of Annual Conferences are seminary graduates, and of those coming in since 1937, 77.4 percent are graduates. Adds valuable information to the subject matter through extensive data, charts, and maps, helping to establish the need for construction of two new seminaries (in Ohio and the Kansas City area).

1133.   *A Survey of Ten Theological Schools Affiliated with The Methodist Church under the Auspices of the Commission on Theological Education, The Association of Methodist Theological Schools.* Nashville, TN: Board of Education of The Methodist Church, 1948.

Provides background and current (as of 1948) data for each of ten Methodist seminaries.   Includes history, administration, admissions policies, faculty, curriculum, library, sources and number of students, physical plant, and finances. Includes: Boston, Candler, Drew, Duke, Gammon, Garrett, Iliff, Perkins, University of Southern California (later Claremont), and Westminster (later Wesley).

1134.   Sweet, William Warren. *Methodism in American History.* New York: Abingdon Press, 1954.

Contains information on theological education in Chapter XI, "Begins Her Educational Task." Notes early opposition by Methodist leaders to theological education and a trained clergy; studies were considered a waste of time; yet the growth in numbers of college-trained laymen led to an increased demand for educated ministers. Identifies John Dempster as the "father of theological education in The Methodist Episcopal Church," noting his accomplishments at Boston and Garrett. States that the Methodists were the last major Protestant denomination to begin a theological school, but soon moved to the forefront. Notes other developments in theological education as they relate to the historical story being told.

1135.   Taylor, Price A., Jr. "A History of Gammom Theological Seminary." Ed.D. dissertation. New York University, 1948.

Provides extensive background on the need for theological training for blacks, resulting in the development of a seminary curriculum through the Religion Department of Clark University in 1883. Gives a thorough account of Gammon's development prior to the merger with The Interdenominational Theological Center in 1957. Offers data on enrollment and funding sources through a helpful appendix.

1136.   Thomas, Mary Martha Hosford. *Southern Methodist University: Founding and Early Years.* Dallas, TX: Southern Methodist University Press, 1974.

Tells the history of Southern Methodist University and its School of Theology from its beginnings in 1940, based primarily on records of the Office of the President and on oral histories. Provides the most extensive written record of the early years of Perkins School of Theology (the name was changed in 1946).

1137.   Tipple, Ezra Squier, ed., *Drew Theological Seminary, 1867-1917.* Cincinnati, OH: Methodist Book Concern, 1917.

Traces the history of the Drew Theological School back to the General Conference of 1864 and the generous gift of its benefactor and namesake, Daniel Drew, in 1866. Focuses on the location of the school, not in Carmel, New York, at Drew's request, but closer to New York City in Madison, New Jersey, incorporated there in 1868. Follows the school's development in some detail in 1917.

1138.   Vail, Stephen M. *Ministerial Education in The Methodist Episcopal Church.* Boston, MA: J. P. Magee, 1853.

Provides an historical context for the very early emphasis on education as ministerial training. Argues for practicality in ministerial training and affiliation of seminaries with existing

Methodist colleges and universities. Places Methodist ministerial
education in a broader historical context, dating back to biblical
times.

1139.   Vernon, Walter N. *Methodism Moves Across North Texas*. Dallas,
         TX: Historical Society, North Texas Conference, The Methodist
         Church, 1967.

         Contains recent history of the North Texas Annual
         Conference, including significant sections on Perkins School of
         Theology and Southern Methodist University.

1140.   Vernon, Walter N., et al. *The Methodist Excitement in Texas: A
         History*. Dallas, TX: Texas United Methodist Historical Society,
         1984.

         Contains a recent and valuable history of Texas Methodism,
         including important sections on Southern Methodist University and
         Perkins School of Theology.

1141.   Wicke, Myron F. *The Methodist Church and Higher Education,
         1939-64*. Nashville, TN: Board of Education, The Methodist
         Church, 1964.

         Provides a brief historical sketch and then surveys Methodist
         investment in higher education from 1939 (formation of The
         'Methodist Church from several antecedent bodies) to the present
         (1965). Focuses also on the development of the Conference Course
         of Study and the growth of existing seminaries.

1142.   Williams, Katherine Sidney. "A History of the Candler School of
         Theology Library of Emory University." M.L.S. thesis. Emory
         University, 1961.

         Describes the growth and character of the School of
         Theology's library and, in so doing, sheds light on the development
         and nature of the theological school itself. Includes a bibliography
         and tables.

CONTRIBUTORS

Contributors are listed in order of their appearance in the book.

THOMAS C. HUNT received the Ph.D. from the University of Wisconsin. He is Professor of Foundations of Education at Virginia Tech. His major interest is history of American education with an emphasis on religion and schooling. He is the co-editor of *Religion and Morality in American Schooling* (1981), and co-edited, with James C. Carper, *Religious Schooling in America* (1984), and *Religious Colleges and Universities in America: A Selected Bibliography* (1988), and (with Carper and Charles S. Kniker) *Religious Schools in America: A Selected Bibliography* (1986). His articles have appeared in *Educational Forum, The Journal of Church and State, Momemtum, The Catholic Historical Review, Paedogogica Historica, Journal of Presbyterian History, Religious Education, Methodist History, National Association of Episcopal Schools Journal,* and *High School Journal.* He received the Thayer S. Warshaw award in 1986 for his essay on "Religion and Public Schooling: A Tale of Tempest."

JAMES C. CARPER earned the Ph.D. from Kansas State University. He recently returned to his position at Mississippi State University after serving two years as Director of the Education and Society Division in the Office of Research of the U.S. Department of Education. His articles have appeared in *Kansas Historical Quarterly, Mid-America, Educational Forum, Journal of Church and State, Review Journal of Philosophy and Social Science,* and *Journal of Thought.* He recently co-edited (with Thomas C. Hunt) *Religious Schooling in America* and (with Hunt and Charles R. Kniker) *Religious Schools in America: A Selected Bibliography,* and (with Hunt) *Religious Colleges and Universities: A Selected Bibliography.* His scholarly interests include the history of American education and religious schools, particularly Christian day schools.

RALPH D. MAWDSLEY, Administrative Counsel at Liberty University, is a graduate of the University of Illinois College of Law. In addition, Dr. Mawdsley holds a Ph.D. in Educational Administration from the University of Minnesota where he holds Adjunct Professor status and teaches a course, Tort Liability for Vocational Educators. He has written extensively in Legal periodicals and is a frequent conference speaker on educational law topics. Dr. Mawdsley is on the Board of Directors for the National Organization on Legal Problems of Education (NOLPE) and the Society of Educators and Scholars, and is a member of the Editorial Advisory Committee of West's Education Law Reporter. His book *Legal Problems of Religious and Private Schools* has been used as a textbook in graduate school law courses and his monograph, *Legal Aspects of Plagiarism*, has become a model for designing university policies on plagiarism.

JERRY M. SELF is Assistant Director of the Education Commission of the Southern Baptist Convention, Nashville, Tennessee.

MARY A. GRANT is Director of the Health Education Resource Center, College of Pharmacy and Allied Health Professions, St. Johns University, New York. She has earned a Master's degree in Library Science and a Ph.D. degree in Educational Administration and Supervision from St. John's. In her professional career Ms. Grant has been a classroom teacher and a director of secondary library media centers in the New York and Philadelphia areas. She has served as a library consultant for Winston Prep School in New York City.   Her professional activities include serving as Vice-President and President of the national Catholic Library Association from 1983 to 1987. As immediate past president of the Association, she continues to serve on its Executive Board.

KENNETH M. SHAFFER, JR. is director of the Brethren Historical Library and Archives in Elgin, Illinois. Prior to coming to his present position, he was director of the Seminary Library (Oak Brook, Illinois), which serves both Bethany Theological Seminary and Northern Baptist Theological Seminary. He received his M.Div. from Bethany and his M.A. in library science from Northern Illinois University.

JOHN M. IMBLER is Vice-President for theological education with the Division of Higher Education of the Christian Church (Disciples of Christ) in St. Louis, Missouri. Additional portfolio responsibilities include management of the Division's scholarship program and oversight of the higher education personnel service.   Dr. Imbler is a member of the Disciples Task Force on Ministry, serves as treasurer of the Association of Disciples for Theological Discussion, and is associate editor of *The Disciples Theological Digest*.

DONALD S. ARMENTROUT received the B.A. from Roanoke College in 1961, the B.D. from the Lutheran Theological Seminary, Gettysburg, in 1964, and the Ph.D. from Vanderbilt University in 1970. In 1967 he began teaching church history at the School of Theology, where he has served as Director of the Advanced Degree Committee since 1974, and was interim dean, 1985-1986. He has written *The Quest for the Informed Priest: A History of the School of Theology* (1979), *James Harvey Otey: First Episcopal Bishop of Tennessee* (1984), and *Episcopal Splinter Groups: A Study of Groups Which have Left the Episcopal Church* (1985). He has compiled *A DuBose Reader: Selections from the Writings of William Porcher DuBose* (1984).   He has published articles in the *Historical Magazine of the Protestant Episcopal Church*, the *St. Luke's Journal of Theology*, *The Living Church*, and the *Lutheran Quarterly*.   He is a member of the Board of Trustees of the University of the South and is on the board of editors of the *St. Luke's Journal of Theology*.

GEORGE C. PAPADEMETRIOU received his Ph.D. from Temple University. He is Associate Professor and Director of the Library at Hellenic

College/Holy Cross Greek Orthodox School of Theology. Since 1960 he has served the Greek Orthodox Archdiocese as a priest. He is the author of *Introduction to St Gregory Palamas* and has also written numerous articles for scholarly journals. Reverend Papademetriou is currently President of the Massachusetts Commission on Christian Unity.

WILLIAM C. RINGENBERG is Chairman, Department of History and Director of the Honors Program at Taylor University, Upland, Indiana, where he has been a member of the faculty since 1968. He is the author of *Taylor University: The First 125 Years* (1973) and *The Christian College: A History of Protestant Higher Education in America* (1984) both published by Eerdmans Press of Grand Rapids, Michigan. He presently serves as president of the Conference on Faith and History.

HAROLD S. WECHSLER is director of higher education publications for the National Education Association. He is the author of *The Qualified Student: A History of Selective College Admission in America* (Wiley-Interscience, 1977), and many articles on the Jewish encounter with American higher education. His most recent monograph is *The New Look: Ford Foundation and the Revolution in Business Education* (Graduate Management Admissions Council, 1988).

RICHARD W. SOLBERG is a retired Lutheran pastor and educator living in Thousand Oaks, California, where he serves as Adjunct Professor of History at California Lutheran university. He is a graduate of St. Olaf College and Luther Northwestern Theological Seminary, and holds a Ph.D. in American history from the University of Chicago. He taught at St.Olaf College, Augustana College (South Dakota), served as Vice President for Academic Affairs at Thiel College in Pennsylvania, and until his retirement, was Director for Higher Education for the Lutheran Church in America. He is the author of *Lutheran Higher Education in North America*, published in 1985, *How Church-Related are Church-Related Colleges?* (1980), *God and Caesar in East Germany* (1961), an account of church/state relations in East Germany, 1945-59, and *As Between Brothers* (1957), a history of world Lutheran relief efforts after World Wars I and II.

JON DIEFENTHALER received his Ph.D. under Sidney Mead in American Religious History in 1976 at the University of Iowa. Prior to this, he graduated from Concordia Seminary, St. Louis, and was awarded his M.A. by Washington University. In 1981-1982, he worked with Timothy L. Smith as a postdoctoral fellow in the Department of History at the Johns Hopkins University. Over the course of his career, Diefenthaler has served as both a seminary professor and parish pastor. For three years he was a member of the Department of Historical Theology at Concordia Theological Seminary, Springfield, Illinois. More recently, he has been a visiting professor at Lutheran Theological Seminary in Gettysburg, teaching courses in American Lutheranism. He is currently pastor of Bethany Lutheran Church, Waynesboro, Virginia. Published in 1986 by Mercer University Press is his book, *H. Richard Niebuhr: A Lifetime of Reflections on the Church and the World.* Work on Niebuhr still in progress involves an anthology that collects essays and articles from his early years. Diefenthaler's research in the area

of American Lutheranism has focused on education, and his essay on
"Lutheran Schools in America" was published in 1984 as a chapter in
Religious Schooling in America, edited by James C. Carper and Thomas C.
Hunt.

HAROLD E. RASER is Associate Professor of the History of Christianity
at Nazarene Theological Seminary, Kansas City, Missouri. He is an ordained
minister in the Church of the Nazarene and is a member of the American
Academy of Religion, the American Society of Church History, and the
Wesleyan Theological Society. He is the author of *Phoebe Palmer, Her Life
and Thought* (The Edwin Mellen Press, "Studies in Women and Religion,"
1987) as well as articles and reviews appearing in several church publications
and scholarly journals.

WILLIAM J. WESTON is a Research Associate with the Office of Research
of the U.S. Department of Education. He is a graduate of Yale Divinity
School, and has recently completed a dissertation in sociology at Yale on
religious pluralism within the northern Presbyterian Church.

PETER DE KLERK received his B.A. from Calvin College, his M.Div. from
Westminster Theological Seminary and his M.Ln. from Emory University.
He is Theological Librarian and Curator of the H. Henry Meeter Center for
Calvin Studies at Calvin Theological Seminary. His areas of special interests
include compilation of bibliographies on publications by and about John
Calvin, and research on Dutch immigration to Colorado in 1892-1893. He is
author of numerous books, articles, and essays on these subjects.

GEORGE R. KNIGHT is professor of Church History at Andrews
University since 1985. Previously he was professor of Educational
Foundations at the same institution from 1976-1985. His major publications
are: *Philosophy and Education: An Introduction in Christian Perspectives*
(1980); *Issues and Alternatives in Educational Philosophy* (1982); *Early
Adventist Educators* (editor, 1983); *Myths in Adventism* (1985); *From 1888 to
Apostasy: The Case of A.T. Jones* (1987). He is also editor of *Andrews
University Seminary Studies* and research editor for *The Journal of Adventist
Education*.

LOWELL H. ZUCK is professor of Church History at Eden Theological
Seminary, St. Louis, Missouri. He received his Ph.D. from Yale University.
He is a member of the Historical Council of the United Church of Christ.
His books include *Christianity and Revolution, 1520 to 1650* and *Socially
Responsible Believers*. His articles have appeared in *Church History*,
*Historical Intelligencer, Bulletin of the Congregational Library, Zeitschrift für
Religions und Geistesgeschichte, Theology and Life, Church School Worker*,
and *Pastoral Psychology*.

LESLIE GLENN TYNDALL serves as United Methodist Campus Minister
at Virginia Polytechnic Institute and State University in Blacksburg, Virginia.
Tyndall, a native of Kinston, North Carolina, received the A.B. Degree in
History from Duke University (1963), and the Master of Divinity from the
Duke Divinity School (1966). In 1977 he received the Master of Arts Degree

in Church History from Wake Forest University. Tyndall is married to LaVina Stevens and they have two children.

AUTHOR INDEX

Abel, Paul Frederick 752
Adams, James E. 814
Adams, John Quincy 911
Addison, Charles M. 439
Addison, Daniel D. 440
Addison, James T. 279
Adler, Cyrus 440, 770-772
Ahlstrom, Sydney E. 1015
Albert, James A. 25
Albright, Raymond W. 280
Alden, Joseph Price 968
Alexander, Archibald 894
Alexander, George M. 548
Allbeck, Willard D. 815
Allen, Alexander V. G. 441, 442
Allen, Michael 404
Allen, Yorke 1016
Allison, Leon McDill 871
Althausen, Johannes 969
Alvarez, Eliezer 1032
American Jewish Archives 773
Ames, Van Meter 236
Anderson, H. George 816
Anderson, Harry H. 508
Anderson, Park H. 51
Arbuckle, Gerald A. 123
Arden, G. Everett 817
Armentrout, Donald S. 549-554,
  629
Armstrong, Richard 159
Arnold, Charles Harvey 213, 753
Arnold, Frederick S. 673
Arpke, Jerome C. 970
Arseniev, N. S. 699
Athenagoras, Archbishop 700
Athenagoras, Bishop of Elaia 701,
  702
Auburn Theological Seminary
  912
Aulick, Amos Lindsey 52
Austin, Alan Kenneth 754
Averky, Archbishop 703

Baars, Conrad W. 124
Bacon, Leonard 971
Bailey, Kenneth K. 1088
Bainton, Roland H. 755, 1017,
  1018
Baird, J. H. 908
Baird, Samuel 855
Baker, Robert Andrew 53
Barnds, William J. 666-668
Barnes, C. Rankin 693
Barnhart, Joe Edward 54
Barron, Jack 199
Bass, Dorothy C. 972, 1019
Bauer, Francis C. 125
Baum, William W. 126
Baumer, Fred 127
Beale, David O. 55
Beardsley, E. Edwards 405
Beardsley, William A. 406, 482
Beher, Linda 249
Behney, J. Bruce 1089
Bennett, Anita Cole 200
Bentwich, Norman 774
Bernardin, Joseph L. 128
Berry, Joseph B. 443
Beull, Lawrence 1020
Bigham, Thomas J., Jr. 281
Bird, Wendell R. 9
Blackburn, Imri M. 509, 510
Blackburn, John Glenn 56
Blackman, George L. 444
Blackmore, James H. 57
Blakemore, William Barnett 214
Blandy, Gray M. 476
Bloodgood, Francis J. 483
Blusin, Basil M. 704
Board of Control, Concordia
  Seminary 818
Board of Theological Education
  282
Bone, Winstead P. 875

Roach, Corwin C. 421
Robertson, Charles F. 662
Robinson, David 1069
Robinson, Kenneth 852
Robinson, William C. 867
Rockwell, Hays H. 462
Rodenmayer, Robert N. 375
Rodgers, John H. 590
Rogers, Arthur 463
Ronk, Albert T. 272
Rooks, Charles S. 1070
Roozen, David A. 376
Ross, Bob 377
Rothkoff, Aaron 807
Rottenberg, Isaac C. 952
Routh, Eugene Coke 102
Rowe, Henry K. 1000
Rubinstein, Aryeh 808
Ruger, Anthony 1001
Russell, James S. 617
Ryan, John Henry 186
Ryan, Michael Daniel 1126
Rynbrandt, Abraham 953

San Francisco Theological
    Seminary 910
Sandusky, Fred 103
Sanford, Louis S. 435
Saunders, Robert S. 874
Sawyer, Kenneth 764
Scanlon, Arthur J. 187
Scarborough, Lee Rutland 104
Schaff, Phillip 1002
Schechter, Solomon 809
Schermerhorn, William E. 628
Schmemann, Alexander 743
Schneider, Carl E. 1003, 1004
Schnucher, Calvin 870
Schoenherr, Richard A. 188
Schreiter, Robert J. 189
Schroeder, Oliver C., Jr. 233
Schroeder, W. Widick 1005
Schuler, Richard J. 190
Schultz, Joseph R. 251
Schwalm, Vernon F. 105, 273,
    274
Sciarrino, Alfred J. 45
Scott, David A. 378
Scott, Donald M. 1071
Sellars, Ovid 884
Sharp, S. Z. 275

Shaw, Henry King 210, 234
Sheatsley, C. V. 842
Shelton, Charles 191
Shepherd, Massey H., Jr. 436, 437
Sheppard, E. L. 580
Sherman, Arthur M. 380
Shewmaker, William O. 381, 1006
Shipps, Howard Fenimore 765,
    1129
Shires, Henry H. 438
Shockley, Grant S. 1073, 1074
Shriver, Donald W. 1072
Shultz, Joseph R. 263
Shuttleworth, Frank K. 347
Siegenthaler, David 452
Silverman, Debra A. 46
Simpson, James 543
Sister, Victoria, Sister 745
Sitterly, Charles Fremont 1130
Skillrud, Harold C. 843
Slattery, Charles Lewis 464
Smith, George W. 646
Smith, Horace Greeley 1131
Smith, Jane I. 1075
Smith, John Talbot 192
Smith, Kenneth B. 1019
Smith, Laura Chase 422, 655
Smith, Warren H. 625
Smythe, George F. 423, 424
Snow, John H. 452
Snyder, Graydon F. 108, 276
Snyder, Lester B. 48
Sorensen, Annemette 188
Southwestern Baptist Theological
    Seminary 110
Spielmann, Richard M. 425
Spindle, Oran Randall 853
Stadius, Arnold 844
Stanley, Clifford L. 604
Steiner, Bernard C. 412
Stephens, John Vant 885
Stevenson, Dwight E. 211, 212
Stibitz, George 1007
Stob, George 955
Stoffer, Dale Rupert 277
Stoltz, Karl Ruf 1076
Storr, Richard J. 220
Strategic Planning Committee 382
Strider, Robert E. L. 383
Sumner, David E. 384
Swartzbaugh, Constance H. 656

SUBJECT INDEX

Absalom Jones Theological Institute 610, 611
Accreditation 28
Adler, Cyrus 770-772, 780, 802
Advanced Bible School 962, 967
Alcoholism and drug abuse, ministry 1127
Alexander, Archibald 899, 900, 902
Alexander, Caleb 646
Alexander, William 901
Allen, Alexander V. G. 463-466
American Association of Theological Schools 358, 445, 1129
American Baptist Convention 121
American Education, An Overview of 1024, 1025
Ames, Edward Scribner 213, 236
Amos v. Corporation of Presiding Bishop 1, 36
Andover-Newton Seminary 971, 982, 995, 1000, 1010, 1011, 1045
Appleby, James 922
Arkansas Theological Chautauqua School 612
Asbury Theological Seminary 752, 765, 1129
Ashland Theological Seminary 251, 263, 268, 272
Associate Mission and Brotherhood 531
Athinson, Bishop 678
Auburn Theological Seminary 911, 912, 914
Augsburg Seminary 820
Augustana Theological Seminary 817
Austin Presbyterian Theological Seminary 860, 861

Ball, Charles T. 96
Bangor Seminary 978, 979, 984
Baptist Bible Institute 63-67
Baptist Seminaries 51-122
Barnes, W. W. 96
Bauman, L. S. 262
Beach, John 303
Bedell, Gregory T. 423
Berkeley, George 411
Berkeley Divinity School 338, 404-413
Beth Medrash Goudhi 786
Bethany Seminary (Baptist) 60, 77, 88, 105, 108, 116
Bethany Seminary (Lutheran) 828
Bethany Theological Seminary
  history of 252, 255, 258, 266, 274, 275, 278
  life at 249, 254
  objectives of 257, 271
  pastoral training in 256, 271
  peace tradition at 265, 269
  teachers and leaders at 250, 259, 273
Bexley Hall 285, 354, 414-426
Bishop Payne Divinity School 396, 595, 613-617
Black theological education 1022, 1027
Bloy House 693, 694
Bob Jones University v. U.S. 29, 37, 47
Bonis, Professor C. 705
Booty, John E. 382
Borromeo College of Ohio 133
Bosher, Robert Semple 488
Boston University School of Theology 1092, 1093, 1097, 1098, 1115
Breck, James Lloyd 427, 432, 438, 511, 527, 573, 575

222

Subject Index

Chicago Theological Seminary
973, 987, 990
Christ the Savior Seminary 719,
734
Christian Church (Disciples of
Christ) 199-248
education of ministers in 230,
232
history of 235
Illinois, in 228
Indiana, in 234
Kentucky, in 225
Oklahoma, in 224
Tennessee, in 231
Texas, in 222, 227
theological education in 229
Christian-Jewish Relations 146
Christian Reformed Church 943,
944
Christian Theological Seminary
201, 203, 207
Church autonomy 34
Church Divinity School of the
Pacific (formerly the
Missionary College of St.
Augustine) 354, 427-438
Church of the Brethren Higher
Education 267, 276, 277
Church of the Brethren Seminaries
249-278
Chyet, Stanely 788
City and County of Denver v.
Colorado Seminary 2
Clark University 1091
Clarke, Joseph Morison 529
Clarkson, Robert 672
Coburn, John B. 462
Coffin, Henry Sloane 759
College of St. John the Evangelist
338, 618
College of the Bible 208, 211
Columbia Bible College and
Seminary 756
Columbia Theological Seminary
758, 862-867
Concordia College (Ft. Wayne)
819
Concordia Seminary (St. Louis)
814, 818, 823, 826, 838
Concordia Theological Seminary
(Springfield) 831

Cone, James H. 759
Conference of Theological
Seminaries 289
Congregational Ministerial
Patterns 1041
Congregational
Theology/Philosophy 988
Conner, W. T. 81, 94, 96
Conservative Baptist Theological
Seminary 87
Cooke, Giles B. 613
Copas, B. A. 96
Crawford, Angus 597
Criswell Center for Biblical
Studies 78
Crommett, Eugene E. 632, 633,
637, 638
Crowder, J. W. 96
Cumberland University 875; see
also McCormick 885

Dallas Theological Seminary 763,
769
Dana, H. E. 81
Danish Lutherans 821, 827
Danville Seminary 872
Dawley, Powell Mills 484, 506,
507
DeLancey, William H. 619, 622,
623
DeLancey Divinity School 338,
619-626
Decent, Bryon H. 66
Dehon, Theodore 492
Dempster, John 1093, 1121, 1134
Denver Theological School 618
Dewey, John 988
Disciples Divinity House of the
University of Chicago 214,
215
Discrimination 9, 30, 32, 41, 47
Divinity Department of
Burlington College 627,
628
Divinity School of the Protestant
Episcopal Church 338
Dixon, John 688, 692
Doane, George Washington 628
Drachman, Bernard 782
Drew, Daniel 1121, 1137
Drew University Theological

Episcopal Theological Seminary in
Kentucky 639-643
Episcopal Theological Seminary
of the Southwest 321,
476-479
Equal Employment Opportunity
Commission (EEOC), 3, 12
*Equal Employment Opportunity
Commission v.
Southwestern Baptist
Theological Seminary* 3
Erskine Theological Seminary 871
Evangelical Lutheran Theological
Seminary 824
Evangelical School of Theology
1089
Evangelical Theological Seminary
1089, 1102

FCC 25
Faculty dismissal 20
Fairfield Academy 621, 644-646
Farley, Edward 189
Federated Russian Orthodox
Clubs (F.R.O.C.) 735
Federated Theological Faculty
973
Financial crisis 20, 31, 39
Finkelstein, Louis 780, 789
Fleese, G. Allen 756
Fosbroke, Hughell Edgar Woodall
489, 497
Fuller Seminary 762
Fund raising 16, 25
Fundamentalism 762

Gambrell, J. B. 86, 102
Gammon Theological Seminary
(Part of
Interdenominational
Theological Center) 1091,
1094, 1124, 1125, 1135
Garrett, Samuel McCray 431
Garrett-Evangelical Theological
Seminary 1089, 1097,
1098, 1102, 1114, 1119,
1128, 1131
Garrison, J. H. 246
Gavin, Frank 483
*Gay Rights Coalition v.
Georgetown University* 32

General Theological Seminary
285, 290, 338, 354, 386,
480-507
Geneva College 621, 624, 625
George B. Mercer Jr. Memorial
School of Theology 695
German Evangelicals 1003
German Reformed Church 949,
985
German Reformed in Wisconsin
970, 986, 1008, 1009
Gettysburg Lutheran Theological
Seminary 849
Gibson, Robert F., Jr. 568, 594
Ginzberg, Louis 780, 789, 800
Golden Gate Seminary 82
Gordis, Robert 789
Government regulations 34, 38,
42, 50
Government relationships to
seminaries 1-50
Grace Theological Seminary 253,
260, 261, 264, 270, 277
Grand View Seminary 827
Grant, Frederick Clifton 576
Greek Orthodox Seminary 706
Griffiss, James E., Jr. 638
Grindez, John A. 154
Griswold College 647, 648

Haag, John E. 154
Hall, Francis J. 378
Hamma School of Theology 833
Handicapped Act of 1973 12
Harper, William Rainey 239
Harper's University 220
Hartford Theological Seminary
1037, 1044, 1063, 1065,
1076
Hartwick, John Christopher 830
Hartwick University 830
Harvard Divinity School 767,
995, 1015, 1028, 1049,
1052, 1075, 1079, 1082
Haugaard, William P. 634, 638
Hawks, Bishop 660
Hebrew Union College/Jewish
Institute of Religion 773,
775, 785, 788, 790, 794,
800, 805, 806
Heidelberg Theological Seminary